Explore office strategies...

- keeping a scrapbook on the boss
- looking like a success on the way to becoming one
- acting as the company hatchet-man
- coffee-making to cultivate friends and gain information
- performing for an audience
- simplifying your boss's life
- helping someone else to succeed

WINNING AT OFFICE POLITICS

will enlighten, stimulate, even shock you. You owe it to yourself and to your career.

Winning at Office Politics

Andrew J. DuBrin, Ph.D.

College of Business
Rochester Institute of Technology

BALLANTINE BOOKS • NEW YORK

Library of Congress Catalog Card Number: 78-8935

ISBN 0-345-29532-3

This edition published by arrangement with
Van Nostrand Reinhold Company

Manufactured in the United States of America

Second Ballantine Books Edition: September 1980

To Marcia, my wife,
and Gertrude, my mother-in-law

Preface

Office politics finally is coming out of the closet. A number of writers about general-interest business topics —including myself—have begun to expose the previously hush-hush tactics people use to gain advantage in all areas of work. To ignore office politics is to ignore those underlying forces that account for the differences in success between equally talented people. The person who understands and uses office politics to his or her advantage is much more likely to succeed than his or her politically naïve counterpart.

Most general and technical books about management concentrate on what *should* be done rather than what *is* done in the world of work. A recently published handbook of business administration contains over 2,000 pages of documented facts and expert opinion. Yet a person who applies only those ideas, techniques, and strategies to his job probably never will receive more than one promotion. Unless you practice some form of sensible office politics, you are doomed to a lifelong purgatory of entry-level assignments. As a 55-year-old messenger boy said when he was forced into early retirement (because it was felt he was overpaid for the job): "I can proudly say I never played politics one day in my life."

Books and articles written about office politics seem to have a common bias. They assume that the reader is male and already an executive—or aspires to become one. In reality, office politics is practiced at all levels in all places of work. Volunteer organizations also have their share of politicking for plum assignments! *Winning at Office Politics* is a unisex guide for practicing sensible politics at every job level—no matter what the organization.

Although the art and practice of office politics is becoming more public, it is still a topic surrounded by secrecy and denial. The large number of business executives who either refused to be interviewed about the topic or contended that "very little of that kind of thing takes place in our company" helped underscore the importance of conducting research about office politics. Similar reactions of secrecy and denial are forthcoming when company officials are questioned about expense account cheating, payola to choice customers, or extramarital affairs in the office.

The reader might be concerned about following the suggestions and advice in this book since other people, including your boss, will be privy to the same information, and your advantage in using this information might, therefore, be diminished. Such concerns are ill-founded for three important reasons. One: If other people read this or similar information, you will need to be knowledgeable about office politics as a defensive tactic; being naïve merely will place you at a severe disadvantage. Two: Only a few people who read valid information about self-improvement or career management actually apply the information. Thousands of people—in the process of job hunting—mail out atrociously prepared résumés, despite all they have read about the importance of an effective summary of qualifications. Three: Even if one half a million people buy this book (a fantasy I share with my publisher) and another half million people borrow and read their copies, less than 1.5 percent of the work force will have read this book. Why not join the ranks of that small minority who win at office politics rather than become its victim?

ANDREW J. DUBRIN

Acknowledgments

My students and research assistants, who have uncovered hundreds of examples of office politics, receive my primary thanks on this project. Many of these students—career people—have provided me insights about the machinations taking place in their companies. Those younger and less job-experienced, have been particularly helpful in exposing the operation of office politics at the bottom of organizations. A number of managerial and professional people contributed directly to this project in their candid discussions with me about the practices of office politics—in which they have both participated and witnessed. An even greater number of managerial and professional people receive my gratitude for their indirect contribution to this project. (I have unobtrusively observed them practicing both sensible and devious office politics.)

Because of the comprehensive nature of this book, some of my ideas are borrowed from other writers and researchers, many of whom are named at the back of the book. It would be impossible to accurately trace the origin of every non-original idea contained in the following pages as political strategies are hundreds—if not thousands—of years old.

Nancy Davis, my editor at Mason/Charter, and her colleagues encouraged my undertaking this project. K. Lois Smith worked on this manuscript with her usual efficiency and enthusiasm. Kathy Kulp once again helped me with essential secretarial and clerical chores.

My wife, Marcia, my sons, Drew and Douglas, and

my daughter, Melanie, individually and collectively, gave me an added inducement to undertake the writing of another book.

Rochester, New York   ANDREW J. DuBRIN

Contents

Preface   vii
Acknowledgments   ix

PART I   UNDERSTANDING OFFICE POLITICS

1   The Inevitability of Office Politics   2
2   How Political Are You?   22
3   Sizing Up the Political Climate   36

PART II   STRATEGIES FOR GAINING FAVOR

4   Cultivating Your Boss   62
5   Cultivating the Higher-ups   91
6   Cultivating Your Peers   112
7   Cultivating the People Below You   128

PART III   STRATEGIES FOR GAINING POWER

8   The Information Game   146
9   Boosting Your Career   165
10   Power Grabbing at Lower Levels   191
11   Power Plays at the Top   213

PART IV   MISFORTUNE, MISTAKES, AND MISDEEDS

12   Coping with Defeat   230
13   Organizational Taboos   244
14   Devious Tactics   265

PART V   ANTIDOTES

15   Stemming the Tide of Office Politics   294

     Notes   307

     Bibliography   313

     Index   315

PART I

Understanding
Office Politics

The Inevitability of Office Politics

In an ideal world, everybody would get promoted, receive salary increases, be assigned his or her share of desirable and undesirable assignments, and, in general, receive other goodies strictly on the basis of merit. Nobody would need to curry favor, do handstands to impress the boss, cultivate little people in order to gain their cooperation, smile at the boss despite a hangover, purchase stock in one's own company (even though it's a bad investment), or send a St. Patrick's Day card to a boss named Clancy O'Leary. People would be assigned work and rewarded strictly on the basis of merit. To be successful in business, all one would need would be talent, hard work, and a share of good breaks.

As the world is and has always been constituted, you need one more vital ingredient to get your share of the rewards the world of work has to offer: political knowhow, or the ability to practice sensible office politics. To some, the term office politics connotes deceit, deception, and self-interest. To others, it is an awareness—of the subtle ways of winning favor, advancing your career, and gaining power—inevitable parts of organization life.

Office politics is practiced everywhere. Many a junior executive has joined a golf club with the hope of worming his way into a foursome that includes a key company executive. Many a sales clerk has worn a dress she could not afford (bought from her own store) in order to impress her store manager. Many an intern has complimented his or her chief on the brilliance of his or her diagnostic skills in order to facilitate receiving a favorable future reference. Many a college student has cultivated an outside-of-class friendship with his or her professor in order to create a favorable climate for not receiving a poor grade. Who would downgrade a friend?

Why office politics is omnipresent [1] can be revealed through the case histories of Derek, Mildred, Olaf, Vince, Tom, and Les. Each of these people resorts to politics for one of the six fundamental reasons that office politics is inevitable:

> Power seeking; the existence of jobs for which results are difficult to measure; the emotional insecurity of people; self-interest; people's hunger for acceptance; people's tendency to imitate the behavior of power holders.

DEREK, THE POWER SEEKER

Derek, a 45-year-old sales manager for a tire manufacturer, has a thirst for power that expresses itself in many subtle and some not-so-subtle ways. A visitor to his office can immediately sense Derek's almost immature desire to appear powerful and important. In a company where most managers conduct their work in short sleeves and no jacket, Derek wears a vest and jacket even during the summer. His shirts are French-cuffed; his boots have three-inch heels. Derek's office is uniformly furnished in leather, chrome, and glass. Instead of the ashtray fashioned of a miniature tire found on the coffee tables of his colleagues, he utilizes oversized decorator trays.

Derek's desk consists of a six-foot-long piece of heavy glass placed on top of two chrome sawhorses. Guests have no choice but to sit in chairs set at a level six inches lower than the two chairs Derek uses. Several photos and plaques adorn Derek's wall: One photo shows him—wearing a captain's cap—seated at the helm of a large speedboat; another, shaking hands with the Mayor of Cleveland; a third depicts him standing while his wife and three children are seated. One plaque attests to the extraordinary number of miles he has traveled on one commercial airline. Another plaque gives Derek the accolade, "Outstanding Alumnus Award," based upon both his community activities and his contribution to the alumni fund of his college.

In the 3 years that Derek has been in charge of sales for his company, his total number of subordinates has grown from less than 50 to more than 100. As Gloria, the company personnel manager explains it, much of the growth of Derek's empire is for legitimate business reasons.

> Derek might be accused of being an empire builder, but you cannot justifiably say he is feather-bedding. The marketing and sales department is very efficient. It seems that everybody has a worthwhile function to perform. We get no complaints in the personnel department that people in his area are being under-utilized. It's just that Derek keeps on picking up activities and functions that it could be argued should be reporting somewhere else.

> A case in point is the advertising department. We used to make extensive use of advertising agencies and their facilities. Now we do a good part of our advertising with in-house people. We use agencies more for special promotions and innovative campaigns. Before Derek took over, we had three people in the advertising department. We now have ten. In Derek's defense, our total expenditure for advertising is less than before he revamped our approach to advertising.

A presentation Derek recently made to the president and board of directors of his company further illustrates his mode of operation. Accompanied by his assistant and a neatly organized set of flip charts, Derek tried this gambit:

Ladies and gentlemen, I wouldn't have requested an audience with you unless I thought I had a plan for reorganization that would pay enormous dividends to Superior Tire. As you may know, I have been a student of organization design for many years. The reason I have not asked that the other vice-presidents attend this meeting is that some will be personally affected by my proposed changes. Therefore, they would lack the objectivity necessary to judge my proposal. Self-interest and subjectivity can destroy any sound business proposal. I have seen it happen all too often in the past.

On to the specifics of my proposed reorganization. Everybody in this room realizes what a problem it is to be held accountable for something over which you have too little control. To make a simple analogy, let's assume the coach of a baseball team was reprimanded every time rain forced a postponement of a scheduled game. He would feel frustrated, confused, and helpless. How can you hold a baseball coach responsible for the vagaries of the weather? I ask you, similarly, how can you hold a vice-president of marketing responsible for the whims of the distribution department? My sales force might outsell Hercules tires in a given month, but if we can't get them delivered to where they are needed, when they are needed, our good efforts are nullified. Cancellations because of late delivery are disastrous to our business.

The one logical way to prevent this lack of coordination between sales and distribution is for my department to control distribution. Distribution should report to marketing. When the distribution people boggle a shipment, I want to personally lay them out on the carpet. To make our business run smoothly, they must report to me. Distribution should be working for us. As things stand now, they sometimes try to tell us how much to sell and when to sell it. Ladies and gentlemen, let's put some realism back into the tire business.

Malcolm Bardwell, Chairman of the Board, was the first to speak: "Please, Derek, let's hear your next proposal before we comment on the first one. We need the total picture of what you are proposing to do before we comment on each proposal separately."
Said Derek:

My second proposal is again in the interests of business efficiency. Admittedly, it will increase the stature of marketing, but this is a secondary consideration. As marketing prospers, so does the entire corporation. Remember, we're in business to sell tires and related products to the public. No sales, no company.

From what I can gather, the deal has almost been consummated to acquire a small battery manufacturer in Michigan. We have all agreed that they have a good product that could gain its share of the market and turn in a profit for Superior Tire. My analysis is that they have limped along for several years with a good product, but badly lacking sales support. The tentative plan we have agreed upon is for our tire sales representatives to also sell batteries once the acquisition is consummated. Since Superior will not be altering the battery company except to add sales support, let's make the logical organizational move. I propose that the new subsidiary, Atco Battery, report to the marketing division of our company.

High Level Politics. Derek may or may not get these two sweeping proposals accepted by the board, and thereby add to his empire. What is significant for our purposes is that Derek is making a large-scale political maneuver designed to enlarge his sphere of influence.

He is playing office politics at the highest level. It is precisely this drive for power that is responsible for much of the politicking that takes place in most organizations.[2] Power in an organization is limited. Only so many people can share the power that exists. Derek is trying to increase his power by taking control of another important part of the business—distribution. Recognizing that only so many resources exist at Superior Tire, Derek is cleverly trying to gain control of a new resource—the proposed acquisition, Atco Battery.

UNMEASURABLE MILDRED

Mildred works busily as the public affairs coordinator at Riverview Hospital. Her job description reads, in part, "The public affairs coordinator will foster constructive relationships with influential groups in the community. He or she will insure that the appropriate agencies and individuals recognize the function of Riverview Hospital and appreciate the scope of services it offers." Mildred contends that in practice she is the linking pin between the hospital and the community. Her boss, Chief Hospital Administrator Fred, believes her job is to publicize the hospital in such a way that Riverview gets its share of patients and donations. However, Fred recognizes that it is very difficult to measure the extent to which Mildred is carrying out her function.

Mildred also recognizes that it is difficult to measure her contribution to the hospital. As one antidote to her dilemma, Mildred sends a monthly activity report to Fred, which can be disseminated to other officials at Riverview who care to know what activities the public affairs coordinator is conducting. Last month's activity report included these entries:

- *May 3:* Had lunch with Mrs. Theresa Birdwhistle, local president of the Junior League. It is apparent that the Junior League is seeking to perform for another worthwhile community service activity. I think we have established a climate quite favorable for Birdwhistle and her friends to seriously entertain the possibility of taking on a project of mutual benefit to both Riverview Hospital and the Junior League. Since we are currently over-committed with volunteers, the exact nature of their contribution will have to be determined at a later date.

- *June 22:* Attended a dinner given by the County Medical Society to honor the retirement of 85-year-old Dr. Wendell Watkins, the oldest general practitioner in the county. The after-dinner speaker, Dr. Emily Sparks, introduced a topic concerning the cash position of Riverview. Dr. Sparks said that she believed too many people are using the emergency room facilities of private hospitals in lieu of making daytime appointments with their family physicians. From her standpoint, this is an alarming trend that could affect the future of family medicine. It was apparent that many of the doctors at the meeting concurred with Dr. Sparks.

  I intervened directly, making a minority comment. I expressed the thought that only in a small proportion of cases, according to our hospital records, were essentially healthy people with routine medical concerns using our emergency room facilities at night. In my opinion, I gave both Dr. Sparks and the other members at the meeting a new perspective on the problem.

Mildred has found supplementary ways to cultivate her boss, recognizing that her activity report does not always speak for itself. Asked what special things she does to foster a good relationship with her boss, Mildred was quite specific:

You have to recognize that I would never do anything unprofessional or unethical to help me get along well with Fred. I have enough common sense to realize that there are limits to what I would do to win favor from my boss. A friend of mine was asked by her boss how she liked his new outfit. The man was wearing plaid pants and a striped jacket with a multicolored knit shirt. The combination would have made most people seasick. She replied, "I like your choice of bold colors. It makes you stand out."

My approach to pleasing my boss is not too different from my approach to pleasing the community served by the hospital. I try to establish a favorable climate between my boss and myself. In this way, Fred will view my work with a positive frame of mind. If your boss is neutral or negative toward you as a person, he may fail to appreciate the full extent of your contribution. You might even call the process preconditioning.

One tactic I use is to help Fred with vexing personal problems that might spill over to the job. Through casual conversation, I learned that Fred and his wife were planning a big weekend trip to New York. Their baby-sitter changed her mind at the last minute about taking care of Fred's two children for the weekend. I quickly got in touch with my younger sister who said she would enjoy a weekend baby-sitting assignment. I then told Fred of my sister's availability. He was delighted. Fred and his wife had a wonderful weekend and their children were well taken care of for the time they were gone. As you might imagine, Fred was very appreciative of my efforts. It seemed to add something to our working relationship.

I like horseback riding. It's a truly beautiful sport and not nearly as dangerous as most people think. Fred and his wife are nonriders, but I learned through Fred that his 9-year-old daughter, Phyllis, liked horses. I asked if I might take Phyllis horseback riding as a special treat for her birthday. Fred agreed and Phyllis was thrilled. We've gone riding together three times since. She refers to me as "Aunt Mildred" when she talks about me to her parents.

As Chief Administrator of the hospital, Fred is so busy that he is not always as observant of his subordinates as he should be. My impression is that he needs a little feedback now and then about who is loyal to him and the kind of contribution the people in his department are making. I'm not overly concerned about what others are doing, but I may have found a good third party for getting through to Fred—his wife, Alice.

One day, I called Alice at her home and recommended that we have lunch together. We set a date. At the first lunch, we just exchanged pleasantries and found that we had good rapport. She initiated the next luncheon meeting. At that lunch and the next one, I talked about Fred and the hospital. I mentioned to Alice how much I enjoyed working for a professional administrator like Fred, and what a sense of loyalty I had developed toward him in the 2 years I had been working in his department. Undoubtedly, Alice fed this information back to Fred. I'm sure my comments made him feel good.

There was nothing deceptive in what I did. I do feel loyal toward Fred and I do admire his professionalism. But how do you tell those things directly to your boss? You obviously need a third party to pass along the message.

Perhaps my most constructive approach to winning Fred over to my side was to appeal directly to his professional ego. As part of my normal duties, I meet with representatives of the Rotary, Lions, and Elks clubs. Once, I was introduced to the program chairperson of our downtown Rotary Club, a group with several hundred members. I recommended Fred as a potential luncheon speaker. The program coordinator did contact Fred, who was flattered at the opportunity to make a presentation. Fred performed admirably and was very appreciative that I had recommended him for such an honor.

What Other Step Might Mildred Have Taken. Industrial psychologists who have studied office politics are convinced that unmeasurable jobs lead to the kind of favor-currying activity engaged in by Mildred. When your job results do not speak for themselves, you are placed in the position of trying to convince other people that you are doing a good job. When this does not work (and it usually does not), your alternative is to seek approval from your boss through a variety of not-strictly work-related methods. Mildred's tactics are not properly considered devious. A better approach for Mildred would have been to supplement her politicking by coming to an agreement with Fred as to her specific job duties. For instance, one such job objective might have been to increase the number of donations to the hospital from business and industry. Her performance could then have been measured against that standard.

INSECURE OLAF

Olaf is worried. He worked as a middle manager in a giant corporation, and he is concerned that he is not making a big enough contribution to the corporate effort to be considered a valuable organizational member. Olaf, in fact, thinks he could be squeezed out in the next company retrenchment. His reasoning is not totally unfounded. Olaf is far from being considered a "comer" or "fast tracker" in his company. Instead, his superiors and colleagues consider him to be an average, albeit somewhat insipid, person. He makes few major mistakes but does not come forth with creative contributions.

Olaf has had a lifelong pattern of worrying about whether he is performing well. As a youngster, while playing Little League baseball, he would often glance at the coach for a sign of approval that he had just made the right play. In college, Olaf frequently would ask his professors if he might submit a preliminary draft of a paper to learn if he had a correct understanding of the assignment. When Olaf dated a woman for the first time, he would not kiss her without first asking for, and receiving, her permission.

In his present job as Manager of Spare Parts, Olaf looks for opportunities to gain approval from as many higher-ranking managers as he can. His most irksome ploy is to ask recipients of any report he generates, "What did you think of my report? Was it just the information you needed?" Rather than disappoint Olaf and reply, "Sorry, I haven't read it," most people respond to Olaf's standard question with a reply such as, "Oh, sure, Olaf, it was just what I needed." Such answers give Olaf some relief from his pangs of insecurity.

Olaf's insecurities on the job are best revealed through his use of body language in his contacts with his boss and other individuals of high rank. During a staff meeting, Olaf nods approval and smiles whenever his boss speaks. To Olaf, the boss is always right. A co-worker of Olaf's commented that he would nod more vigorously and smile wider in proportion to the importance and power of the person speaking. In contrast, he usually remained expressionless when a peer or clerk spoke.

Ben, Olaf's immediate boss, soon became annoyed with the latter's insincere smiles and nods. One day, he asked Olaf why he found it necessary to nod with approval at almost everything a manager had to say. Olaf's smile converted to a worrisome expression. He explained, "I don't think I give approval to everything. But it certainly is a good policy to agree with management. If your own subordinates don't agree with you, who will? I'm here to back you up, not tear you down. And one way I can prove that is by showing my appreciation for your words of wisdom. Don't worry, when you or any other manager does say something that I think is unsound, you'll hear from me. Do you understand my reasoning?"

Olaf Is Shortsighted.   In truth, Olaf never would express disagreement with a boss. He is too insecure to be anything but a "yes" person. Olaf's form of office politics has become almost a reflex action. When he spots a person of rank higher than his, his brain sends a message to his body to express approval. Until Olaf becomes a more confident person, he will probably continue to practice his naïve form of office politics. In the long run, his pitiful ploys will be self-defeating. His unwillingness to express approval of what peers have to say is in sharp contrast to his approval of the words of those above him. Because of this tactic, Olaf is on the way to losing the support of his peers—a fatal mistake in any team effort.

SELF-INTERESTED VINCE

Fifty-year-old Vince has worked hard for many years to become a plant manager. Similar to many other people, he is much more interested in his own welfare than that of others in his corporation. Yet, if someone asked Vince if he were more loyal to himself than he is to the company, he would reply, "Count on me, I'm strictly a company man." What Vince says, however, does not dovetail with what he does. Vince's penchant for keeping his own welfare paramount in his business dealings is illustrated in his selection of an assistant manager. A manager who formerly worked for Vince describes the incident in this manner:

My first inkling that Vince was self-protective came about during an expansion phase of our business. At the time, our company had landed a big contract to build small motors for two of the biggest appliance manufacturers. Things were looking good for everybody. When business is booming, people tend to forget their petty grievances; everybody seems to focus on the big problems facing us. If you want to do some bobbing and weaving, it's easier to pull off when things are going well. Management doesn't critically analyze every personnel action you take. My comments lead to the scenario with Vince.

Vince's boss suggested to him that the plant was busy enough to warrant having an assistant plant manager. After some hesitation, Vince agreed that his work load had increased to the point where he could use some assistance. Vince was told that the company reserved assistant plant manager slots for people who seemed to have high potential for holding down executive responsibility in the future. Therefore, Vince was given a choice of hiring Larry or Norm, two younger men in the plant, as his assistant plant manager. Both Larry and Norm had entered the company through the management training program.

Vince told his boss that he would need 30 days to reach a final decision as to whether to hire Larry or Norm. Both men were industrial engineering graduates with both staff and supervisory experience. Vince had some interaction with the two men and had been favorably impressed by both. In his usual systematic approach, Vince began to collect information about the capabilities of the two candidates for the new position.

When Vince asked me about the younger men, I told him quite candidly that I thought Larry was the much stronger individual. I explained that, although Norm made a better appearance and was more articulate, he wasn't a person of great substance. I noticed that Norm tended to back down in any dispute with the union steward. Besides, he didn't seem to be able to establish good working relationships with the supervisors. Despite those criticisms, I did not regard Norm as an incompetent; in my estimation, Larry had more promise.

The next day I had a casual conversation with Jim, the plant superintendent. Jim had worked closely with both Norm and Larry. He shared my opinion. In his words, Norm was more "sizzle" and

Larry was more "steak." It was logical to assume that Larry would become the assistant general manager. Jim and I were both wrong. Three weeks later, Vince announced that Norm was the new assistant plant manager.

It dawned on me as to why Vince had made this move. An assistant plant manager in our company usually had a good shot at taking over the plant manager position. Once in that position, a strong person like Larry might quickly become as capable as his boss. Larry posed a threat to Vince, while Norm did not. As things worked out, Norm became more of a flunkie than a true assistant plant manager.

My suspicions about Vince being more interested in himself than he was in the welfare of the company were further confirmed by an incident involving the manager of quality control, Pete. In my evaluation, Pete was a truly professional quality control manager. He called problems as he saw them. At the time, he was making a big pitch for tighter quality standards on the motors we were building. Because Vince had been responsible for setting the quality standards of the plant in his previous job, Pete's claims were indirectly a criticism of Vince. Therefore, it was in Vince's best interests not to agree that the plant's quality standards were low.

Vince began his anti-Pete campaign with a soft-sell approach. During a luncheon meeting at which Pete was present, Vince smilingly said, "If Pete gets his way, we'll be building motors that will last for 50 years in washing machines built to last 5 years. Our junkyards will be filled with perfect little motors."

Vince's innuendoes about Pete became more vitriolic. I overheard a telephone conversation between Vince and his boss, the division general manager. Vince said something to the effect that Pete was losing perspective—that he was becoming an unrealistic nit-picker just to make a name for himself. Vince's comments had some impact. The final set of quality standards was a compromise between what existed and the new standards suggested by Pete.

Vince's penchant for self-glory finally gave him a corporate black eye that may have leveled off his career for good. The division general manager announced that a new company policy was to take up the slack in any unused manufacturing capability by performing subcontract work for other manufacturers. In other words, we would take on odd jobs for other companies who lacked the capacity to build all the motors demanded by their customers. I attended the meeting in which the division manager asked Vince how interested he would be in taking on some of this subcontract work. Without realizing the implications of what he was saying Vince replied, "That's not exactly the type of activity I prefer for my plant. We could do it in an emergency, but I prefer that we be associated with something a little more glamorous. You can't develop a reputation as a top-flight plant manager by taking on subcontract work." You could see the disdain on the division manager's face from across the room.

Where Vince Went Wrong. Vince's self-interest led him to play office politics. Unfortunately for him, the political strategies he chose were ill-advised. Vince might have fared better if he had chosen a strong assistant plant manager. Subsequently, he might have recommended that the man was ready to manage another plant. Bad-mouthing Pete, the quality control manager, was immature; a better political strategy would have been to admit that times have changed and that tighter standards were in vogue. Adapting to the times is good office politics. Finally, Vince should have grabbed the subcontract assignment. Pleasing your boss is a much surer path to glory than accepting only those assignments you regard as glamorous.

ACCEPTANCE-HUNGRY TOM

In his early years, Tom was a mediocre fellow with few friends and few admirers. Intuitively, almost unconsciously, he recognized that he was never going to be accepted for his feats of accomplishment in business, on the sports field, or in bed. Tom needed other ways of being appreciated, loved, or just plain accepted. The mechanisms he chose to gain acceptance are evident at the office. Over a 15-year time span, Tom has worked his way up the ladder from office boy to supervisor of central duplicating. Tom's department is responsible for all in-house reproduction of reports. He also negotiates with outside printers about his company's printing requirements.

Bev, a machine operator in Tom's department, calls him the Candy Man. She notes:

> I don't know who gave Tom this nickname, but it fits. The guy is lovable. Who can refuse a Candy Man, especially when his candy is free? Every Friday afternoon, Tom comes back from lunch with bags of candy. He keeps some on his desk, just lying there for the freeloaders. But he also flits around to all the desks in our department, handing out candy. The people who smile the most get the most expensive candy. But even if you half-ignore Tom, you're likely to wind up with a sour ball or a lollipop on your desk.
>
> On Valentine's Day, Halloween, and around Christmas time, the Candy Man is at his busiest. He must spend 2 days' pay on his candy collection. So as not to offend anyone, Tom has also added some Chanukah food treats to his collection.
>
> Randy, one of the three supervisors reporting to Tom, calls him the Yankee Clipper. I asked Randy why somebody would call a person in charge of the duplicating department the same nickname as that given to Joe DiMaggio, an all-time, great baseball

player. Randy replied, "It's kind of a nice little joke. A Yankee is supposed to be frugal. A clipper could also be somebody who clips things. Well, Tom clips coupons to save money. He doesn't cash in these coupons himself. Instead, he provides this coupon-clipping service for women in the office who are interested in saving these coupons. The women who use his coupons think Tom is the kindest man in the company. By rotating the most valuable coupons among different women, Tom avoids being accused of favoritism."

The name Yankee Clipper has another important connotation in reference to Tom. He also clips magazine and newspaper articles that he thinks might be of interest to key people in the company. I suppose it's kind of a valuable service. Let's assume that Tom learns that our company is thinking of opening a branch in Düsseldorf, West Germany. The executive in charge of that project will soon find in his office mail—neatly mounted on a sheet of paper—several timely articles about West Germany. Tom isn't pushy about the matter. He makes a notation that the clipping is just for the reader's potential interest.

I heard that one of Tom's clippings led to a giant sales contract for our firm. Tom discovered that the Postal Service was going to have a large, new building constructed sometime in the future. The clipping led our company to being the prime contractor on the piping for the building.

Is Tom So Foolish?   An acceptance-hungry person such as Tom is an easy target for castigation. Yet, is Tom practicing sensible or senseless office politics? In my opinion, Tom's approach to gaining acceptance from others is naïve, yet harmless. Passing out candy and coupons on company time may not be in the best interests of company efficiency; however, it is doubtful that he wastes more time than others during the work day. His news clipping service seems to serve the corporate good. Recognizing that Tom will never be an executive or a prominent person, his approach to gaining favor is suited to his life-style. Psychologically, Tom is a little person. His political strategies for gaining favor are suited to such an individual and he is choosing office politics suited to his aims. All he wants from the office is a decent job, a regular pay check, and the acceptance of his co-workers.

IMITATIVE LES

Les is a survivalist. He apes behavior patterns that he thinks will keep him in the good graces of the power-holders in his company. Imitating the office politics practiced by his company's executive is not the primary factor that has promoted Les to director of financial services. He is talented and hard-working. But Les believes that copying certain accepted actions (by the company's executives) prevents him from drawing unfavorable attention to himself.

Michelle, the company recruiter for professional and technical personnel, uncovered an interesting manifestation of Les's political ploys. Part of Michelle's job was to recruit into the corporation young college-trained accountants, many of whom were targeted for Les's department. Les rejected two consecutive candidates Michelle submitted for his approval. Concerned, Michelle invited Les to lunch to discuss the situation. Before they had finished the first martini, Les confided in Michelle:

"You've worked very hard on behalf of my department, and I like you as an individual. So I'll be honest with you, Michelle. You are sending me the wrong type of job candidates. I have no doubt that the two last candidates you sent me could perform the job. They seemed bright enough and I am sure they can get along with people."

"Then what are your objections to them? Has it anything to do with their ethnic backgrounds? Do they have any annoying habits or mannerisms?"

"Not at all, Michelle. It's just that I want to recruit into my department the same type of people the people in power around here are looking for. The president believes that only people with MBA degrees from the top five business schools should be invited into our company in beginning professional jobs. One of these fellows lacked an MBA and the other came from a school in Pennsylvania that I had never heard of."

A person who meets Les for the first time in his office might be perplexed by his appearance. Les wears expensive Italian-style suits with broad, upturned shoulders and Italian-style shoes to match, accompanied by flamboyant silk ties. Les's attire would be stunning if worn by a well-built IBM salesman or an equally well-built clothing designer. Yet on roly-poly Les, this high-fashion clothing is wasted. Out of curiosity I asked Les how long he had been wearing his present style of clothing. Nondefensively, he said:

> Ever since I became director of financial services. I don't much care for these suits myself and my wife says I look much better in more traditional suits. However, if you'll notice, every executive in this company wears Italian- or French-styled suits. I wouldn't enter the office in a suit that I bought for less than $300. Why wear clothing that contrasts sharply to the style favored by our executive team?

Les Is a Borderline Case. Les is playing politics by imitating what he sees taking place in the executive suite. He is playing it safe by attempting to recruit only those people who would have been recruited by his superiors. Instead of blindly following the lead of his superiors, Les might have asked a few key executives if they had any particular hiring policies for young professional people. These executives might have welcomed a questioning of their present informal policies.

Les's attempt to dress in a manner similar to his superiors was a sensible strategy, poorly implemented. He was dressing expensively, not appropriately.[3] He was draping himself in clothing that did not fit his physique. A workable compromise for Les would have been to *modify* his clothing in the direction of the style worn by his superiors.

Derek, Mildred, Olaf, Vince, Tom, and Les all practice office politics. Each uses a different set of tactics. Each achieves slightly different results. It might be time for you to take a candid look at your own proclivities toward office politics. Self-examination in this area might heighten your chances of winning at office politics.

How Political Are You?

A predisposition to play office politics can best be measured in degrees. Some people are totally political. Everything they do at work has the ulterior motive of making them look good or advancing their cause. At the other extreme are completely ingenuous, non-political individuals whose primary concern is getting the job done. Most people fall somewhere between these two extremes. I have constructed a 100-item questionnaire to help you measure your tendencies toward being an office politician. Every question contained in the Office Politics Questionnaire relates to some important facet of office politics.[1, 2] The more candid you are in filling out this form, the more accurately you will be able to measure your tendencies toward being a power seeker or an office politician.

THE OFFICE POLITICS QUESTIONNAIRE

Directions. Answer each of the following statements mostly true or mostly false. We are looking for general trends; therefore, do not be concerned if you are uncertain as to whether you answer true mostly or mostly false on each one of the questions. In answering each question, assume that you are taking this questionnaire with the intent of learning something about yourself. Only you will see the results. *Do not* assume you are taking this questionnaire as part of the screening process for a job you want.

	Mostly True	Mostly False
1. The boss is always right.	———	———
2. It is wise to flatter important people.	———	———
3. Power for its own sake is one of life's most precious commodities.	———	———
4. If you are even one-eighth American Indian, mention it on your resume (assuming you believed it would increase your chance of getting the job you wanted).	———	———
5. I would ask my boss's opinion about personal matters (such as life insurance or real estate) although I didn't need his advice.	———	———
6. If I had the skills, I would help the president of my company with his or her furniture refinishing hobby on a Sunday afternoon.	———	———
7. Dressing for success is a sham. Wear clothing to the office that you find to be the most comfortable.	———	———
8. If I were aware that an executive in my company was stealing money, I would use that information against him or her in asking for favors.	———	———
9. I would invite my boss to a party in my home even if I didn't like him or her.	———	———
10. A woman shouldn't flirt with executives in the company just to gain advantage.	———	———
11. One should know why people are one's friends.	———	———
12. If my boss were a prominent person, I would voluntarily start a scrapbook about him or her.	———	———

	Mostly True	Mostly False
13. Given a choice, take on only those assignments which will make you look good.	____	____
14. I would never tell my boss what some of my co-workers really thought about him or her (if the opinion was negative).	____	____
15. If someone higher-up than you on the organizational ladder offends you, let him or her know about it.	____	____
16. I like the idea of keeping a "blunder file" about the competition for potential future use.	____	____
17. I would have an affair with the company president's spouse if I were attracted to that person and he or she was willing.	____	____
18. Most people at work cannot be trusted.	____	____
19. One should tell the truth, or not, depending on how others are affected.	____	____
20. Honesty is the best policy in practically all cases.	____	____
21. Don't tell anyone at work anything that he or she could conceivably use against you in the future.	____	____
22. One should personally select the subordinates upon whom one's success greatly depends.	____	____
23. If you have to punish somebody, do it all at once.	____	____
24. Act and look cool even when you don't feel that way.	____	____
25. Bluffing, in the long run, is self-defeating.	____	____
26. If I worked for a shirt or blouse manufacturer, I would never wear a competitive brand to the office.	____	____
27. If you disagreed with an action		

	Mostly True	Mostly False

taken by your boss, it would be a poor strategy to complain to an acquaintance on the board of directors. ___ ___

28. Given the opportunity, I would help my boss build some shelves in his or her den. ___ ___

29. Why bother cultivating the minnows in my company? It's the big fish I'm after. ___ ___

30. Before taking any action at work, think how it might be interpreted by key people. ___ ___

31. People will remember you longer if you do nice things for them. Therefore, I try to be as nice as possible to everybody. ___ ___

32. I would attend a company picnic even if I had the chance to do something I enjoyed much more that day. ___ ___

33. If necessary, I would say rotten things about a rival in order to attain a promotion. ___ ___

34. If a customer was pleased with the way I handled his account, I would ask him to write a complimentary note to my boss. ___ ___

35. Even if you make a poor showing, it is worthwhile to compete. ___ ___

36. It is necessary to lie once in a while in business. ___ ___

37. If you have important confidential information, release it to your advantage. ___ ___

38. Accept advice willingly; don't obscure the issue by questioning why you are being given advice. ___ ___

39. The best way to handle people is to tell them what they want to hear. ___ ___

	Mostly True	Mostly False
40. It is important to have lunch with the "right people" at least twice a month.	——	——
41. How you accomplish something is much more important than what you accomplish.	——	——
42. Do not simply wound an enemy. Shoot to kill.		
43. If your rival for a promotion is making a big mistake, why tell him or her?	——	——
44. A person who is able and willing to work hard will succeed in business most of the time.	——	——
45. If I wanted to show up someone, I would be willing to write memos documenting his or her mistakes.	——	——
46. If I had a legitimate gripe about my place of work, I would air my views publicly (such as writing a letter to the editor of a local newspaper).	——	——
47. Before you write a final report to your boss, find out what he or she really wants to see included in that report.	——	——
48. I would be willing to say nice things about a rival with the intent of getting him or her transferred away from my department.	——	——
49. I would stay late in the office just to impress my boss.	——	——
50. Why teach your subordinates everything you know about your job? He or she could then replace you.	——	——
51. All in all, it is better to be humble and honest than to be important and dishonest.	——	——
52. Do not enter into a cooperative venture if it means that you are going to risk personal advantage.	——	——

	Mostly True	Mostly False
53. I have no interest in using gossip for personal advantage.	——	——
54. While on vacation, it's a smart idea to pick up a small gift for your boss.	——	——
55. Don't be a complainer. It may be held against you.	——	——
56. Past promises need not stand in the way of success.	——	——
57. It is necessary to keep some people in place by making them afraid of you.	——	——
58. It is wise never to let one's reputation be fully tested.	——	——
59. I would get drunk with my boss if I thought it would help me get ahead.	——	——
60. Reading about office politics is as much fun as reading an adventure story.	——	——
61. Jack wants to be a hero so he creates a crisis for his company and then resolves it. His strategy is, at least, worth a try.	——	——
62. I would go out of my way to cultivate friendships with powerful people.	——	——
63. I would never raise questions about the capabilities of my competition. Let his or her record speak for itself.	——	——
64. Keep a few secrets in your head. It is a bad idea to put everything in writing.	——	——
65. If you have an acid tongue, display it proudly at the office.	——	——
66. If I were a tournament-level golf player and my boss were a duffer, I would gladly team with him or her in a golf match.	——	——
67. I would have an affair with a		

	Mostly True	Mostly False
powerful person in my company, if I thought it would help my career.	___	___
68. I am unwilling to take credit for someone else's work.	___	___
69. If someone compliments you for a task that is another's accomplishment, smile and say thank you.	___	___
70. If I discovered that a co-worker was looking for a new job, I would inform my boss.	___	___
71. Even if you made only a minor contribution to an important project, get your name listed as being associated with that project.	___	___
72. It is only necessary to play office politics if you are an incompetent.	___	___
73. If you have injured a rival, get him or her removed from the scene if it is at all possible.	___	___
74. There is nothing wrong with tooting your own horn.	___	___
75. It's a good idea to use the same jargon your boss does, despite the fact that you dislike jargon.	___	___
76. I like to keep my office cluttered with personal mementos such as pencil holders and ashtrays made by my children. By doing so, my office doesn't seem so cold and businesslike.	___	___
77. Once you have offended someone, never entrust him or her with something important.	___	___
78. One should take action only when sure that it is morally correct.	___	___
79. Only a fool would correct mistakes made by the boss.	___	___
80. I would purchase stock in my company even though it might not be a good investment.	___	___
81. I would never use personal influence to gain a promotion.	___	___

	Mostly Time	Mostly False
82. If I wanted something done by a co-worker, I would be willing to say, "If you don't get this done, our boss might be very unhappy."	____	____
83. Even if I thought it would help my career, I would not take on a hatchet-man assignment.	____	____
84. It is much safer to be feared than loved by your subordinates.	____	____
85. If I were looking for a new hobby, I would think first of trying out my boss' favorite.	____	____
86. Only a small minority of people act out of self-interest.	____	____
87. Although you have to resort to speculation, make up some financial figures to prove the value of your proposal.	____	____
88. Once you become the boss, transfer from your department anyone who you suspect does not like you.	____	____
89. If you dislike a particular man in your firm, don't send him a congratulatory note when he receives a big promotion.	____	____
90. I laugh heartily at my boss's jokes even when I think they are not funny.	____	____
91. It is difficult to get ahead without cutting corners here and there.	____	____
92. I would first learn of my boss's political preferences before discussing politics with him or her.	____	____
93. If you do somebody a favor, remember to cash in on it.	____	____
94. I would be careful not to hire a subordinate with a more formal education than my own.	____	____
95. Never tell anyone the real reasons you do something unless it is useful to do so.	____	____

	Mostly True	Mostly False
96. A wise strategy is to keep on good terms with everybody in your office.	___	___
97. People are generally trying to win favorable comparison over others.	___	___
98. All forms of office politics boil down to ass-kissing.		
99. If apple-polishing helps me, I'll polish apples.	___	___
100. My primary job is to please my boss.	___	___

SCORING YOUR ANSWERS

Give yourself a plus one for each answer you gave in agreement with the keyed answer. Note that we did not use the term *correct* answer. Whether an answer is correct is a question of personal values and ethics. Each question that receives a score of plus one shows a tendency *toward* playing office politics or grabbing for power. The scoring key is as follows:

Question Number	Political Answer	Question Number	Political Answer
1.	Mostly True	17.	Mostly False
2.	Mostly True	18.	Mostly True
3.	Mostly True	19.	Mostly True
4.	Mostly True	20.	Mostly False
5.	Mostly True	21.	Mostly True
6.	Mostly True	22.	Mostly True
7.	Mostly False	23.	Mostly True
8.	Mostly True	24.	Mostly True
9.	Mostly True	25.	Mostly False
10.	Mostly False	26.	Mostly True
11.	Mostly True	27.	Mostly False
12.	Mostly True	28.	Mostly True
13.	Mostly True	29.	Mostly True
14.	Mostly False	30.	Mostly True
15.	Mostly False	31.	Mostly True
16.	Mostly True	32.	Mostly True

Question Number	Political Answer	Question Number	Political Answer
33.	Mostly True	67.	Mostly True
34.	Mostly True	68.	Mostly False
35.	Mostly False	69.	Mostly True
36.	Mostly True	70.	Mostly True
37.	Mostly True	71.	Mostly True
38.	Mostly False	72.	Mostly False
39.	Mostly True	73.	Mostly True
40.	Mostly True	74.	Mostly True
41.	Mostly False	75.	Mostly True
42.	Mostly True	76.	Mostly False
43.	Mostly True	77.	Mostly True
44.	Mostly False	78.	Mostly False
45.	Mostly True	79.	Mostly True
46.	Mostly False	80.	Mostly True
47.	Mostly True	81.	Mostly False
48.	Mostly True	82.	Mostly True
49.	Mostly True	83.	Mostly False
50.	Mostly True	84.	Mostly True
51.	Mostly False	85.	Mostly True
52.	Mostly True	86.	Mostly False
53.	Mostly False	87.	Mostly True
54.	Mostly True	88.	Mostly True
55.	Mostly True	89.	Mostly False
56.	Mostly True	90.	Mostly True
57.	Mostly True	91.	Mostly True
58.	Mostly True	92.	Mostly True
59.	Mostly True	93.	Mostly True
60.	Mostly True	94.	Mostly True
61.	Mostly True	95.	Mostly True
62.	Mostly True	96.	Mostly True
63.	Mostly False	97.	Mostly True
64.	Mostly True	98.	Mostly False
65.	Mostly False	99.	Mostly True
66.	Mostly True	100.	Mostly True

INTERPRETING YOUR SCORE

Your total score on the Office Politics Questionnaire provides you a rough index of your overall tendencies toward being an office politician. The higher you score, the more political you are in your dealings at work.

The lower your score, the less you are inclined toward political maneuvering. A more precise method of interpreting your score is to place it in one of the five categories: Machiavelli, Company Politician, Survivalist, Straight Arrow, or Innocent Lamb.

Machiavellian. If you scored 90 or more points on the questionnaire, you have an almost uncontrollable tendency toward doing things for political reasons. A Machiavelli is a power-hungry, power-grabbing individual. People who fall into this category are often perceived by others as being ruthless, devious, and power-crazed. It would not be out of character for a Machiavelli to use electronic surveillance devices to gain advantage over rivals. Machiavellis will try to succeed in their careers at any cost to others.

A Machiavelli is often a sycophant during his or her climb to power. If it appears to be advantageous, a Machiavelli will fawn over a superior whom he or she hates. A person with strong lust for power will voluntarily discredit the rival of a boss. One such sycophant hired a detective to uncover derogatory information about a new company manager who posed a threat to his boss.

A person falling into the Machiavellian category of our questionnaire lives in constant peril. He or she usually has created a number of enemies on the way to the top. If you are a Machiavelli, there are probably people right now who are plotting revenge. When a Machiavelli begins to slip from power, there are a number of people lurking in the background to give him or her that last definitive shove.

Suppose you scored 100 on the Office Politics Questionnaire. This would indicate an obsession with power and politics so overwhelming that it would be crippling. It would be difficult to get your legitimate tasks accomplished because of your preoccupation with weighing the political consequences of your every action. For example: Unless you established an elaborate record-keeping system, you would soon forget what self-serving lie you told to whom.

Company Politician. If you scored between 75 and 89 points, you fall into the Company Politician category. A person of this nature might be described as a shrewd maneuverer and politico: someone who, typically, lands on both feet when deposed from a particular situation. Many successful executives fall into this category. A Company Politician is much like a Machiavelli, except that the former has a better developed sense of morality. A Company Politician lusts for power, but it is not an all-consuming preoccupation. Many Company Politicians will do whatever they can to advance their cause except to deliberately defame or injure another individual. You have to be insightful to be a Company Politician. Before utilizing a political strategy such as keeping a blunder file on others, you would have to determine if the organization would tolerate such shenanigans.

If you want to climb the organizational ladder, your chances would generally be best if you were a moderate Company Politician—someone who scored in the 75-85 range. A score of 89 suggests that you might ultimately trip over your own ruthlessness.

Survivalist. A person with a score of 50-75 falls into the Survivalist category. If you placed here, you probably practice enough office politics to take advantage of good opportunities. You are not concerned about making any obvious political blunders such as upstaging your boss in an interdepartmental meeting. You laugh at your boss's jokes when salary review time rolls around. If your boss invited you to a church breakfast you would not say, "No, thanks, I'm an atheist." As a survivalist, you probably practice enough office politics to keep you out of trouble with your boss and other people of higher rank than yourself. A Survivalist would send a gift to a boss's newborn baby, even if he or she did not care for babies. But a Survivalist would send a gift to a boss's newborn baby, godmother or godfather. Such antics are practiced by the Machiavelli.

Straight Arrow. A score of 35-49 places you in the Straight Arrow category. Such an individual would not be perceived by others as being an office politician. Nor would he or she be seen as a person intent on committing political suicide. A Straight Arrow fundamentally believes that most people are honest, hardworking, and trustworthy. A Straight Arrow's favorite career-advancement strategy is to display job competence. In the process, a Straight Arrow (particularly one who scores in the 35-40 range) may neglect other important career-advancement strategies such as cultivating key people.

Innocent Lamb. Scores of less than 35 place you in the bottom category of political savvy. An Innocent Lamb believes all organizations to be meritocracies; that good people are rewarded for their efforts and thus rise to the top. His or her only political strategy is "By Their Works Ye Shall Know Them." Thus the Lamb keeps his or her eyes focused clearly on the task at hand, hoping that someday his or her hard work will be rewarded. Innocent Lambs with an abundance of talent do—occasionally—make it to the top. (Star athletes and inventors are sometimes Innocent Lambs.) Unless you happen to have such extraordinary aptitude, it is difficult to advance in your career by practicing the Innocent Lamb philosophy of life.

The aged messenger boy referred to in the Preface to this book was an Innocent Lamb. Forced into retirement at age 55, he boasted of never having practiced office politics a day in his life. A person who scored zero on the Office Politics Questionnaire is best suited for work that is 100 percent technical, involving no interaction with people. A geological engineer who makes one yearly visit with his or her boss might fit this description.

Few readers of this book are likely to be Innocent Lambs for, if you were, the very subject of office politics might be so repugnant to you that, instead of this book, you would choose one about business ethics or management science.

If you happen to be an Innocent Lamb, you need to read this book for self-protection. As a Straight Arrow, Survivalist, or Office Politician you might want to read the rest of this book to become even more knowledgeable about winning (and losing) strategies of office politics. If you are a Machiavelli, you might want to finish this book to find out if there is any strategy someone else is using that you have missed.

Sizing Up the Political Climate

Before jumping head first into the political fray, it is imperative that you size up the playing field. Office politics is always played within the context of an organization. You must understand that context to choose winning political strategies. In one company, it might be considered wise political strategy to purchase a house in the same neighborhood as the chief executive officer. In another company, that same maneuver might be considered pushy and offensive. In the former situation, you have improved your chances for success; in the latter, you have decreased them.

Sizing up the political climate to determine what types of political strategies are likely to work best for you is an important—but not sufficient—condition for becoming a first-rate office politician. You also have to apply your political ploy with sensitivity and tact. Suppose you discover that your boss is receptive to feedback from you about the attitudes of other members of the department toward him. It would be inadvisable to provide him a five-page document about how the other people in the department see him. Your best chances for capitalizing on this strategy would be if you used offhand verbal comments rather than written reports. A cagey manager would not want there to be written evidence that he or she engages in this kind of intrigue.

FIRST CHECK OUT NEPOTISM

Ideally, the best time to size up the political climate of an organization is before you become a member. If your aspirations are high, it is wise to determine if nonfamily members have an equal chance for success. Believers in a meritocracy think that only small family businesses and the governments of tiny municipalities still practice nepotism. How could a large organization find enough family members to staff its key jobs? The answer is that the ranks of blood relatives and those through marriage are combed to find reasonably competent people for important positions. Often a distant relative is recruited into the fold if his or her services are needed by the organization.

Toby Checks Out Nepotism.   Toby, an ambitious and forthright young man, was offered a position as a sales representative with Farnsworth Metal Fabricating Company. Said Toby, gleefully:

> This is the opportunity I've been waiting for. Farnsworth is a medium-sized company specializing in low-priced, foreign steel products. They will shortly be expanding into new markets in the Midwest, Ontario, and the East Coast. Within a few years, I expect to become a sales manager. But before I accept an offer, I'm going to check out if anybody but a Farnsworth can get ahead at the company.

Toby's next step was to find, and peruse, a company telephone directory. He reported back to his wife:

> Honey, I think I've found the right company. I could locate only three people named Farnsworth in the company. One person is Byron Farnsworth, the president, whom they tell me is aged 66 and overdue for retirement. The second is Elton Farns-

worth, the manager of manufacturing. He is 45, but since he works in manufacturing and not sales, I can hardly consider him a potential competitor for future openings in the sales area. Gail is the third Farnsworth. She is a kindly, white-haired woman in charge of the company books. I doubt that, at her age and with her experience, she will be in line for key jobs in the future of the company.

Toby Should Have Asked More Questions. After three months on the job, Toby discovered some good and bad news. The good news was that he correctly sized up Farnsworth Metal Fabricating as an aggressive company with a bright future. A new $4 million facility was planned for Ontario within the next year. Business was booming. The bad news was that three senior people in the company would be retiring within a year. Replacements for all three executives were announced. Each replacement was married to a Farnsworth daughter.

Toby's analysis was too superficial. He neglected to inquire about the number of family members—through marriage—who worked for the company. Old Mr. Farnsworth had four daughters, one of whom was a college senior interested in business. Either she or any man she might marry could, conceivably, block opportunities for outsiders. Toby relied exclusively on a telephone directory as a source of information about nepotism in the company. Before he joined them, Toby should have questioned several company employees or suppliers about the extent to which it was a family company. Toby's career was not doomed, but he was losing precious time in his quest to move up the ladder.

SIZING UP YOUR BOSS

Office politics begins with making a favorable impression on your boss, once you have determined what impresses him. If you work for a boss long enough, you will (most likely) learn what pleases him or her, but long *enough* may be *too* long. You are better advised if early in your relationship, you find answers to ten significant questions about your boss. Answers can be found through direct observation, gentle questioning of your boss, or by asking the questions of co-workers and his or her secretary. If you intend to win at office politics, find answers to these questions soon.

1. *What mission is my boss trying to accomplish?* The key to creating a favorable impression upon your boss is to help him or her accomplish the most important task facing the department. In some fields, the answer to this question is straightforward. If you were a professional hockey player, it would be safe to assume that your boss was trying to win hockey games. In other situations, your boss's true mission may be less obvious. In some instances your boss may be intentionally inefficient. Efficiency might lead to a cutback in funds.

Bud, a training director, presented a proposal to his boss, Myra, which, on the surface, seemed quite logical. It described a training program in transactional analysis for first-line supervisors that could be conducted by members of the existing training staff.

Enthusiastically, Bud said to Myra, "I casually mentioned my proposal to the vice-president of Personnel the other day when I met him in the cafeteria. I could see his eyes light up when I emphasized that our own staff could conduct the program."

Myra eyed Bud with a concerned expression on her face, saying:

How nice that you prematurely spoke to Mr. Gray about your proposal for a completely in-house program. What you failed to realize is that I'm trying to obtain a 100 percent increase in our budget for the next year. We need an enlarged staff and the funds to hire some outside consultants to lend status to our programs. Your proposal runs counter to what I'm trying to accomplish for the year. In short, Bud, the program you proposed is not what I had in mind for our department.

2. *What practices by subordinates usually irritate my boss?* Avoid annoying someone you are trying to impress. If your boss prefers telephone conversations rather than memos, keep memos to the absolute minimum. If your boss prefers that people do not smoke in his or her office, get your nicotine fix before you visit the boss's office.

Alison, a young reporter, landed a job with her local newspaper, the *Observer Dispatch*. She and her school friends had always affectionately called the newspaper, "The O.D." Her first day, Alison noted that her boss cringed when a visitor to the office asked, "What is the circulation of the O.D." The boss replied, "The latest figures indicate that the *Observer Dispatch* reaches 95,000 families."

When asked by her boss how she enjoyed her first full day working for the newspaper, Alison replied without a wince, "So far, it looks as though I'm going to enjoy being a reporter for the *Observer Dispatch*." Her boss smiled and Alison had started her journalism career on a positive note.

3. *Does your boss accept compliments graciously?* Psychologists repeatedly have demonstrated that virtually all people enjoy receiving compliments. But "virtually all" does not mean everybody. It is to your political advantage to observe how your boss receives compliments before praising his or her ordinary actions. It is not unknown for a boss to sometimes be rebuffed by a compliment. Gordie, a factory accountant, worked for Larry, a gruff plant superintendent. In order to prepare his weekly report, Gordie needed to obtain some production figures from Larry. Trying to establish a favorable relationship between himself and Larry, Gordie commented to the latter, "You sure look great today, Larry. You're sun-tanned and your suit is the latest style." With a gruffer-than-usual look on his face,

Larry retorted, "Stop kissing my ass and get on with your work."

4. *Who are your boss's enemies?* [1] An astute office politician learns early in the game not to make favorable comments about the boss's enemies. Assuming you are on good terms with your boss's secretary ask her (or in a few instances, *him*) who the boss likes the least. Or, ask your boss which departments cooperate least with your department. Usually, "lack of cooperation" means that your boss is involved in a continuing conflict with that department head.

Tim, an account executive in an advertising agency, noted in a staff meeting that his boss, Jerry, and Gunther, another account supervisor, clashed. Hoping to foster a good relationship with his boss, Tim asked Jerry if he had a moment to spare.

Said Jerry, "What's up, Tim?"

"You may not have heard this yet, Jerry," said Tim, "but just in case you didn't, I thought you might get a charge out of it. Gunther's department seems to have gone off the deep end. I think they want to either set back advertising ten years or put us out of business. Maybe both. Gunther is proposing that our agency set up a product-testing laboratory at our expense. We would then subject each product that we are currently advertising, or propose to advertise, to extensive product testing. We would then advertise only those products that survived our scrutiny. I wonder if Gunther thinks we are the Environmental Protection Agency instead of an advertising agency."

"That *is* a good one, Tim," said Jerry. "At times, I wonder about Gunther myself. If he keeps thinking like that, I may have to talk to our president about him. Any other tidbits?"

5. *What is the most vexing problem facing my boss?* An astute career-minded person gives top job priority to those problems of biggest concern to his or her boss. It makes both political and common sense to tackle those problems. If you find a solution, you will be highly valued by your boss. If you find no solution,

you will still be well regarded for having tried, providing you do not exacerbate the problem in the process. When your boss fails to tell you his or her biggest problem, it's up to you to find out.

Ed, a middle manager in a government agency, joined his boss, Jim, for lunch. Having read about the importance of becoming a crucial subordinate, Ed asked Jim, "What should I be doing to help the agency run more smoothly?"

"Truthfully," replied Jim, "We are facing a rather bizarre problem that can be best described as an embarrassment of riches. We have an $8,000 surplus in our budget. If I turn it in at the end of the fiscal year —which is 2 months from now—our budget for next year will probably be shot down by that amount. Of course, we can't do anything frivolous with the surplus—such as purchasing some elaborate new furniture or a special vehicle for our department—and hiring another clerk is out since there is now a hiring freeze in our branch of the government."

"Give me 24 hours," commented Ed, "I may have an honorable solution to our problem." Immediately after lunch, Ed made a phone call to an acquaintance whose agency had faced a similar problem. The next morning Ed reported back to Jim with his findings. His recommendation: Spend the $8,000 for a consulting study of the effectiveness of Ed's department in carrying out its mission. The money in the budget would then be used in an acceptable way that had considerable precedent in government. Jim accepted Ed's idea, and it worked. The consultants made their study, the department used up its budget almost to the penny, the results of the study were useful, and Ed received a superior rating on the next performance review.

6. *What are important personal facts about my boss?* The smaller your boss's mind, the more important it is to remember personal facts about him or her such as his or her birth date, names of family members (including household pets), favorite sports, hobbies, personal gifts, and colors. You have to tread lightly in capitaliz-

ing on this information; otherwise, you will appear to be a servile flatterer.

Luke was a work shirker in a glass factory. He played office politics to avoid work rather than to advance his career. Luke's idea of nirvana was to sack out in the cool store room on a hot summer's day. Bothered by a bad back, Luke also tried to avoid assignments that required heavy lifting. To stay on the payroll without having to put in a full day's work, Luke did what he could to cultivate the friendship of Walt, his boss.

Luke's ploy was to be extra nice to the Doberman pinschers Walt proudly owned. Almost monthly, Luke would bring Walt a small gift for his two prize animals. The gifts were inexpensive but thoughtful, including a teething ring and a rubber cat. Luke became convinced that the interest he showed in Wolfgang and Beethoven (the two Dobermans) helped him avoid having to carry a full work load.

7. *What does my boss regard as good performance?* A serious practitioner of office politics finds a good answer to this question early in a relationship with the boss. The answer may not always be as obvious as it sounds. Your analysis of what constitutes good performance does not always coincide with that of your boss. Subjective judgment is called for in evaluating many types of higher-level jobs.

Mandi graduated in the top third of her class in law school. Her best job offer was from the small legal department within a large business firm. After a 1-month orientation on the job, enterprising Mandi swung into action. She began to cultivate clients throughout the corporation, extolling the capabilities of the company legal department. She sent clippings from legal journals and newspapers that illustrated the legal implications of business decisions to various executives. Within 3 months, business was booming in the company legal department. Executives were asking questions such as "Are there any legal consequences to offering price reductions for customers who receive shipments direct from our factory?" and "Is it legal for the company not to list a gay marriage in the section of the company newspaper that lists employee marriages?" In addition, executives throughout the company were now asking questions such as "Can I write off part of my summer cottage as a business expense if I use it to demonstrate our line of motor boats to customers?"

Pleased with her performance, Mandi asked her boss, "How do you like the results I have been achieving? It's obvious from the activity of our department that our executive team is becoming much more sensitive to legal problems."

Her boss replied, "Please Mandi, stop your public relations campaign right now. We have a small department that is supposed to work on only a handful of intricate legal questions faced by the corporation. Certainly we are not a company-sponsored legal clinic. If you don't slow down your public relations activity, we'll soon have a waiting room full of employees wanting to discuss their pending divorces with us."

8. *What forms of office politics does your boss practice?* A cautious guideline is to assume that the type of office politics practiced by your boss is the type of office politics he or she considers acceptable and would consider acceptable for a subordinate to use. Smart politics should include those practices condoned by your boss. He or she may use a particular political strategy, probably considering it good human relations rather than office politics. Therefore, to strengthen your relationship with your boss, a good starting point is to practice his or her brand of office politics.

Ray was placed in charge of conducting company attitude surveys for both managers and nonmanagers with the idea of uncovering the morale problems within the management ranks. Ray's department would then alert top management to these problems with the intent of taking constructive action on the most pressing issues. Ray excitedly told Perry, his boss, about a new form of attitude survey he planned to conduct: one that was elaborate and scientifically developed.

Perry said, "Not a bad idea, Ray. Run your survey if it pleases you. But remember, the best way of finding out what's disquieting our management team is to increase your bar bill."

"I don't understand. How can increasing a bar bill help uncover morale problems?"

"Simple," explained Perry, "I systematically invite a large number of managers, one at a time, for a drink after work. I do this about three late afternoons per week. The results of the survey can then be used to verify the problems I have uncovered in the bar. Besides, I cultivate a lot of supporters for our programs this way."

Ray joined in the fun without sacrificing his professional scruples. He did conduct his scientific-type surveys. Ray's new wrinkle was to flush out the results of his survey with the alcohol-facilitated comments made by managers who joined him regularly for after-work cocktails. When Ray and Perry were finished with their respective informal interviews, they would frequently join each other for a final cocktail before heading home to the suburbs.

9. *Does your boss welcome conferring with subordinates?* Managers vary widely in the amount of time they are willing to spend in conference with subordinates. Some managers feel busy and productive when placed in one-on-one relationships with the people they supervise. Others enjoy calling frequent small meetings to confer about both important and trivial problems. Still other managers believe that mature and competent subordinates spend most of the time working independently. It is to your advantage to learn of your boss's stated or unstated position on this important matter.

Mike, a middle manager and second-rate office politician, was apprehensive about the arrival of Dave, the new vice-president of manufacturing, to whom he would report. "I had better get a relationship going with him right away before the barracudas in my department get to him first," Mike told his wife. A barracuda himself without realizing it, Mike began his campaign to cultivate a good relationship with his boss. He made two trips a day to his new boss's office. Once, the excuse was to hand-deliver an important message to Dave's secretary. (Its contents were so consequential, thought Mike, that interoffice mail was too slow to do it justice.) Twice the excuse was "Dave, I just happened to be in the area. Do you have a moment to chat?"

After 15 minutes of conferring with Mike about Mike's perception of the problems within the manufacturing division, Dave forthrightly noted that he had another appointment. After Mike left, Dave said to his secretary, "Who is this pest and why is he bothering me?" Mike unwittingly had put one foot in the company bucket and it would take him many months to extricate himself. If Mike had been patiently observant, he would have discovered by Dave's actions that Dave only wanted to confer with subordinates when he initiated the conference.

10. *What are my boss's mood cycles?* If you want to favorably impress your boss, approach him or her with your proposal at the right time. Ask your boss's secretary about the best time to discuss these (and new) proposals. Most executives (that I know) are most approachable after they have had time to sort through the major problems facing them during the working day. Monday afternoon, and Tuesday mornings, generally, are good times to gain a boss's favorable attention on work-related matters.

If your boss looks terrible, it may be because he or she is on the down side of his or her natural mood cycle. Stay away, except for emergencies. If your boss is mired in some personal problem, wait until he or she has things under control before making your thrust. Karen, a public relations specialist, had a wonderful idea (she thought) about how her company could win more favor in the community. In an optimistic mood,

Karen asked for an appointment to confer with Ned, the president (and her boss).

"Ned, I know that you've been out sick for 3 days with the flu and that your whole family has also been ill. But this won't take but a few minutes of your time. Why don't we donate a machine shop to the state prison, about 40 miles north of here. By doing so, we could certainly endear ourselves to community groups who feel that our prisons aren't doing a proper job of rehabilitating prisoners. We could then hire the first graduate—or two—of the program as soon as they were released."

"Good God, Karen," snapped Ned, "I have enough problems facing me without you telling me how we can spend another $25,000 on public relations. Who should we lay off to hire those ex-cons? We don't have enough work for our people to do. Why don't you stick to speechwriting for a while?" Karen's poor timing did no good for herself, the company, or the prisoners who might have benefited from her progressive thinking.

FIND OUT WHAT YOUR BOSS THINKS YOU SHOULD BE DOING

You may have your own interpretation of what you should be doing on your job.[2] An important part of sizing up the political (office) climate is to discover what your boss thinks you should be doing. Sensible office politics begins with pleasing your boss. Max, a first-rate office politician and an adequate plant manager is a case in point of the importance of discovering what your boss thinks you should be doing. He told us:

> Sure I have my own ideas about what a manager should be doing. I've also taken some management courses which have been helpful. But when I take on a new job, I get a clear picture of what my boss really wants to do. Now, I'm working for a professional manager. He wants me to do things for the

troops that they can't do for themselves. This means I spend a lot of time haggling over budgets and bringing their gripes up to management.

My last boss looked upon a manager as just another pair of hands in the department. He really wanted me to be an administrator ten percent of the time and just another worker the other 90 percent. When I did what he expected, he told me how great a manager I was. When I acted like a true manager, he thought I was goofing off.

Rick, an intelligent and organized manager, was replaced by one of his subordinates and reassigned to a staff job. I asked his boss why Rick was replaced. He said, "Rick wasn't really doing the work of a manager. He spent all his time reviewing reports and shuffling papers. To my mind, a good manager spends most of his time with people."

IDENTIFY THE TRUE POWER

An important objective of sizing up the political climate is to figure out who the real powerholders are in your organization.[3] These are the people you must impress (in addition to your boss) in order to gain advantage. Use subtlety and tact in making your power analysis; otherwise, you will be branded by others as a brash office politician. Four techniques for identifying the true power are particularly recommended.

Ask Innocent Questions.   An unwise question to ask, particularly if you are a newcomer to a place of work is, "Who are the most influential and powerful people around here?" You are better advised to ask innocent-sounding questions; make it appear you are merely interested in getting your work accomplished. Baxter, a newly recruited junior executive, was intent on becoming a full executive. He knew that he had to impress key company officers in order to reach his objective.

Baxter developed a workable plan to get through to the executive vice-president.

He noticed that a distinguished-looking older gentleman was nicknamed "Mr. Secretary." This same individual was often seen at lunch with either the company president or the executive vice-president. When Baxter saw Mr. Secretary in the parking lot one day, he introduced himself and queried Mr. Secretary as to his position. "I'm the president's chief secretary. I take care of correspondence and arrange travel for Mr. Goldfarb, our president."

"How interesting," answered Baxter, "That job must keep you pretty busy. I look forward to seeing you again." Baxter made a mental note to learn more about this situation.

The next day, Baxter asked the same question of three people. "As you may know, I'm new here and am trying to understand the company as best I can. I'm trying to learn who does what. Could you please tell me what that kindly gentleman, Mr. Secretary, does? I'm not familiar with that job title." Barney, the man in charge of the automatic elevators, gave Baxter the most complete (and useful) answer. "Be nice to that guy, my lad. He may look harmless enough but he about runs this place. The president trusts him like Mr. Secretary were his family doctor and lawyer. They tell me the old fellow makes all the recommendations for promoting people. Mr. Goldfarb usually endorses what he says. Get on Mr. Secretary's bad list and you might as well quit."

Baxter then proceeded to cultivate Mr. Secretary by making enthusiastic comments about the company and his job whenever they met. Before long, Mr. Secretary had put Baxter on the promotable list in his secret dossier of lower-ranking managers.

Check Out the Organization Chart. We all have to get back to basics once in a while. Whatever the nature of your organization, it will probably serve you well to study the most fundamental document about the political structure of your firm—the organization chart. An up-to-date chart gives you a graphic description of who reports to whom and the relative rank of each person named. You will also discover which departments are higher ranking than others and, therefore, most likely to contain a larger number of powerful people. An organization chart will never reveal things such as the amount of influence held by a person such as Mr. Secretary, but you will learn how things are *supposed* to work.

Gus, a prolific memo writer, was newly arrived on the scene as an audit manager in a state agency. Three months into the job, Gus thought it time he began sending memos to appropriate parties, advising them of his suggestions for the improvement of state auditing procedures. Gus's memos were concise, well written, and factually based. Unfortunately, their lack of political astuteness led to their rejection. Gus explains his mistake:

> What a chowderhead. I won't repeat that mistake again. I was sending out memos with about five copies for each memo. I was naïve enough to rank the recipients according to those I thought could use the information the most. In this way, I sometimes placed a lower-ranking official's name above that of a higher-ranking official. In another instance, I implied that a person of lower rank should take exception to the audit procedures of a person of higher rank.
>
> If I had checked out the organization chart, I would not have made those errors. Now I'll have to wait for people's ruffled feathers to become unruffled before I try to correct my mistakes. You simply cannot violate protocol in our agency if you want to get something important accomplished.

Talk to Oldtimers. The worst person to approach for information to give you political advantage would be a man or woman who sees you as a potential rival for a promotion. An older person in the company (one comfortably placed on a plateau for a number of years) is unlikely to be threatened by a person snooping around for information about the informal power structure in the company.[4] (As just described, the organization chart tells you the formal power structure in the company.)

Beth wanted to sell her company on a program of recruiting female executives that would go beyond the bounds of the minimum compliance required by the Affirmative Action plan implemented by the federal government. Her plan was well reasoned and had worked for two other companies. Beth's problem was that she needed a sympathetic ear who would help her sell her plan to the president. Before moving ahead with a frontal assault, Beth decided to get the advice of the kindliest person in the company, Mr. Portland, the head of payroll.

"Believe me, Beth," said Mr. Portland, "the president will not go ahead with any new plan unless it is approved by Mr. Lawson, the company controller. Mr. Lawson may be two steps below the president on the organization chart, but it was Mr. Lawson who brought the president into the business as a sales manager. Mr. Lawson is the wisdom behind the throne.

"I have seen many a good idea discarded simply because Lawson vetoed it. We computerized the company 5 years after our competitors because some wiseacre computer salesman tried to sidestep Mr. Lawson and sell directly to the president. I can't tell you how to sell your plan to Mr. Lawson, but I can tell you that if he is on your side, the president will buy your plan for bringing more women into the company."

Beth was inspired by her conversation with Mr. Portland. She made some calculations about the possible financial benefits to the company of hiring more women for key spots. She pointed out that a truly equal opportunity employer might receive a good share of government contracts. Lawson agreed to meet with Beth, considering her plan had financial implications for the company. He liked the idea and mentioned it favorably to the president. Beth was made coordinator of the program. Simultaneously, she had scored an important political victory early in her career.

Ask Your Boss an Indirect Question. Your boss is a logical source of information about the power structure of the company or your department. Asking him or her an indirect question about the Right People to impress could pay dividends. A direct question such as "Who are the powerful people around here that I should try to impress?" is tacky. A better approach is to ask your boss which executive in the company is the most interested in your department or makes the best use of the reports your department generates.

Charlie, a management scientist, is a case in point. He worked in a staff department, titled Operations Research. Charlie and his colleagues conducted a series of studies about how to make the organization run more smoothly. Concerned that all his hard work was increasing his visibility in the corporation, Charlie asked his boss, "I note that ten executives receive copies of our research reports. But who at the top of the organization really cares about Operations Research?" His boss answered, "Ed Boswell, the senior vice-president of planning."

Charlie had the hubris to write a handwritten note (no copies required of unofficial correspondence) to Boswell stating how glad he was that the planning vice-president was interested in Operations Research. Charlie is now assistant to the general manager—a promotion that may have come about because a senior executive became aware of Charlie's presence in the organization.

DO I FIT IN WITH THE POWERFUL PEOPLE?

After you have taken the time and trouble to identify the powerful people in your organization, it is important to estimate how you fit in with them. If it appears that you are too radically different in personal style or background characteristics, it is highly probable that you will not be invited to join the power elite.[5] How well you fit can be attributable to a wide range of factors including age, education, race, sex, ethnic background, major personality characteristics, or your area of expertise. It is often more important to determine if you have a *disqualifying* rather than a *qualifying* characteristic. The former frequently are more well defined than the latter. In many companies, for example, it is difficult to rise to the top unless you have a laboratory or engineering background. The qualifying characteristics, aside from the proper technical background, are much less tangible. Among these qualities are a good problem-solving ability and the ability to work under pressure—very difficult-to-measure qualities.

Laird Is a Victim of Reverse Discrimination. Six-foot-five Laird enjoyed a glorious career as a high school and college basketball player. His record as a sales representative and then a sales manager for a large business equipment company was equally impressive. At the age of 30, Laird joined a smaller company —as the manager of its largest branch—and thought he was headed right for the executive suite. The deep-rooted prejudices of Gabe, the company president, represented an obstacle Laird had not anticipated.

Five-foot-four Gabe grew up in a world that practices heightism—discrimination against people, particularly males, who are several inches shorter than average. Gabe promised himself early in his adult life that he would do something to combat the rampant prejudice in business against short males. At 30, Gabe invested a substantial inheritance in a fledgling business that manufactured a computerized cash register and appointed himself president. The inventor of the machine became the number two executive. Gabe's aggressiveness and hard work applied to a technically excellent product led to a rapid growth of the company. Each person that Gabe appointed to an executive post—in-

cluding a woman controller—was no taller than five-
foot-six.

In a moment of candor, Gabe admitted why he had
hired Laird. "I had nothing personal against the guy.
I knew he could do a great job for us. But in no way
was this giant going to occupy a chair in my executive
suite. Big men get all the breaks in the other companies.
In my shop, a tall man will bump his head against the
ceiling early in his career."

ANALYZE THE POLITICS BELOW YOU

Sizing up the political climate in your organization
involves figuring what type of politics your subordinates
are using.[6] The better you understand the political
ploys taking place below you, the more effectively you
will be able to guard against being the victim of office
politics. Many of the maneuvers designed to please you
are harmless; some are not so harmless. No sure-fire
procedure exists for uncovering the type of office politics your subordinates are using, but it helps to speculate
on the answers to a few probing questions. The answers
to these questions may suggest countermaneuvers on
your part.

Why Is He or She Telling Me This? A subordinate
may bring information about other people to your
attention for genuine business reasons. At other times,
the information may have the political motive of attempting to unfairly discredit another person. A subordinate might casually mention to you, "We're all
rooting for Jasper. It seems as though he's made great
strides in overcoming his marital and financial problems." You then have to ask yourself whether Jasper
really has a problem or the informant is merely trying
to remove Jasper from consideration as a serious contender for a promotion.

What Methods Are They Using to Depose Me? Without becoming a company paranoid, it is worth taking

stock of whether people in your department are formulating devious schemes to have you removed from office. A bizarre case of character defamation took place in a large bank. A graffiti buff wrote the following message on the walls of the men's executive lavatory: "Brad Jones makes Idi Amin seem like a pussycat." Brad's reaction was first shock; the second, laughter. His third reaction was self-protective. During their next scheduled business get-together, Brad commented to his boss, "I think I am becoming an important person in the bank. People are now writing nasty things about me on the lavatory walls. It's nice to know I'm being noticed."

Is Politics Being Used to Cover Up a Lack of Results? Many forms of office politics are used for the sole purpose of bringing favorable attention to a person who is doing a satisfactory or better job. At other times, politics are played to cover up a poor performance. As the boss, you have to recognize the difference because you are held accountable for the performance of your *total* department. Buck passing is a common form of politics used to cover up for poor results. One subordinate complained to his boss, "I would have gotten my report out on time except for those damn delays in the computer department." When the boss investigated, she discovered that the computer department had detailed logs indicating that no report had been sent back late to computer users in the previous 3 months. She then knew precisely where the blame lay for the late report.

What Methods are Being Used to Impress Me? Part of your job as a boss is to sort out a good from a faked good performance. Therefore, when a document passes your desk relating to the productivity of a subordinate, it behooves you to ask, "Is this document a reflection of good performance or is it an exercise in puffery?" Clark, a faithful civil servant, found out the difference quite by accident. He explains the incident:

> One morning, I received a memo from another department praising the virtues of Cynthia, a woman who works for me. The other department pointed out what an important contribution Cynthia had made while she was on loan to their department. I was pleased that one of my people had performed so well in a special assignment. I made a copy of the note and placed it in Cynthia's permanent personnel file.
>
> Three days later, I was having lunch with Sam, the head of the department in which Cynthia carried out her temporary assignment. I commented about the complimentary memo. He, in turn, told me about a remarkable coincidence. Maggie, a woman who was on loan to my department, had received an almost identical note from my department praising her virtues while on her temporary assignment. Undoubtedly, the two women had been writing "heroine" notes about each other. I simply destroyed the memo and forgot the matter.

WHAT TYPE OF POLITICAL BEHAVIOR IS FAVORED AT THE TOP?

The conservative office politician attempts to learn what type of political actions are in vogue at the top of the organization. It is a reasonably safe generalization that, if key people in the organization favor a limited number of strategies for holding them in good stead with the company, these strategies are worthy of your consideration. In some organizations that are not considered political jungles, the top executives still use strategies other than strictly of merit to improve their standing. Such tame types of office politics include involvement in prestigious community activities or active support of political (government) parties. Country club memberships often fit into the same category.

By observing what is going on at the top of the organization, you can help avoid using a variety of office political ploys that will backfire. Empire building has become so widespread that many top managements are ready to pounce on a lower-ranking manager who makes even one attempt to expand his or her jurisdiction without sound business justification.

Tony was one such would-be empire builder in a public accounting firm. He had worked himself up from a junior accountant to supervisor of other accounting supervisors. Because he handled several large clients, Tony had more professional and clerical people reporting to him than any other manager in the firm at his level. Recognizing that he was on his way toward building an empire, Tony made his next move. He explained his plan to the two highest ranking partners in his branch.

"It seems that my group is now making the most use of the management advisory services (not related to accounting) we offer clients. You'll note that my clients accounted for over 75 percent of the activity engaged in by our management services department. As you probably know, I'm quite interested in the management services aspect of our business. I'm suggesting that management services now report to me. I'll leave the entire unit intact. Thus, the current manager will not be displaced. As business expands, his job will become bigger."

Tony's power ploy did not work. He was upbraided by the top partners for being too pushy. By the end of the year, two of Tony's accounts were reassigned to another manager in the firm. Furthermore, Tony did not receive the promotion he was seeking.

WHAT ARE THE INFORMAL STATUS SYMBOLS?

A superficial way of impressing other people at work is to use the status symbols associated with successful people. The most impressive status symbols—the *formal* ones—are conferred on people by the organization.

Using them is tantamount to stealing. Thus you cannot put a sterling silver or gold-plated thermos decanter in your office if these accoutrements are handed out only to people at, or above, the rank of vice-president. You cannot claim squatter's rights to a vacant office next to the president nor can your car occupy a place next to his in the executive parking lot. Nor can you give yourself the job title "vice-president of regional operations" when you are the mailroom supervisor. If the company personnel department does not authorize your having a personal secretary, you cannot intimidate two women to serve as your secretarial team. Nor can you order the public relations department to prepare a speech for you to present at a Brownie banquet.

What you can do is make judicious use of *informal* status symbols. At best, such symbols will help you attract followers who are impressed by your status, thus enhancing your power. Before such a strategy can be implemented, however, you must be shrewdly observant of what constitutes an informal status symbol in your firm. A good place to start is to learn what status symbols are in vogue with the company fast trackers—those people who are destined for big things at an early age. Older executives who have reached their plateau are less inclined to be concerned about status symbols.

A disconcerting characteristic of status symbols in executive life is that they are not universal. What gives you status in one company might be considered in poor taste at another. Status symbols are also subject to flux. Fifteen years ago wearing a homburg to the office gave you distinction. Today, it gives you the appearance of shopping for clothes at garage sales. One of my researchers reports on the latest informal status symbols at the home office of a major corporation:

Playing squash and/or tennis is definitely in. Golf is on the wane. Thus, keeping a copy of a magazine such as *World Tennis* on your office coffee table impresses people. If you can bring a trophy you've won to the office, your last name might as well be that of the president's. Boats are definitely in, particularly when some physical activity is associated with their use. A photo of you fixing your sailboat is very helpful.

In the company under investigation, sporting *The Wall Street Journal* is no longer an effective status symbol. Today, some of the messengers and higher level clerks carry around the *Journal*. It is still important to read that paper, but carrying something shocking like the *National Enquirer* carries more status. It gives top management the impression that you are trying to understand the mental make-up of little people. After all, they are consumers of the company's products.

Older female secretaries or a young male secretary are the latest power symbol in the executive suite. It's mostly younger middle managers who are overly concerned about hiring a physically attractive, young woman. Marketing people are particularly obsessed with finding "chicks" for secretaries.

Plants have also become widely used status symbols. The company gives the tallest and rarest plants to the highest ranking executives. To give the impression of being powerful, some lower-ranking managers bring their own plants to the office. One middle manager brought a five-foot fig plant. It was so impressive that the company president ordered it removed.

The ultimate power symbol for male executives at this company is to walk into a meeting without an attaché case or memo pad. It's as though you are beyond carrying papers. It's the little people who practically back-pack into a meeting.

PART II

Strategies for Gaining Favor

4

Cultivating Your Boss

Impressing your boss is the most basic strategy of office politics. If you cannot gain favor with him or her, it will be difficult to have a successful career (in that company). Should you clash with one particular boss, you can sometimes be gracefully transferred to another department or find another job in another firm. You will then have one more shot at impressing the person who recommends you for a salary increase and evaluates your work performance.

To help you in your campaign to culivate your boss, and to get your share of the organizational goodies, I have assembled 30 suggestions and strategies. Some of them, like Help Your Boss to Succeed, represent an all encompassing philosophy of winning office politics. Others, like Getting a Freebie for Your Boss, are minor and specific—still, an important part of your political game plan. Pick and choose from the political maneuvers presented in this chapter. Decide which strategies are suited to your skills and your boss's personal style. If your favorite strategy is missing, it is conceivable that you will find it included in the chapter on devious strategies.

HELP YOUR BOSS TO SUCCEED

When you are caught up in the pressures of pursuing your own ambitions, it is easy to forget the primary reason you were hired: Your boss (or the person who hired you originally) thought you could make a positive contribution to helping him or her accomplish the department's mission. Even if you were hired on the basis of nepotism, the person who accepted you into the department believed that you would contribute directly or indirectly to his or her success. Most of your job activities should be directed to this vital success strategy—help your boss succeed.

George Conducts a Clean-Up Campaign. George learned through the grapevine that a representative from company headquarters would be visiting the plant where he worked as chief manufacturing engineer. He also learned from casual conversation with his boss, Gus, that the home office was concerned about the physical appearance of some of the company plants. A few stockholders had complained that the company image was suffering because of the filthy conditions at some of its mills and plants.

George swung into action without first conferring with his boss. He organized a clean-up committee to remove trash and repaint badly smudged doors and walls. The entire clean-up operation took 4 days— precisely the 4 days that Gus was out of town on a business trip. When Gus returned, he was pleasantly surprised to see the good housekeeping that had taken place in his absence. When the inspection team visited the plant shortly thereafter, Gus was praised for keeping up the company image.

Gus then asked his secretary who had initiated the clean-up campaign. Learning that George deserved the credit, Gus said to his secretary, "Write a note of commendation for George's personnel file. After I sign it, we'll send one copy to George and place one in his personnel file. We need more company-minded people around here."

Beth Does Some Bidding for Her Boss.   Beth enjoyed her position as an assistant store manager for a chain of appliance stores. She and her boss, Tallulah, both agreed that, although they now operated one of the most successful stores in the Southeast, more success would be on the way if only headquarters would cooperate. The two women ardently believed that by doubling the physical capacity of their store, their business would also double—a difficult plan to sell to top management. So far, Tallulah had not convinced management that expansion would pay a suitable return on investment. Too often in the past, store managers had wanted a larger store more for appearance than for legitimate business reasons.

At the next regional meeting of store and assistant store managers, a home office executive asked Beth how she liked her job. "Terrific," answered Beth, "In these uncertain economic times, it's nice to be working for a store that's going places in a city that's going places. Another thing I like about my job is Tallulah's attitude. Most managers would grumble having to squeeze all the merchandise and all those customers into such little space.

"Last week we were practically selling TVs off the manufacturer's truck. If we had more room, many of those customers might have browsed around the store some more. But so be it. We do the best we can with what we have."

Within 3 weeks, preliminary plans had been formulated to put an additional wing on the appliance outlet run by Tallulah and Beth. Before 6 months had passed, the appliance store had been enlarged 40 percent. Sales had increased by one-third, and Beth had been recommended by her boss to participate in the company profit-sharing plan.

DISPLAY LOYALTY

A loyal subordinate expresses his or her loyalty in many ways other than by being a sycophant. One such expression is to defend the boss when he or she is under attack by people from other departments. A defense under such circumstances does not necessarily mean that you think your boss is entirely correct. You can defend the merit of what your boss says without agreeing with his or her entire position.

Brian, an educational coordinator in the evening school division of a college, was invited to a curriculum development meeting which was also attended by a number of high-ranking college officials. At one point Steve, a representative from another division of the college, fired a few salvos at Arden, the evening school director (and Brian's boss).

Said Steve, "It's apparent to everybody here that the evening school has been suffering from declining enrollment. I suspect that the evening school is not shifting with the times. The courses you offer are too old, too out of date. Where are your modern courses? When can the public get its appetite whetted for courses in laser technology? Or in energy conservation? Or in Transcendental Meditation?"

Arden looked solemn and concerned. Brian spoke for him:

> Hold on, Steve. I can see the merit in your argument. But let's hear the other side of the story. In my position as education coordinator, I get a careful look at the enrollment for new courses. It's been our experience in the past that so-called modern courses have a very short shelf life. By the time they are offered, the public is usually not very interested in the topic. Even if the course does run once, there may not be a sustaining interest.

A few years ago, we offered a career guidance seminar for homemakers who wanted to get back into the job market or who wanted to enter it for the first time. We thought we would have 400 people registering for the course. When it came right down to women putting their money on the line, about 25 registered. The second time we offered the seminar, only four women registered. Offering modern courses to the public is not as easy as it sounds.

A sigh of relief flashed across Arden's face. After the meeting, he commented to Brian, "I thought your comments were well taken. I wish I had said that about the women's seminar. Yet coming from you, it was more convincing than if I had defended myself."

AVOID DISLOYALTY

Disloyalty takes many forms. Attacking your boss publically, going out of your way to admit that your department's position is wrong, or emphasizing the virtues of a competitor's products are common forms of disloyalty. You may not get fired, but one sign of overt disloyalty to your boss and he or she may never again be concerned about boosting your career. Seemingly trivial situations are often tip-offs about your loyalty or disloyalty.

Kristen had a promising career in the personnel department of a giant food company. Working as a wage and salary specialist, Kris was also assigned a few miscellaneous tasks. Among them was the coordination of the annual company-sponsored family picnic. Up to 500 people were known to attend the picnic, particularly if the weather was favorable. Recognizing that a good company person never turns down an assignment considered important to top management, Kris never publically expressed her true feelings about the annual picnic. Private, she was less guarded. One day while having lunch in a restaurant with a friend from another company, Kris was asked how things were going at the office. She replied:

Yeech. I'm assigned to that dreadful company picnic again. I wish the company would send every employee who wanted a picnic the $12 per head it costs us. That way they could have a cockamamie hamburger and frankfurter roast in their own backyard or balcony. I have never seen so many people make such fools of themselves at once. You get these pasty-looking, out-of-shape people clumsily playing softball and volleyball. Hundreds of children run about shrieking and, at the same time, stuffing themselves with ice cream, soda, and hot dogs.

I don't think the whole damn affair contributes anything to company morale. Only creeps attend a company picnic. And here I get the assignment of organizing it every year. Maybe I could bribe the concession people to contaminate a few of the hamburgers. The furor it would create would end company picnics for all time.

Three days later, Bill, Kristen's boss, sent her a message over the intercom to report to his office immediately. Bill wasted no time with a warmup. Face reddened, Bill said, "Kris, I'm both disappointed and irritated. A friend of mine overheard your conversation in the restaurant about our annual family picnic for employees. You undoubtedly misunderstood the importance of what this department is trying to do for the company. Perhaps a person of your values should not be a member of the personnel department. Never, in my 26 years of corporate experience, have I heard such a blatant display of disloyalty to the company. It's too late to pull you off the assignment now, but rest assured you will never be asked to coordinate the company picnic again."

Bill was true to his word. Kris was never again asked to coordinate the company picnic. Nor was she given any other important assignments in addition to her regular duties. After 2 years, it became apparent to Kris that she was going to be a career wage and salary administrator in her company and nothing more. People

were promoted around her when she was not even
aware that an opening existed. Kris now faced the decision of looking for employment elsewhere despite
her general liking for the company.

DOCUMENT YOUR BOSS'S ACCOMPLISHMENTS

An infrequently practiced, but potentially valuable,
method of cultivating your boss is to keep a scrapbook
of his or her accomplishments. As will be discussed later
in this book, documenting your own accomplishments
is an important way of improving your career. Documenting your boss's good deeds, helps two people: you
and your boss. Your boss can use the documentation at
performance review time or when the department is
seeking its share of the budget for the forthcoming year.

Laura, a college graduate aspiring to executive position, began her climb to the top from a frequently used
starting point, that of department secretary. Her boss,
Max, was the manager of safety engineering. He and
his staff were responsible for preventing accidents in
both the factory and office. People assumed Max was
doing a good job without giving much thought to the
matter. His colorful safety posters were the primary reminder that a safety department existed.

Laura recognized that her boss's contribution to the
corporate welfare was somewhat nebulous. Without
seeking her boss's concurrence, Laura kept a daily log
of the department's accomplishments. Many of the
items were mundane listings of department activities.
Some entries in the log were of greater significance.
Quarterly, Laura would compare accident-frequency
information of before and after certain programs were
initiated. One entry read:

> In the year before we placed nonskid pads around
> the food and beverage vending machines, there were
> five reported cases of lost-time accidents due to peo-
> ple slipping over spilled coffee, soda, or soup. After
> the nonskid pads, no such accidents were reported.

Laura's most impressive documentation dealt with the decrease in parking lot collisions since one-way traffic lanes were installed. Fender-bumping accidents were reduced from 35 to four in a 12-month period. Laura brought her dossier of good deeds to Max just prior to budget preparation time. Max was overwhelmed.

"Laura, this is wonderful. The four of us in this department have been working away, doing our jobs, and often being unappreciated. Now we can tell the rest of the world what we've really accomplished. It also tells me that you have really caught on to the safety concept. This department might have room for an administrative assistant, and you would be the logical choice."

PRAISE YOUR BOSS TO TOP MANAGEMENT

Executed with aplomb, the praising of your boss in high places can cement the relationship between you. The benefits may be direct—should your boss hear about your praise. He or she might recommend you for a generous salary increase. Or they could be indirect, because, as your boss prospers, so do you—providing the two of you have a good working relationship. A compliment about your boss to upper management should be couched in specific terms that make sense to administrators. Avoid the use of nebulous flattery such as labeling your boss, "a saint among sinners," "a truly outstanding North American manager," "an inspired leader of people," or "an ideal model for learning about the mysteries of management."

Sean, a hospital administrator, had an excellent idea. At a hospital board meeting, Sean was asked by the hospital executives how he enjoyed working at Hillside General. Sean assumed they were familiar with management terminolgy. He noted:

Things are going rather well for me at Hillside. Hospital administration is my career so it's important

for me to work for a real pro. So often the chief
executive office at a hospital is a physician who has
little regard for the administrative process. He or she
runs the ship as if he or she were royalty. Not Dr.
Jacobs. The man knows how to manage. He keeps a
careful eye on what you might call productivity in a
hospital. He is very concerned that we keep the
hospital beds filled and that we stay within the
budget. He prefers good patient care to philosophiz-
ing. But at the same time, Dr. Jacobs has concern for
the feelings of people. I have seen him personally
intervene in a situation where it appeared that a
Mexican orderly was the victim of an ethnic slur.
And the person Dr. Jacobs upbraided was a resident
from Harvard Medical School.

One week later, Dr. Jacobs commented casually to
Sean, "It's good to know that my top administrator and
I have compatible management styles. Let me know if
I do anything that interferes with your performance of
your job."

DISCOVER YOUR BOSS'S OBJECTIVES

One way to your boss's heart is through the attainment
of his or her objectives. If you help your boss reach
these department objectives, you will be on your way to
cultivating a good superior-subordinate relationship.
Your task would be simplified if managers routinely
and explicitly pointed out what it is they are trying to
accomplish, but more often, you have to dig for a clear
statement of what your boss is trying to accomplish.
Reggie, a sales representative for Comfort Mills, a textile company, discovered the importance of getting a
true picture of his boss's objectives.

Reggie was proud of his sales performance in his
competitive, lower Manhattan territory. Reggie would
excitedly explain to his boss how hard he had worked
to convince a clothing manufacturer to buy goods from

Comfort Mills. Sara, his boss, would nod with faint approval.

After two more such ungracious compliments from Sara after he had opened new accounts, Reggie confronted her. "Why am I beating my head against the wall? Aren't we in business to sell textiles to clothing manufacturers? Don't you like my customers? Are we trying to lose money in order to avoid taxes? Have we already made too much money this year?"

"No" said Sara. "I've hinted at it before Reggie. Comfort Mills is no longer interested in the little customer. We are trying to become the big chopper on the block. Your specialty is the little manufacturer who costs us too much to supply. I think we actually lost money on your last two sales. Forget the little guy and concentrate on the big enchiladas who can order over 3,000 yards at a time."

Reggie got the message, and also a few extra dollars in his pocket. Now, he turns over the customers his company does not want to a jobber with a small sales force. Reggie gets a small commission. More importantly, he is helping Sara reach her objective of cultivating major customers for Comfort Mills.

UNCOMPLICATE YOUR BOSS'S LIFE

A potent way of developing a good working relationship with your boss is to take problems away, not add to his or her burden. As you take care of the petty ones, your boss has more time to work on major problems. The payoff to you is that your boss develops more confidence in you. Matt, a systems analyst, violated this principle; consequently, his relationship with the boss suffered.

Matt pleaded with Ken's (his boss's) secretary. "Are you sure I can't see Ken today? I've got a devil of a problem with one of the foremen that has to be resolved today."

The secretary wearily replied, "I suppose I could arrange it. Toward the middle of the afternoon, but only for a brief time. How about 2:45?"

At 2:45, Matt plunked himself down in Ken's office and began rattling off his problems. "Old Jeb won't let me into his department. He said he's not going to allow any wise guy staff person snooping around. The guy is afraid I'm going to discover that he's doing something wrong. What he doesn't realize is that we're here to help him.

"I have to get in Jeb's department. I need information from his department to make my report complete. What can you do to help me?"

Ken retaliated, "Right now your problems seem small to me. Top management is now pulling another reorganization that I have to work on. Why can't you and Jeb work out your differences over a couple of beers? Why do I have to fight your petty battles for you? Are you a systems analyst or a factory mouse?"

Matt became a better office politician after that, but he had already damaged his relationship with his boss.

BECOME A CRUCIAL SUBORDINATE

Several of the strategies for cultivating your boss discussed so far point to the importance of performing well for your boss on his or her crucial tasks—make-or-break factors in the job.[1] Discovering your boss's objectives is a step toward becoming a crucial subordinate. "L.T.," a production assistant in a southern furniture company became a crucial subordinate to his factory superintendent and boss, Ronald. In so doing, L.T. took the big first step in his journey toward becoming an executive in that furniture company.

The company was faced with a serious problem. Small bubbles were surfacing on the finish of tables and desks when they were exposed to temperatures above 80°. Customers by the dozens were demanding refunds or refinishes on the company products. Furniture retail stores, in turn, were demanding credit from the company and threatening to discontinue as customers unless there were guarantees that the bubbling problem was conquered. Managers and specialists alike devoted as much time as possible to the mysterious problem that posed potentially disastrous consequences to the company.

After 4 days of frantic searching for causes and much buck passing, no logical reason for the bubbling had been isolated.

L.T. came up with a plan. He telephoned all his acquaintances and former classmates who worked for furniture makers. He asked each of them if they ever had a seemingly unresolvable technical problem at the factory and what they did about it. One acquaintance said his factory had a similar baffling problem (of laminate that became unglued) and that they hired a chemical engineering consultant from Atlanta who solved the problem in 3 days. L. T. told his boss about the consultant; the consultant was hired; and the cause of the bubbling was discovered. Apparently, one large batch of solvent was contaminated when the wrong acid was used in its preparation. L.T.'s boss was enthusiastic about the consultant's efforts, and equally enthusiastic about L.T.'s judgment in recommending him.

APE YOUR BOSS

Imitation and quotation are two of the most genuine forms of flattery. When you imitate or quote your boss you are sending out a message—that you like what you hear or see. Done with selectivity, imitating your boss's activities or quoting favorite phrases will improve the relationship between you. For example: Michelle enhanced her chances for promotion to a desirable job by having the insight to use a few of her boss's favorite phrases.

Michelle was the manager of a small branch of a casualty insurance company. She and the other four branch managers (in the area) would meet at least twice a month with the regional manager, Vance, to discuss plans, problems, and new business developments. After these gatherings, the managers usually held an informal meeting over cocktails where Michelle often was chided for purposely copying Vance's interests and favorite expressions.

Gil, one of Michelle's cohorts, said to her,

"How curious that you have taken a liking to bowling and professional hockey since Vance took over as regional manager. I wonder how many books you had to read about hockey to make you sound like a hockey fan. Another thing, when did you start using that expression that Vance uses ad nauseam, 'Let's see what comes out of the woodwork'? When are you going to start wearing the same cut of suit he wears?"

The not-so-good-natured kidding by her peers did not daunt Michelle. She persisted—performing to the best of her ability as a branch manager and copying certain of Vance's interests and expressions. Four months later, a new position opened up for an industrial accounts manager. The person chosen for this position would personally handle several major accounts. He or she would still function as a branch manager, but an assistant would be appointed to deal with the more routine administrative aspects of the position. Michelle, who had worked so hard to cultivate her boss, was the first industrial accounts manager for her region.

LISTEN TO THE BOSS

A remarkably simple strategy of cultivating your boss is to be a patient listener. Few people are listened to, or taken seriously enough, at home or on the job. Active listening to your boss can take a number of forms: listening to personal problems, asking for suggestions and then following them, nodding with enthusiasm and smiling when the boss speaks, or taking notes during a staff meeting.

Tim, a mechanical engineer, facilitated a good relationship with his boss by demonstrating that he listened carefully to his boss's suggestions. On one occasion, Alex, his boss, made comment when he stopped by

Tim's cubicle, "Say, that looks like an interesting way to reinforce a valve. Where did you learn about that?"

"Alex, indirectly, the credit must go to you. Remember? One day over coffee, we were talking about the strength of valves. You mentioned that a researcher named Schwartz had written the most comprehensive paper on valves. I sent for a reprint and found the exact information I needed. Did I forget to thank you for that suggestion?"

MAINTAIN MAXIMUM CONTACT WITH THE BOSS

Many of the people I interviewed to collect information for this book believed that a good way to cultivate your boss is to keep in frequent contact with him or her. Office politicians frequently develop a reason for seeing their boss even if a legitimate reason does not exist. Their tactics include bringing in telephone messages, getting his reaction to a routine memo, or asking for clarification on a problem. Of course, you do run the risk of becoming a pest if you overdo the principle of maintaining maximum boss contact.

Herb, a man who now has the top marketing job in his company, describes his approach to maintaining contact with the boss:

When I was a sales manager, I made an effort to travel with my boss. For example, if I heard he was going to St. Louis on a business trip, I would try to arrange some appointments in St. Louis. I would then casually mention to him that he and I were traveling to the same town. Inevitably, he would invite me to sit next to him on the plane. That's where a lot of business is conducted. My boss learned more about my hopes for the future there than he did at the office.

Once in town, we would agree to meet for dinner. There is a certain intimacy about having dinner together out of town. It's a good way to develop an edge over rivals and to get management support of your programs. I owe much of my rise to the top to talent, but talent is not enough. Unless your boss really understands you as a person, you are just another worker in the department. Traveling together adds the personal touch.

CATER TO YOUR BOSS'S IDIOSYNCRACIES

Marlene, a gracious entertainer, scheduled a Sunday afternoon party at her townhouse, inviting among the guests, her boss and his wife. Two bowls of punch were available for the guests, one labeled "With Gin," the other "Without Gin." Asked by a co-worker why she bothered having a nonalcoholic punch, Marlene replied, "Don't you realize that Jerry and his wife are Mormons? Why not be considerate of their feelings?"

Marlene had a point. A helpful method of cultivating your boss is to cater to his or her idiosyncracies and whims. Nadine, a bank teller (who later became a head teller) kept about three dollar's worth of change in her handbag. She knew that her boss had a fetish for exact end-of-the-day balances—no shortages, no overages. Nadine would add a few cents or dollars if she were short or subtract a few cents or dollars if she had a surplus. Nadine kept track of her juggling. At the end of one year, she had contributed $5.78 to the bank out of her pocket. Nadine thought this was a small investment for helping her land the position of head teller.

PAY ATTENTION TO YOUR BOSS'S PERSONAL LIFE

At lower levels in the organization, a particularly effective strategy for cultivating your boss is to recognize his or her personal interests. An *extreme* use of this technique is to arrange an introduction of your boss to a person of the opposite (in some instances, the same) sex. Other techniques include helping to repair a car, lending your season's pass to a professional football game, or merely sending birthday and holiday cards.

Paul might be placed in our Machiavelli category for pulling a stunt—that worked. Looking for a way to cultivate his boss, Paul noted that he had an avid interest in winemaking. While at a garage sale one day, Paul found an ancient wine press that was still functional. It looked like a bargain at $15. Paul said to his boss on the next Monday morning: [2]

"I just inherited something that might be of interest to you. An aunt of mine willed me an old wine press along with a host of much less valuable articles. I know you are interested in winemaking. How would you like to buy this press from me for $2?"

Paul felt that if he offered the wine press as a gift, his boss would be hesitant. By purchasing it from Paul, the boss would not feel he was taking advantage of a subordinate's generosity or that he was being manipulated.

GET A FREEBIE FOR YOUR BOSS

You might argue that there is no such thing as a "free lunch." Still, your boss might like to believe that he or she is getting something for nothing. A minor tactic for cultivating your boss is to arrange for an occasional freebie. Sal, an electrical engineer, explains how he uses the freebie principle:

Since I work in a small company, I have the power to recommend purchases of equipment and supplies for our company. The purchasing agent usually goes along with my suggestions. Because I am a potential customer, a good number of prospective vendors invite me to lunch. Occasionally, I have suggested to the vendor that he invite my boss, who likes to be involved in making major purchases, for the luncheon sales conference.

The salesman usually agrees that my idea is a

good one, and I know my boss likes to get out of
the office for a fancy lunch once in a while. The
fringe benefit is that my boss, who rarely has a
chance to observe me directly involved in negotiating with another individual, has the opportunity to
see me in action.

MAKE GOOD USE OF TIDBITS

Gossip columnists are not the only ones who gain
through the use of tidbits. Gossip is used in the office
to relieve the tedium of routine work. If you can come
up with an occasional tidbit, you may be able to improve your relationship with your boss. Passing on a
malicious tidbit is a devious tactic. It makes far more
sensible office politics if you can find *informative* but
not *defamatory* tidbits. Mary, a legal secretary in a
law office, describes how she "tidbitted" her way to an
improved relationship with her boss.

Mr. Muir, my boss, likes to feel he is on top of
what is happening both in our office and in the
community. It makes sense since we serve both individuals and companies. I collect tidbits by asking
my friends and getting a few juicy morsels from the
local papers and our local legal newspaper. Mr.
Muir is too busy to carefully read the papers himself. Some tidbits are better at arousing my boss's
attention than others.

Mr. Muir is particularly appreciative when I tell
him about bankruptcies, divorces, and the sale of
major real estate properties. He also appreciates
hearing about the cancellation of big business contracts. One day I told him that a junior lawyer in
our firm had recently purchased a Mercedes Benz
sports convertible. That really got to Mr. Muir. He
drives a car worth about one fifth as much as the
junior lawyer's Mercedes Benz. I guess Mr. Muir
doesn't like being upstaged by a junior lawyer.

The payoff to my supplying Mr. Muir with tidbits

is that he considers me an invaluable member of his staff. There are many other women around who could function just as well as a straight legal secretary.

BE THE DEPARTMENT WATCHDOG

Conceptually similar to the purveyor of tidbits is the department watchdog. The difference is that the watchdog keeps the boss informed about big problems within the department (such as who is out to knife him or her and conflicts between people). If you are a watchdog, make sure your information is correct or you will soon be written off, appropriately enough, as a son of a bitch or just a plain bitch. An insurance company manager explains why he was forced to recommend that a watchdog in his department be transferred to another kennel:

At first, I trusted Ted. He was a valuable ally. He would tell me if two of my department heads were too much in conflict with each other. I would poke into the matter and try to get things straightened out. Once, he told me that one of my managers was saying nasty things about me to the personnel department. I confronted the man, without identifying the source. The accusations to the personnel department stopped.

Ted told me that Alice, my claims manager, was mailing out her résumé to about half the insurance companies in the business. I asked her if she was discontented with the company since she was exploring the job market. Alice told me she hadn't looked for a job in years. Furthermore, she told me to contact any insurance company I wish to see if she had written them. She also invited me to search her desk.

My conclusion was that Ted was using desperate tactics either to get rid of Alice or impress me that

he was highly loyal to me. Whatever the real reason,
I fired him.

VOLUNTEER FOR DELICATE ASSIGNMENTS

The owner of an insurance agency incurred the wrath
of a major client—the owner of a large furniture store.
A fire had done an estimated $350,000 worth of dam-
age. Unfortunately for the furniture store owner, the
insurance policy sold to the store had a liability limit
of $300,000. In addition to threatening to cancel his
policy with the agency, the furniture storeowner talked
of telling other merchants to dissociate with the agency.
Word of the difficulty facing the owner spread quickly
through the agency. Mitch, a man in his thirties who
had recently joined the agency as a sales representative,
approached his boss (the agency head) with this proposition:

> I know we are facing a nasty situation. But I don't
> think the situation is impossible. Let me make a
> personal visit to the furniture storeowner. I'll calm
> him down and show him how his $50,000 uninsured
> casualty loss can be used to reduce his income tax
> liability for this year. I'll see if we can sell him the
> right type of policy to fit the size of his inventory.

Mitch proved to be a hero. His visit to the furniture
store owner was a success. The owner was still upset
over his loss but Mitch tactfully pointed out that one
year ago the agency had tried to increase the size of
his coverage. Mitch sold the owner a policy with
$500,000 fire coverage plus an escalation clause for
inflation. In gratitude for having taken care of this
delicate problem, Mitch was befriended by the agency
head. From that point forward Mitch was given choice
leads for new business, many of which resulted in
substantial size commissions for him.

Not everybody can be as fortunate as Mitch, but the
principle can be applied to your own situation. Perhaps

your boss will ask for a volunteer to attend a funeral for a company official, or to product-test a line of thermal underwear in subfreezing temperature. It is of no consequence as to whether you perform admirably, the fact that you volunteered should help cultivate your relationship with your boss.

DO YOUR BOSS'S DIRTY WORK

"I'm sorry to have to inform you about this, but upper management has instructed me to tell you about our new coffee break plans," said Marty. "From now on, no coffee pots will be authorized in the office. Anybody who wants coffee will have to use the vending machines located near the company cafeteria. Only under emergency situations are you to bring coffee back to your desk. It is preferable that you drink your coffee at the benches designated for that purpose near the vending machines. Furthermore, coffee breaks are not to exceed 12 minutes."

Marty did not relish being the bearer of bad-news assignments, but he continued to volunteer for them. Marty knew that taking care of your boss's dirty work can help you endear yourself to him or her. Many a company hatchet man has helped to elevate his career by his willingness to implement the decision to fire employees or to announce layoffs or paycuts.

BE A RUNNER OF ERRANDS

Running errands for your boss can be the sincerest form of apple polishing. Most people have more errands to run than they can comfortably manage. My personal calculation is that a person with a career, family, house, and two pets could easily spend 35 hours per week just running errands. The job responsibilities of many executive secretaries include errand running (purchasing gifts, making medical appointments, and so forth). Most managers are not so privileged. You might be able to cultivate a good relationship with your boss if you become the unofficial errand runner or substitute spouse.

Dick, a first-level office supervisor, survived three layoffs, partially because of the good relationship he had established with his boss, Oscar. Dick explains:

> My job is to serve my boss. Right? So I help Oscar out all I can without turning into a lackey. Oscar once had to obtain plates for a classic auto he had recently purchased. That could easily take 3 hours at the Motor Vehicle Bureau, particularly if you consider the number of times you will be sent to another line or back for more information. I mentioned to Oscar that I would help him register his car, providing he didn't mind if I came back late from lunch. I didn't mind taking the whole afternoon off to do the job. After all, I was being paid. I passed the time by reading the month's mail that had accumulated on my desk.
>
> Oscar was most appreciative the time I picked a bucket of Kentucky Fried Chicken for him. He is all thumbs in the kitchen and his wife was away for the weekend, so that Friday afternoon, I asked if I could get him a bucket of chicken that would last through the weekend. He said something about my being such a thoughtful person.

ASK YOUR BOSS'S ADVICE ABOUT PERSONAL MATTERS

"Naomi, if I recall, you once said something about purchasing a condominium instead of renting an apartment when you are single. I am looking into that matter myself right now. Could you tell me what your final decision was and why?"

Rhonda, Naomi's subordinate, is asking her the question about buying a condominium for a dual reason. Rhonda *is* interested in finding a way to avoid paying rent, but she is also trying to enhance her relationship with her boss. Asking your boss a question about a personal situation implies that you respect his or her general judgment. Asking about financial matters or consumer purchases is preferable to asking about personal-social matters (such as family relationships and marital problems). Most skillful managers are hesitant to become involved in the personal problems of subordinates.

Many younger managers have found it to their advantage to appeal to the father-figure urge in older managers. Said Rick, explaining how it works:

A number of younger managers at our company use the same method to impress the boss. If your boss happens to be an older man, he would probably enjoy giving you fatherly advice. Some of the younger men have gone outside their departments to find a patron—by appealing to the fatherly instincts of an older executive. You have the best chance of impressing the boss if he came up the same route you are now using. If he was, and you are, a salesman, it helps form a natural relationship.

Asking your boss's advice about your career is very helpful. A friend of mine asked his superior as to whether to purchase individual stocks or mutual funds. Another asked his boss whether to give his son an original name or to make him a "junior." So long as you seem genuinely interested in his answers, it doesn't really matter what type of advice you ask a boss who wants to be a father figure.

BE DEFERENT

In almost every place of work outside of medical settings, some universities, and a few conservative banks, subordinates are encouraged to call superiors by their first name. Despite this superficial manifestation of informality, most bosses enjoy a show of respect for their positions. By being appropriately deferent you might be able to improve your relationship with *your* boss. Here are a few deferent statements that might appeal to a boss's sense of authority without your appearing obsequious:

"Yes, sir, that sounds like a good idea."

"Yes, ma'am, that sounds like a good idea."

"Okay, coach, what do I do now?"

"You're the boss."

"From your vantage point as the manager of this department, how do you see this problem?"

BECOME A STRAIGHT MAN

I am not being unintentionally sexist. So far, no good unisex synonym exists for the term straight man— someone who plays his part straight, usually "straight man" for an entertainer. A "straight" person now refers to somebody who is heterosexual or not a drug abuser. The type of straight man to whom I refer is the subordinate who sets up his or her boss in a meeting to make the boss look good. Rudy improved his rating with his boss by playing the role of straight man. In his own words, here is how he operates:

First of all, you must know your boss's capabilities and areas of knowledge in order to pull off this stunt with finesse. Jack, my boss, had spent considerable time doing an analysis of the actual cost of some of our manufactured products. His pitch was that our company would be better off—in many instances— using subcontractors instead of building some components ourselves. In a meeting with a couple of representatives from the financial department, I asked the rhetorical question: "Do we really know how much it costs us to build our own parts?" This was the perfect cue for Jack to display his newly found knowledge.

Another time, I was at a party with Jack after his return from a summer vacation in Greece. The conversation turned to vacation talk and I said to the group, "I hear the Beautiful People are vacationing at the luscious Greek beaches." A smile flashed across Jack's face, and he launched into the topic of his recent experiences at Greek beaches.

ALLOW YOUR BOSS HIS OR HER PRETENSE

Kathleen noticed her boss looking more haggard than usual one Monday morning. His bloodshot eyes and fatigued expression were strong indicators that he was hung over from a drinking bout. Kathleen said, without a snicker, "Tom, might I get you a cup of coffee or tea? It seems as if almost everybody has a touch of the flu these days."

Kathleen was allowing Tom his pretense that he was ill without his having to initiate the pretense. Kathleen's behavior made sense. It was not her role to criticize her boss for being a problem drinker. If Tom's behavior became too deviant, perhaps Kathleen could have a serious discussion with him about how his actions were making it difficult for her to properly do her job. As a last resort, Kathleen could ask for a private conference with Tom's boss to discuss the gravity of the problem. In the interim, it would help Kathleen's cause to support her boss. Tom might then remember her support when she needed a special favor (such as time off to register for a course or to take a long weekend without cutting into her vacation time).

COVER YOUR BOSS'S BLOOPER

Being human, your boss may make a blooper as well as the next person. Why try to show him or her up? Instead, cover for your boss, your relationship might be all the better for your act of self-interested kindness. Kurt, a supervisor, was the only other person in the office with his boss, Allan, one evening.

Noting that Kurt was still there, Allan said, "Kurt, I know this is after hours, but I would like you to take care of something important for me. I have left a few memos on my desk that I would like Doris to type in the morning. I'll be out of town tomorrow. Will you see that Doris gets them? You might go over the memos to make sure the figures I have used check out with those we discussed the other day."

Kurt dutifully reviewed the figures. In the process, he saw an item that, if incorrect, could be a source of embarrassment to Allan, Doris, or both. One memo mentioned that an executive from a customer company, M. F. Badass, would be visiting the department. Early the next morning, Kurt telephoned the customer company, inquiring if there was anyone by that name in the company. The switchboard operator said, "I'm sorry, sir, we may have a bad connection. Do you mean Mr. M. F. Bandrass? May I connect you with his office?"

Kurt corrected the error; a month later he told Allan the story. Both men chuckled about what might have happened if people in the department had read the original version of the memo and had greeted the visitor, "Hello Mr. Badass, so nice to meet you."

TEACH YOUR BOSS A SKILL

Even an Innocent Lamb would not object to the political strategy of cultivating your boss by teaching him or her a valuable job-related skill. Helping your boss in this way should help your relationship. Lou, a young man interested in scientific approaches to management, noted that his boss, Heath, was having difficulty deciding whether to make station-to-station or person-to-person calls. Lou volunteered to help his boss find the best answer by use of a payoff matrix—a relatively uncomplicated, mathematical way of making these types of decisions. Heath used Lou's results. After a 6-month trial period, the amount of money paid for toll calls decreased. Lou explains:

"Heath was really excited about my little payoff matrix. I told him the matrix could be applied to a variety of well-defined business problems. Heath then asked me how he could go about learning this technique. I volunteered to teach him the method, figuring an informed boss is a happy boss. I could feel my stature rise in Heath's eyes once he learned how to calculate on a payoff matrix."

INTRODUCE YOUR BOSS TO IMPORTANT PEOPLE

If your boss is ambitious, he or she would enjoy being introduced to an influential person. If you make the introduction, it means one more positive step in cultivating your boss. Althea, a sales representative in a company that manufactured business forms, enhanced her influence in her department by just such a maneuver. She notes:

It's not easy to impress your boss when you're out selling business forms. If your orders are better than average that can be impressive. However, the amount of orders you receive are often out of your control. If a customer uses up his forms, he'll order some more. If machines are changed, some new forms may be needed. It's tough to make a quick impression on the boss.

It occurred to me that I had a relative my boss might like to meet. My uncle is the vice-president of a machine distributing company. It would have been presumptuous of me to try and sell directly to my uncle. It's usually the sales manager who makes the first contact with a company official. I arranged for my boss and my uncle to have lunch together. It worked out to their mutual benefit. My boss made a large, profitable sale and my uncle received a few good leads on potential customers from him.

CULTIVATE YOUR BOSS'S SECRETARY

Why neglect one of the most obvious ways of cultivating your boss? If your boss's secretary is a competent and trusted person, her (or his) opinion of you can weigh heavily in your boss's evaluation of you. Conversely, if you fail to cultivate—or you alienate—the boss's secretary, you will be doing harm to your own cause. Ann explains how she retaliated against Pete:

Pete thought he was a star mathematics professor. He may have been a genius in math, but he was a moron in human relations. I'll give you an example of what I mean. He would tell me at 10 A.M. on a Friday that he needed a paper typed for him by Monday morning. It would usually contain a large number of complicated equations. I would try to explain to Pete that a department secretary does not ordinarily type papers for assistant professors, but he would become obnoxious and tell me I was being picayune.

If I were talking to a student, he would often barge right into the conversation and tell me that he had to see Professor Reston (the department chairperson). When Pete and I passed each other outside the department he would scarcely acknowledge me. From the offhand comments the students made, I don't think they were too impressed with Pete's manners either.

Finally, I got my sweet revenge. Professor Reston was making plans for his annual evaluation of the faculty. He mentioned that although he was not aware of any major problem in the department, the student evaluations are always of some value. I told Reston, that from the scuttlebutt I heard, we did have a major problem. Reston, of course, pressed me for more details.

My answer was, "Pete is the only professor the students seem to dislike intensely." Within 1 year, Pete obtained a job at a lesser-known college.

CULTIVATE YOUR BOSS'S SPOUSE (WITHIN LIMITS)

"Roger is such a nice person," said Mildred to her husband. "At the party the other night, he was telling me about how involved he is with his wife, children, and his job. Another thing about Roger you should know—he enjoys working for you. He finds his job so stimulating."

On the basis of this conversation, Mildred's husband may not rush to the office and increase Roger's salary or offer him a promotion. But a second-party endorsement—through a spouse—can be helpful in your cultivating a good relationship with your boss. A delicate line, however, must be drawn between cultivating your boss's spouse and making it appear that you are trying to cultivate an affair with him or her. In short, send your boss's spouse a get-well card, but not a Valentine's Day card.

PRESENT ALTERNATIVES TO YOUR BOSS

An indirect way of cultivating your boss is to find ways of blaming others for wrong decisions! To the extent that you are blamed for bad decisions, it detracts from your boss's opinion of you. A technique to circumvent this problem—as practiced by a number of shrewd office politicians—is that of presenting your boss with alternatives when you are faced with a difficult decision. It works this way:

YOU: We have a difficult problem facing us. A company with a bad credit rating wants to place a $10,000 order on 90-day terms. We can readily fill the order from current inventory, but it could prove very expensive if the customer doesn't pay. The way I look at it, we have three alternatives for dealing with this problem:

One, we could tell the customer to take out a loan and then come back to us when he has the cash.

Two, we could request that the customer make a substantial down payment and give us the balance due in 90 days.

Three, we could demand a 30-day payment because the customer is not a first-rate credit risk.

BOSS: I like the first alternative. Let's deal with them on a cash basis.

As Murphy's Law predicted (if anything can go wrong, it will), the prospective customer does not wish to borrow money to purchase goods from your company. Irritated, they find another supplier. Your boss is upset about the lost sale, but he or she accepts most of the blame because he or she chose *what appeared to be the wrong alternative.*

SHARE YOUR ACCOMPLISHMENTS WITH YOUR BOSS

Most jobs in organizations are team efforts. If you make a contribution, it is usually a shared one. If you are an advertising copywriter and you think of a slogan that catapults your client's product to the top, it is not solely your accomplishment. It's easy to forget that the artist who prepared the layout on which to present your slogan made an important contribution. It's also easy to forget that you tried out the slogan on the office boy (his pupils dilated when he heard your sonorous phrase). And did you forget your boss who may have pushed your thinking in the right direction to think of the prize-winning slogan, "We are not Number One for nothing"?

Kevin was creative both as a laboratory technician and an office politician. His suggestion for saving the company $5,000 per year by recycling laboratory wastes netted him a $1,500 suggestion award. As the company photographer took a picture of Kevin standing between his boss and the manager of the suggestion system program, Kevin turned to his boss and said, "I couldn't have made it without you."

5

Cultivating the Higher-Ups

Climbing the organizational ladder requires more than
your doing a good job and currying favor with your
boss. You also have to cultivate the powerful people
in your company—from your boss's boss to, conceivably, the president. Cultivating higher-ups is usually
done for the offensive purpose of helping you find a
patron—an influential person who will help pluck you
from obscurity to organizational stardom. A positive
recommendation from on high can do wonders for your
career. Take note, too, that defense is also important in
office politics. Cultivating higher-ups may provide a
hedge against a poor relationship with your immediate
boss. If your boss is unimpressed by you and/or your
performance, you and your reputation can be salvaged
by a higher-up. If a high-ranking official extols your
virtues, your boss's negative opinion of you might be
overruled.

Whether you are cultivating influential people for
offensive or defensive purposes, the 18 strategies recommended in this chapter should be of help. Keep in
mind that many of the strategies and tactics for cultivating your boss (described in the previous chapter)
can sometimes be applied at higher levels.

AVOID BEING ONE OF THE GANG

"Why are you recommending Steve Williams for a branch manager's appointment?" asked Sid, the national sales manager. "Steve is a nice kid, and I admire his salesmanship. As the records show, he was the highest-producing sales representative in our region last year. But don't you realize that he's strictly one of the gang? He'd never get the respect of the other sales representatives. They would see Steve as one of them. We need people with more executive stature in branch managerial positions."

Bruce, concerned that his recommendation of Steve for a promotion was being turned down, countered, "Sid, can you give me a couple of examples of why you think Steve is one of the gang? His sales record would suggest he's a leader."

"Steve is undoubtedly a leader with respect to sales performance. But inside the sales office, he tries too hard to be one of the boys. I've seen him about five times over the past couple of years. Once, I saw him matching quarters with the clerks in the department to determine who would buy the coffee. At a regional sales meeting, I noticed that Steve spent a good deal of time at the bar with other sales representatives. He seemed to have no interest in spending time with members of management. Maybe, when he matures more, we can reconsider him."

The message from this oft-repeated scenario at places of work is clear. An effective strategy for impressing higher-ups in your organization is indicated by your willingness to leave the troops behind. Establishing rapport with people at all levels in the organization is important for your success. But do not overdo it. Guard against conveying the impression that you would feel uncomfortable if placed in an executive environment.

COMPLIMENT INFLUENTIAL PEOPLE

One underused strategy for cultivating the higher-ups is to pay an honest compliment to the *right* people. Paying a compliment to an official of your organization will increase your chances of being remembered by that official, if judiciously executed. Sending "you are great" memos and letters is too transparent a scheme. It is much more effective to make job-related, specific comment. Toni, a chemist in a food company, explains how she complimented an influential person:

My boy friend and I were visiting Toronto. I suspect it's an occupational hazard, but, when on vacation, I have an irresistible urge to visit grocery stores. I enjoy seeing whether some of our company products are being sold in a particular store. One afternoon, we noticed a large Loblaw's supermarket near the downtown area. Inside the store, I was quite happy to see a number of our products on the rack.

I took particular notice of a large display of new seasonings our company was promoting. When I returned from our vacation, I wrote a note to the product manager in charge of seasonings, complimenting him on his penetration of the Canadian market. He sent a brief note in return, thanking me for the information.

Several months later, I received an unexpected promotion to laboratory supervisor when my boss resigned to enter a family business. Part of the explanation given for offering me the job was that higher management thought I was a company-minded person. At that time, I also discovered that the product manager for seasonings was on the selection committee for management promotions.

SHINE AT MEETINGS

Business meetings, justifiably, are sometimes referred to as dog-and-pony shows—people use meetings to display themselves to advantage. At many meetings you attend, at least one person present will be a higher-up. When you are trying to impress a higher-up at a meeting keep in mind that you are not trying to dominate or win control of the meeting. Neither are you trying to resolve a conflict. You should be trying to impress your boss and higher-ups with your good judgment and management potential. Keep four impression-making tactics in mind if you want to shine at meetings.

Ask Set-up Questions.   Bart was present at a meeting attended by Mr. Chadwick, the chairman of the board, who was actively interested in environmental protection and human rights. At midmeeting, Bart turned to Chadwick and said, "Sir, may I ask a question? Your answer may help resolve a few of the issues raised this morning."

"Go ahead, by all means," replied Chadwick.

"Mr. Chadwick, are we in business strictly to make a profit?"

"So glad you asked that question, Bart. Certainly not. As a business organization, we have a social responsibility as well as profit responsibility. . . ."

Avoid Daydreaming.   A major problem facing many people at a meeting is how to stay fully awake. As an alternative to falling asleep, many people begin to drift into a dream-like state. One man confessed that he dreamed about recent sexual experiences during budget review meetings. The danger in daydreaming, of course, is that you will miss out on some important information or be unable to answer a question specifically asked of you.

The executive director of a settlement house turned to a young supervisor during a staff meeting and asked,

"Bill, what do you think of the proposal just advanced by Clara?"

Bill replied, "I'm sorry, I must have been daydreaming. What proposal?" Bill not only missed out on an opportunity to impress the executive director, he left a lasting negative impression.

Take Notes when Influential People Speak. A potent form of flattery is to take notes of important messages delivered at meetings. If you take notes on everything said, others will think you are acting as the meeting secretary. It is better to be selective. Take a few notes when your boss speaks. Take copious notes when a higher-up offers information. Later on in the meeting, or at a future date, these notes can be used to advantage.

Ned attended a production meeting in which the vice-president of manufacturing was also present. Ned brought along his usual yellow tablet and jotted down information he perceived as being important. Toward the end of the meeting, he addressed the vice-president. Pointing to his tablet, he said, "Sir, you mentioned at the outset of this meeting that some of our products were becoming overpriced in comparison to the competition. We at the manufacturing engineering level would certainly agree. Could you give us some more information on that topic? It is of vital concern."

Score one for Ned. All at once, he set up the vice-president as influential, paid him a compliment (by taking notes on the information the higher-up presented), and created a good impression in the process.

Allow Others to Talk. People who dominate meetings often do so because they are tense or trying too hard to create a good impression. Unless you have called the meeting and its primary purpose is for you to dispense information to others, avoid overtalking in meetings. Particularly if you are trying to impress higher-ups.

Ben was a compulsive talker at meetings. It was important to him that everyone be aware of his opinion on every issue raised. Despite his urge to control meetings, Ben was effective in his middle management job. Yet his actions in meetings excluded him from at least one key promotional opportunity. A new assistant general managerial position opened up. Ben was one of the candidates suggested to the general manager. The latter commented, "Sorry, you'll have to do better than that. I've been in meetings with Ben and I find him obnoxious. The guy won't shut up and give other people a chance to talk. How could he ever find the answer to problems I asked him to investigate if he did all the talking?"

TALK BIG, SHUN TRIVIA

Small talk can keep you placed in a small job. If you have a predilection for talking about the weather, your sinuses, or the food in the company cafeteria, save these comments for the right occasion. The right occasion is when you are spending time with people who enjoy small talk. The wrong occasion is when you are trying to impress higher-ups (and also your boss). When you have the chance to talk to an influential, some trivia may be necessary for an initial warm-up, but quickly shift the topic to big talk. Here is an example of the difference between making small and big talk over the same issue, when meeting a high-ranking official from your organization. The person talking is the manager of a branch motor vehicle department. The visitor to the office is the State Commissioner of Motor Vehicles.

MANAGER (using small talk):	Look at that rain outside. It's been like that for 3 days. This sure is the rainiest place I've ever lived. I guess it's fine if you're a farmer or a plant.
COMMISSIONER:	Did you say something?
MANAGER (using big talk):	This rain creates an interesting problem for the Motor Vehicle

Department at the branch level. Common sense would suggest that our work load decreases when it rains. My calculations and those of my staff indicate that we are extra busy on rainy days. I think a good number of people wait for a rainy day to take care of their routine business with us. I wonder if this is a national trend.

COMMISSIONER: You have raised an important issue about our work load. I think the problem warrants further study.

PERFORM A VILE TASK BEFORE AN AUDIENCE

Getting your hands or your body dirty can dramatize your sense of loyalty when physical work is not an ordinary part of your job. The former president of one of the world's largest paper companies is a case in point.[1] Early in his career, this man had a managerial position in one of the company's paper mills. A difficult mechanical problem arose in the mill. In order for the problem to be fixed, it was necessary for a person to climb into a vat of wet paper mulch and turn off a valve.

Not one of the workmen would volunteer to attempt the task. Sensing the urgency of the problem, the manager in question took off his jacket and climbed into the vat himself. He ruined his suit in the process, but upper management became aware of his act of loyalty. His career received a significant boost upward.

Vile, or at least hazardous, tasks that you might perform to impress the higher-ups present themselves infrequently. Nature can sometimes play a hand in their occurrence. A payroll supervisor made himself a hero during the great snowstorm of 1977. At the height of the storm, all roads were closed to automobiles and all offices and factories were shut down. Mark explains his heroics:

> The way things were going, it was obvious that nobody was going to get his paycheck on time. Some more work needed to be done to get the paychecks processed so they would be ready when the storm cleared—probably another 48 hours. I hopped into my snowmobile and got to the factory office about 8 A.M. By 2 P.M. I had all the checks processed. Later, I received a personal letter of gratitude from the controller. People still remember me as the man who rescued the paychecks during the big storm.

DISPLAY COMPANY MANNERS

The proper use of company manners is both an offensive and a defensive strategy for gaining favor with the higher-ups. From the offensive standpoint, displaying manners that are considered desirable by the higher-ups might help you project a favorable image. From the defensive standpoint, displaying manners that are considered unacceptable by the higher-ups will prevent you from gaining favorable attention. To determine what constitutes acceptable manners, you have to observe the fast trackers and higher-ups in your company. If you aspired to a management job with the New York Yankees, it might enhance your image to chew bubble gum or tobacco during a team meeting. But rid yourself of those habits if you want a management position with IBM.

The importance of displaying company manners is underscored by the comments of the president of an insurance company. I was discussing with him the strengths and weaknesses of a manager being considered for the position of a department head, which would have brought him one step away from becoming a vice-president. The president interjected:

"Despite the glowing comments you make about

Mel's inner strengths, he's going nowhere in this company until he graduates from charm school. He's one of the crudest people in management. He talks with food in his mouth, he burps during staff meetings, and he yawns in your face when he's bored. He even has dandruff. Let's keep him where he is until he straightens out."

Mel was subsequently counseled about his impact on people, but it didn't help him in his particular company. Mel changed, but his image lingered on—that of a middle manager with poor manners who would be out of place in the executive suite.

APPEAR COOL UNDER PRESSURE

Beyond not displaying poor manners, a good way to impress higher-ups is to appear in the role of a polished executive. Almost everybody reading this book will say to himself or herself, "That's true. Anybody who works for a living knows that." Yet many people trying to create a favorable impression make no particular effort to appear poised and in control of themselves. In recent years, management has been alerted to the importance of people honestly expressing their feelings. However, it is still to your advantage not to appear unglued when the pressure mounts or to throw childish temper tantrums when things do not go your way.

Bursts of emotion are more permissible on the shop floor and in the field than in the executive office. Such outbursts are better directed at subordinates than at superiors. Eric, now a marketing executive in the machine tool industry, made a big impression on the company president by remaining cool under pressure. Rosie, his executive secretary relates the incident:

Eric had newly arrived as the sales manager at one of our biggest divisions. About the day he finished unpacking, sales in the machine tool industry plummeted. There was a lot of talk about a depression sweeping the world, so naturally people were holding back on buying new machines. It was very difficult to place an order and a number of customers were trying to cancel contracts for new machinery.

Three months after Eric was on the job, not one new order had been placed. The vice-president of marketing from corporate headquarters visited our division. He asked Eric in my presence how things were going. I'll never forget his reply: "Everything is fine except for orders. We have a good sales force and excellent clerical support and equipment repair. Once demand picks up, we'll be in great shape."

You could tell the vice-president of marketing was very impressed. Eric didn't act defensive and flustered; he made a factual statement of business conditions. You have to admit it is unusual for a sales manager to create a positive impression when his department is selling nothing but a few replacement parts.

DISPLAY THE RIGHT READING MATERIAL

A strategy that can do no harm is to display reading material that you think will impress top management. *What* to display is relatively uncomplicated. Among the more influential types of reading material are newspapers: *The Wall Street Journal* or the *Financial Post* (in Canada) and the *New York Times*. Business magazines such as *Business Week, Forbes,* and *Fortune* are impressive. Specialty or trade magazines and journals indicate you are professional in your interests. Examples are *Women's Wear Daily, Advertising Age,* and *Electronic Industry*. Popular books about management and the *Harvard Business Review* give you an aura of professionalism. But don't neglect the caveat offered in the first chapter of this book. In your particular organization, reading the *National Enquirer, New York Post* or *New York Daily News,* could be impressive because the papers indicate you are trying to stay in touch with the pulse of the community.

Where to display your impressive reading material is a more challenging question than *what* to display. Your goal is to have the material on display when higher-ups (and your boss) see you, but you do not want to appear to be reading on the job. A standard approach is to prop the newspaper or magazine under your arm as you enter the building in the morning or leave in the late afternoon. If you travel with a company executive, it is natural to be reading your attention-getting publication.

If you have the luxury of a coffee table in your office, display your reading material there with index cards inserted between pages to suggest that you are in the middle of a chapter or article. Never keep a newspaper placed on your desk turned to a crossword puzzle, comic page, or bridge column. In general, it is better not to have a newspaper on your desk. For the same reason, it looks unimpressive to be carrying around a newspaper during normal working hours. However, as you exit or return from lunch flaunt your reading material.

LAUGH HEARTILY AT HIGHER-UPS' JOKES

It is not necessary to laugh heartily *at all* your boss's jokes. If he or she frequently tells jokes, it will be obvious to your boss that some of his or her jokes are funnier than others. Higher-ups see you less frequently and therefore tell you fewer jokes. Machiavellis and Office Politicians always laugh at jokes told by higher-ups even when they have heard the joke before. Eddie, a Machiavelli, was almost caught.

HIGHER-UP: Eddie, have you heard the one about the politician who visits the Indian reservation? In a speech, he tells the Indians that if he is elected, they will all get improved medical care. The Indians shout "hoya, hoya." He then tells the Indians that if he is elected they will get a special pension from the federal government to pay for some of the wrongs the white man has done to the red man. Again, shouts of "hoya, hoya."

After the speech, the politician says to the chief: "I would like to walk across your fields and see some of your cattle."

"Okay," says the chief. "But I hope you brought your boots. The fields are covered with hoya."

EDDIE: (With a wide grin and a burst of laughter) That's fabulous. It's the best I've heard this year. Where did you learn that joke?

HIGHER-UP: Hold on, Eddie, I think you told me that joke last year. That's where I heard it. What made you laugh so hard?

EDDIE: A good joke is just as funny in the re-telling. Besides your delivery was fabulous.

GET YOUR NAME ON PROJECTS

The modern way of impressing higher management is to be associated with special projects and task forces. It is generally considered a feather in your career cap to be appointed to a project. (An important exception is one glamor company where it is a frequent practice to dump unwanted people into project assignments. You may have to investigate why you are assigned to a particular project.) Therefore, an impression-making technique is to find ways to have your name listed on as many projects as possible.

Karl, a financial analyst, used the project route to bring his name to the attention of the higher-ups in his company. He would ask the chief financial person on a project if he could volunteer his services to take care of an overload situation. Karl would then use his after-hours time to complete the extra-duty assignment. The only recompense Karl asked for (and received) was that his name be listed down at the bottom of the list of project members.

Four months later, a project director chose Karl as the financial analyst on his team, primarily because he was looking for a financial analyst with project experience. Karl's participation in the project eventually helped him land a position in the marketing department. A team member on Karl's project was an executive in the marketing department. Karl had parlayed a footnote into a first-rate assignment.

SEND PHOTOCOPIES TO INFLUENTIALS

The science of xerography has advanced the art of office politics. Now everybody but Innocent Lambs sends photocopies to influential people (to keep them posted of their significant achievements). A typical ploy is to send a higher-up a copy of a memo that indicates how much money you saved the company by completing a particular assignment. A general approach is to send out copies of information that make you look good. Iggy, a product planner, and a Machiavelli, used a semidevious application of photocopy warfare. Iggy explains how:

My technique is based on statistical probabilities. When somebody introduces a new product idea, I write a memo pointing out some of the problems that might be associated with that product. I can always note that consumer demand is uncertain. Only about one percent of new product ideas ever become profitable for a company. Thus, I am almost always right. When a product idea flops, Iggy's memo is right there pointing to its potential pitfalls.

So far, my bit of gamesmanship has earned me the reputation of being a good company critic. I should be able to cash in on this reputation at a later date. My technique is not unique. Reviewers of Broadway plays have been doing that for years. They are negative about most shows. Since few ever have long runs, the critics are right most of the time.

CLIMB THE SOCIAL LADDER

A widely recognized strategy for cultivating higher-ups is to socialize with them. Many an aspirant to more power has joined a country club in order to maintain social contact with influential people. Socializing with the higher-ups can be an effective way of cultivating them if you keep two elementary principles in mind.

First, it is important to use socializing primarily to create a favorable climate of acceptance for yourself. For many a naïve office politician, climbing the social ladder has backfired because he or she tried to pin down an influential politician during a social occasion.

Jimmy Tries a Shower Room Seduction.   After completing a round of golf on a hot humid day, Jimmy headed to the showers. Under the shower next to him stood Badge, a vice-president of his firm whom Jimmy knew primarily through the golf club. Jimmy made his thrust: "By the way Badge, they tell me you are looking for a new department head. I haven't had the chance to tell you this back at the office, but I've been looking for more responsibility. I think a department head position would be ideal for me. Please keep me in mind."

Taken back, Badge mumbled, "Young man, let's keep business out of the locker room. I come here to play golf and relax, not to talk shop." Badge was irritated enough by the incident to carry it one step further. The next day he wrote a memo to Jimmy's boss, recommending that the latter instruct Jimmy about the proper communication channels to be used for requesting transfers and promotions.

Second, it is important to adjust your social activities to the preferences of those people you are trying to cultivate.[2] If paddle tennis is big at the executive level in your organization, then pursue competence in that sport. On the negative side, avoid cultivating higher-ups through social activities that they find uncomfortable.

Roz Takes the Floor Supervisor to Her Private Cave.
Roz, an assistant department head in a department store, wanted to cultivate Barbara, the floor supervisor. Roz realized that Barbara not only had high rank at the store but she was also a person whose opinion counted heavily when promotions and transfers were made. The strategy Roz chose for cultivating Barbara was to extend the latter an invitation to a party at her private "cave." For party purposes, Roz would convert the recreation room in her townhouse into a dark discotheque. Music blared from three speakers, and more than 50 people were crowded together on the makeshift dance floor on a typical party night at the cave.

Barbara graciously accepted Roz's party invitation and brought along her husband. Entering Roz's cave, both Barbara and her husband were appalled and disappointed. Barbara stayed in the cave for 5 minutes. She went upstairs, where she and her husband stayed for an hour before they left the party. As Barbara and her husband left Roz asked them why they were leaving so early. Barbara answered:

"I didn't know this was to be a disco party. I simply don't know how to do that kind of dancing, and it is rather hard on my ears. But other than that, we had a lovely time."

INVEST IN YOUR FIRM

A wise investment in your future—if you work in a business that uses outside funding—is to purchase company stocks or bonds. Few companies would demand that you invest in the firm as a condition of employment, but it impresses the higher-ups when you show enough faith in the company to become an investor.

Investment of this nature is more likely to pay off in a small company than in a mammoth corporation. (In the latter, company executives might not be supplied with the names of small investors.)

Chris Buys a Promotion and a Salary Increase. Chris was the production engineer in a small-sized machine screw company. Two years previously he had left a large corporation to join the smaller company because he felt his chances for recognition and accomplishment were better in a smaller pond. Chris learned through the grapevine that the director of manufacturing position would soon be open and felt he had an even chance to be selected for the position. To increase his chances, Chris took all his savings ($750) and purchased 325 shares in the company.

The investment has paid handsome dividends although the stock has decreased in value since Chris made the investment. The treasurer informed the company president of Chris's investment, which helped bring Chris to the president's attention. Shortly thereafter, Chris was promoted to the director of manufacturing position which included a $2,000-per-year raise. Chris is performing well in that position and would not have received the promotion if he were not seen as a person with potential. Nevertheless, the stock purchase singled out Chris as a person who believed in the company—a fact very impressive to the higher-ups.

CONTACT A NEWLY ARRIVED OFFICEHOLDER

This technique is practiced to excess at the White House. When White House aides are newly installed, the switchboard suffers from electronic overload.[3] The army of well-wishers, sycophants, and some people with the good of the country in mind want to assure themselves that the new broom has not swept them "out of it." Since this technique is used primarily in Washington, D.C. (and by life insurance sales persons all over), it probably has not been over-used in your office. Send your well wishes after the dust has settled. Most of the greetings flood in during the new official's first 30 days in power.

Duane Uses Sensitivity. Duane, a personnel manager in a multi-division company, learned through formal channels that Hal Winters was newly installed as the president of the corporation's largest division. Duane had worked three levels under Hal some years previously. To his knowledge, the working relationship was favorable. Duane carefully mapped out his political ploy. He mailed to the home of the newly arrived president the following hand-written note:

> Dear Mr. Winters,
> Count me as one of the many well-wishers who offer you congratulations on a sterling achievement. I wish you all the success you deserve in your new position.
> Just in case you might be staffing your organization, I have enclosed my résumé. Working for you in the past was a very positive professional experience for me.
> Best of luck,
> Duane Anderson

Hal Winters was impressed by the honesty of Duane's letter. Duane thought highly enough of Hal to want to work for him and did not try to hide the fact. Most people who contact newly arrived office holders are reluctant to admit the real purpose of their greeting.

PROMOTE YOUR COMPANY'S PRODUCTS OR SERVICES

A variation of the loyalty theme sometimes can be effectively used to impress the higher-ups. Find a way to promote your company's products or services and you will endear yourself to many people above you in the company hierarchy. A routine application of this strategy is to purchase goods made by your company when possible. If you work for an aluminum siding company, have your house sided with aluminum by your company. If you work for American Motors, drive a Jeep, a Pacer, or any other AMC vehicle. A nonroutine strategy is to promote your company's goods and services by involving other people.

Louise Starts a Camera Club. Louise, the payroll manager in a darkroom supply manufacturer, decided to start a camera club. Her basement contained a substantial-sized darkroom in addition to a knotty-pine recreation room, thus being a natural for the central meeting place for the club. Louise organized photo-taking field trips and darkroom sessions. She gently suggested that members of the club try darkroom supplies used by her company. Four members of the club started their own darkrooms because of their satisfaction with the equipment displayed in Louise's basement.

Louise's club received a write-up in the company newspaper. Six months later, Louise was offered a promotion to office manager. The favorable attention she had brought to herself through her camera club has facilitated her receiving a promotion.

BEFRIEND AN UNPOPULAR EXECUTIVE

Popular executives, by definition, are those most frequently cultivated by underlings. "Hitch your wagon to a star" is a widely used strategy for climbing the ladder. Befriending an unpopular and less competent executive can sometimes pay bigger dividends. An unpopular executive is more likely to be appreciative of the attention paid him or her from below. Buck, a brash assembly line inspector, explains how this technique worked for him:

I wanted to become a foreman pretty bad. I figured lots of guys wanted to become foreman so I had to do something out of the ordinary. My plan was very simple. One of our superintendents, Jim, was disliked by about everybody. The guy was such a bastard. He would chew out people in front of their friends. I figured anybody this mean must need a friend. Right out of the blue, I invited the codger fishing. His response was, "Why not, I'm not particular about who I go fishing with. You'd better be a better fisherman than you are an inspector." That was Jim's way of kidding.

We got along famously out on the fishing boat. We continued on as fishing buddies. While on the boat, Jim would cuss out all the other people in the company. I actually got to like the man. The payoff was that he made me foreman of the best operations in the plant. Now the other guys are jealous of me.

BEFRIEND A HIGHER-UP'S CHILD

Being nice to your boss's child is an effective political strategy. Although the strategy is more difficult to implement, befriending a higher-up's child can have a big personal payoff. You may have to dig for information about appealing to that particular child. Here are three techniques that have met with some effectiveness:

- One woman brought in hard-to-obtain empty beer cans for an executive to bring home to his 12-year-old son who was an avid beer-can collector. The woman learned of the beer-can collection through a friendship with the executive's personal secretary.
- A Little League baseball coach was extra nice to the awkward son of the vice-president of claims in an insurance company (particularly after he checked out the boy's surname in the company directory). During warm-up time at one of the games, the grateful Little Leaguer said to his father, "Daddy, here is the nice man who has been helping me learn how to throw."

- A facilities manager in a manufacturing company heard, through a friend, that the 17-year-old daughter of the director of manufacturing was looking for summer work. He telephoned the vice-president and said, "Do you think you could persuade your daughter to do groundswork this summer? I have a summer job open for a grounds-keeper and I think it's about time we hired a woman for this kind of job."

MARRY THE BOSS'S OFFSPRING

For sake of completing this list, we are compelled to mention that the ageless strategy of marrying an off-spring of a powerful person can catapult you to a key spot in the organization. However, marrying the boss's daughter or son will probably not help you unless two conditions are met.

First, you must have a good relationship with the person you marry. If your wife or husband complains continually to the Big Boss that you are mistreating him or her, your career may be in jeopardy in that organization. If you split with your spouse, you may also split with your job.

Second, you must be able to work effectively with your prospective father- or mother-in-law. Gil, a manufacturer's representative in a small, prosperous firm, began to date the president's daughter. After a year of seeing each other, they announced their marriage plans. The president said to Gil:

I welcome you into our family, but not into our business. As long as I am president, you will always be a traveling salesman. I may give you a territory that is easy on your home life, but that will be your last concession. I think you will make a fine husband to Diana. She loves you very much.

When I retire, this company will be sold to an out-sider. During the 3 years you have worked for our firm, you have given me no indication that you have what it takes to be the president of our company. It has taken me 25 years to build up this business and I will not see it hurt by handing it over to the wrong person.

But son, don't take my comments the wrong way. I want you to have a happy marriage and a successful career.

Gil had a sinking feeling in his stomach as he pondered whether to back out of his marriage plans, find a new job, or do both. Since he truly wanted to marry the president's daughter, he went ahead with the marriage, but quit the firm. Gil was then forced to take a lower-paying sales position. For Gil, marrying the boss's daughter backfired.

Cultivating Your Peers

Office politics is best played in a step-by-step, logical sequence. It is important for you to gain favor with your peers to later become a powerful and influential person in your organization. The solo artist who neglects to cultivate his or her peers on the way to power may never get to exercise that power. A recently conducted study of power in corporate life showed that individual performers received rewards for their immediate accomplishments, but found their careers mixed because they had not developed the kinds of connections necessary to succeed in higher-level jobs.[1]

What about the person who wants to live a comfortable and secure life, free from the competitive pressures of a higher-level job? Cultivating your peers is still important. You may need their support to help you get your job accomplished or you may need them to come to your defense when you are attacked from above. Developing friendships on the job is also important for mundane reasons such as having an office friend take care of your job properly while you are sick at home.

What about the office curmudgeon who wants to be left alone to carry out his or her chores without having to bother with other people in the office? You still need to cultivate—or at least, not totally alienate—your peers. It is self-defeating to be bad-mouthed by co-workers or recommended as the first person to be axed in times of a cutback.

BE A TEAM PLAYER

An essential strategy for cultivating your peers is to function in your department or task force as a team player.[2] Until you reach the pinnacle of power in your organization, you must work cooperatively with others. In recent years, several books have proposed that a major reason relatively few women do not make it to the organizational top is that they are inexperienced in team play. Men, according to this reasoning, are at an advantage because so many of them played team sports early in their lives or spent time in the armed forces. You may not accept this premise, but it does emphasize the importance of becoming a good team player if you want to succeed in organizational life. Male or female, you can improve your status as a team player if you promote the team concept, give information and opinions to your co-workers, and touch base with them on important issues.

Frank Shares Credit for His Victory. "We won team, we won," said Frank excitedly to his four lunchmates. "The world's largest manufacturer of air conditioners is going to use our new electronic switch in every one of their units. I just got the good news today. Thanks to all of you for giving me so many good suggestions to explain the merits of our switch. I know the big boss will be pleased with our sales department."

It seems as though Frank is reliving in the past glory of his basketball-playing days at college. One interpretation is that, as he closes a sale for an order of electronic switches, he fantasizes that he has thrown the ball through the hoop in the final second of a basketball game. Possibly, but a more parsimonious explanation is in order. Frank—by our scale—is a Survivalist or Office Politician who recognizes the importance of sharing his accomplishments with other people on the team.

When and if Frank should become the boss, the people who shared his credit success will probably accept him as a manager who cares about the welfare of his subordinates. Equally important, the next time Frank needs help in taking care of a customer, his teammates will offer their cooperation.

Tamara Gives Information and Gives Opinions. At a typical staff meeting, Tamara, a public relations specialist, makes comments such as "Let me share with you some important information I've picked up on that topic," "I have some scuttlebutt that might be worth something," or "Let me give you my candid, but very personal, reaction to your proposal." Statements (and actions) like this have helped Tamara to develop her reputation as a good team player in her department and as a woman to count on when help is needed. Tamara was asked why she was so open with, and helpful to, her co-workers. She answered:

> Before getting a job in the public relations field, I was a registered representative, selling stocks and bonds. There were about 15 of us in one large office during the mid-1970s when most of the individuals who bought stocks and bonds seemed to have disappeared. Gradually, we began to guard our tips and leads jealously. The other brokers in the office figured that, if they said something useful about a particular stock, another broker might use that information for one of his own clients. Then the first broker would look bad because the second broker made a bigger sale.
>
> People seemed to forget that if other brokers in the office didn't do well, soon there would be no office left. One incident proved to me that I no longer wanted to work in an office—or in a field—where everybody is looking out only for himself or herself. A woman walked into our office with a prior appointment, asking to buy some stocks and bonds. Something like that happens very rarely. She was

referred to Milt, whose turn it was to get the next "over the transom" inquiry. I thought the woman looked familiar.

As the woman was leaving the office, she stopped by my desk and reminded me that we had been classmates in college. She told me that she had recently inherited some money and decided to invest about $10,000 in blue-chip stocks. I jokingly asked why she hadn't come over to my desk when she recognized me. She claimed that Milt had told her it's not a good idea to purchase stocks from friends because a friend can't be objective. I felt pity for Milt, but I guess he needed the commission pretty badly. Milt helped me learn something about myself. I could enjoy working in an atmosphere only where people cooperated with each other.

Brett Touches Base with His Co-workers. Brett, a computer scientist, had an idea that could conceivably cut down the operating cost of his department by about $35,000 per year. According to his logic, his division really didn't need its own computer since the parent company—some 200 miles away—recently has installed a computer powerful enough to handle more work than the parent company needed computerized. Brett planned to propose that his division sell its own computer and have a hookup installed to the parent company's computer. He realized that if this idea were presented in a staff meeting with no prior warning, it could create a furor in the department. Perhaps other people in the department (including the boss) would think that such a move would shrink their power as a computer department.

Brett decided to pre-sell the idea by holding private discussions with everyone above the clerical level in the department, including the boss. It took Brett six coffee-break conversations, ten luncheon conferences, four cocktail hours, and three beer-drinking sessions following bowling games to gain acceptance for his idea.

When Brett presented his idea, replete with flip charts

and cost figures, everybody at the meeting smiled. They agreed that, in the long run, if Brett's ideas were accepted by top management, the department would be remembered for its contribution to the corporate welfare. If Brett had surprised his co-workers and boss by presenting his ideas in a meeting without forewarning, he might not have received the support he needed. His proposal might have been shot down with a series of distortions and rationalizations. People don't like big surprises in meetings when the surprise might affect *them*.

EXCHANGE FAVORS

"You say that you've tried to glue that garnet back in its setting, but it just will not stay put? We have a new kind of resin-based bonding material here that should do the trick. Why don't you drop by tomorrow? I should have it fixed by then."

The person just quoted is not a public jeweler. It is Rolando, a supervisor in the company's testing facility. The department's primary mission is to test its own products and those of its competitor. Since their laboratory and shop facilities are so well developed, they have a steady stream of company employees who request minor repair jobs. In the last 2 months, Rolando has removed blood stains from a silk shirt, smoothed the burrs from the wheels of a 6-inch-long racing car entered in a Cub Scout Pinewood Derby, and touched up the cracks on an oil painting of an executive's grandmother.

Called "government jobs" in many companies, these quid pro quo arrangements are one manifestation of the importance of exchanging favors in order to cultivate peers. Rolando may need a favor in the future such as making sure his hospital medical insurance claim is handled promptly, or having a kind word said about him to the personnel department. I don't know whether Rolando intends to cash in on his exchange of favors immediately, but he is taking steps to ensure that he will be treated with courtesy, respect, and affection from the people in the office.

ASK ADVICE

Earlier, we mentioned that asking your boss for advice about matters not strictly related to work was a good political strategy. Asking peers for their advice about both work and nonwork problems can also be a sound political strategy—if done with finesse. However, asking for advice sometimes can be misinterpreted if you work in a competitive environment.

Jamie Asks for Too Much Advice.   Jamie worked for a small advertising and sales promotion agency that specialized in putting together gimmicks for trade shows, conventions, and product promotions. Among their creative productions was a screwdriver that in the handle contained a color photograph of a woman clad in a bathing suit. As the screwdriver was turned, the clothing disappeared. As the screwdriver was turned in the other direction, the bathing suit reappeared. Another production was a miles-per-gallon calculator made of cardboard, with an advertising message printed on its face.

Jamie was one of four copywriters assigned the responsibility of writing copy to launch new products. Several times each day, he would ask one of his three colleagues how he might improve on a particular idea he was developing. Finally, one of the other copywriters, Dean, brought a collective complaint to the head of the agency:

"We're going on record with a protest about Jamie. The memo you recently sent us credits Jamie with being the top producer of ideas in the shop. We want you to realize that Jamie's ideas are not uniquely his. His game is to throw a half-processed idea at us for our reaction. One of us will help him with the idea to the extent of reformulating Jamie's thinking. He then takes credit for the whole idea."

The agency head sympathized with Jamie's co-workers but took no action. However, the rate of Jamie's idea production soon shrank drastically. His co-workers were no longer willing to react in a helpful way to his ideas. Jamie was now on his own. He had crossed the boundary from asking people's advice to claiming their ideas as his own.

USE REALISTIC COMPLIMENTS

An effective way of cultivating your co-workers is to compliment their work or something with which they are closely identified (such as their children or their hobbies). Compliments to co-workers are less fraught with misinterpretations of your intent than are compliments to your boss or higher-ups. Nevertheless, three important points about compliments should be kept in mind, as they could make the difference between getting the results you want with compliments versus wasting time with misdirected flattery.

Cora Compliments Concrete Accomplishment. Cora, a real estate broker in a large office, learned—in a human relations course—that it is more effective to compliment a person's actions than a person's traits and characteristics. People generally find it more meaningful for you to point out what a good job they have done than to state what fine people they are. Cora found a number of ways to implement this technique in her real estate office. The payoff to Cora is that the other realtors in her office gave her a helping hand when it was needed. One such instance took place when an out-of-town client wanted to be shown a few homes in the $150,000 range. Unfortunately, the day he chose was the very day Cora's daughter was graduating from high school. Despite his envy, a co-worker of Cora's gave the man a tour of the more expensive neighborhoods in town. Here are two of Cora's most effective compliments:

- Jack received a handwritten message from Cora

stating: Congrats, Jack, on giving us all a lesson on the art of overcoming difficult odds. We all thought it would be impossible to sell a retired couple a home in a suburban neighborhood densely populated with children. Your sales pitch that the young children would give the couple a new interest in life was certainly an ideal bit of salesmanship—particularly because it proved to be true.

- Henry, the office handyman and "gopher," was told in front of the president of the firm, "Hooray for Henry. We're the only real estate firm in the area whose FOR SALE signs didn't blow down during the last storm, and because ours was the only FOR SALE sign standing in the Chestnut Street neighborhood, I received calls from three prospective buyers."

Tony Individualizes His Compliments. The least effective way of complimenting people is to overuse the same compliment. Your co-workers will soon know you are insincere if they all hear the same compliment from you. Tony, a high school teacher, kept a written record of the compliments he paid other teachers on his staff. He wanted to ensure that he would not be seen as the type of person who dispenses insincere flattery. During a high-school open house, he heard complimentary comments about two of his colleagues made by visiting parents.

Rather than accept these compliments at face value, Tony asked the parents for clarification. He asked both parents, specifically how the teacher in question was helpful to their children. Armed with specifics, Tony was able to pass on two penetrating compliments. To Fred, he said, "I heard something very positive about you last night at the open house. Mrs. Gonzalez said that because of you her oldest son is no longer afraid of math." To Doris, he said, "I heard something at the open house last night that might be of interest to you. Mrs. Austin said that you are one of the few teachers who has been able to understand the eccentricities of her son. I know her son, and he surely is difficult to understand."

Marsha Finds Something to Compliment.   Another important point to consider when complimenting your peers is that some people have few praiseworthy actions. Despite this generalization, it is still worth your while to find *something* to praise about every one of your co-workers. People remember compliments for a long time, and even your least competent co-worker occasionally does something that warrants positive attention from you. Marsha, a social worker in a community agency, found a way of complimenting each one of her peers although she had to stretch her imagination to compliment two of them.

- Clyde, a cynical and hostile old-timer, in recent years processed more cases than any other worker in the unit. He was able to process so many because of the abrupt treatment he gave to most of his clients. His opening statement to most people seeking his help was "Okay, what are you trying to get from me?" To compliment Clyde, Marsha said, "You certainly seem to do a good job of frightening away the people who have no legitimate need for our help."
- Priscilla, a marriage counselor in the agency, was the opposite of Clyde. She tended to cling to clients, which resulted in her seeing less than her share of clients. In thinking up an authentic compliment for Priscilla, Marsha said, "Pris, could you help me develop skill in making clients depend on me for advice? I notice that your clients take their relationship with you very seriously."

BECOME A SUPPLIER

Earlier in this chapter, mention was made of Molly who cultivated another woman in the office by being generous with a commodity that was precious at the time—felt-tip pens. Some people systematically cultivate peers by the very nature of their formal authority to hand out supplies—particularly when funds are limited. To capitalize on such a position, you have to treat people *un*equally. In a system where everybody gets a share of supplies based strictly on need, there is no particular advantage to playing the role of office supplier. Supply clerks in the military frequently use their supply power to gain favor with others in their unit. Lucy, a good-natured Survivalist, describes how her job as office supplier has improved her lot.

I have two jobs in my office. I'm in charge of the steno pool; I'm also in charge of handing out office supplies. When I want a special favor from a person, I can be very generous with typing services and office supplies. If somebody is nice to me, or if I figure I may need his or her help later on, I make sure the typing gets done promptly. Manipulating office supplies works even better. The company now has a series of requisition forms people have to fill out to obtain supplies such as yellow-lined pads, paper clips, rubber bands, and staples. If I'm trying to be nice to somebody, I might throw in an extra lined pad or whatever. It's not stealing because the supplies are used on company premises. If somebody gives me a hard time, or I'm not interested in that person doing me a favor later on, I pull the strict-company-policy routine. I might even make a comment that he or she is using too many of a particular item in comparison to others in the office. If I want to be mean, I make sure that there is a written justification for every supply request.

BECOME THE COFFEE BARON OR BARONESS

At lower levels in an organization, you can cultivate people by carrying out such menial tasks as operating the office percolator. (As the price of coffee continues to skyrocket, the status of this informal role may be on the rise.) Few people would be unkind to the man or woman who dispenses morning and afternoon coffee. Some coffee barons and baronesses have gone underground (with percolators kept in filing cabinets or other hiding places) as more companies discourage this time-consuming and fire-hazardous practice. Being the office coffee person has more advantages than would appear on the surface. Chuck, a young coffee baron, explains the phenomenon in this manner:

> It takes about 1 hour per day out of my work routine to take care of the office coffee. This includes counting the money; cleaning the pot, cups, spoons; and wiping the floor where coffee inevitably spills. It's a good investment in time. While serving the coffee, I get a chance to speak briefly to many people in the office. You could say it plugs me right into the office grapevine and people know it. So, when they want some hot information—like who is going to be fired next, or which two people are involved in the newest office romance—I'm right there with the information. People pay a lot of attention to me in my office. That's worth a lot.

MAINTAIN A GOODIE DRAWER OR DESK TOP

Another way to gain favor from peers, pitched at their physiological level, is to supply them with an assortment of candies. A goodie drawer or desk-top dish might contain items such as gum drops, chocolate candy, sticks of gum, or raisins and nuts. The people you cultivate with the goodie-drawer approach tend to be office moochers, but even a moocher may someday be of help to you. Cedric, the keeper of the goodie drawer in his office, illustrates the potential value of such an arrangement:

> Accuse me of going out of my way to please people, if you will, but friendships are important to me.

I keep fresh candies on my desk and in my drawer. Because of it, people often pay me a visit. It is a small token to pay for making friends. Your friendship may be returned when you need it the most. Like the time my mother phoned me one morning at work to tell me that my cat had died.

I was just too upset to work, yet I felt foolish asking the boss if I could go home to make funeral arrangements for my cat. I brought my problem to Jane, a woman who had made many a trip to my desk for an afternoon sweet. I explained my problem. Jane was so sympathetic that she offered to have my calls transferred to her desk and to explain to callers that I was tied up on some important project. By the next day, I felt better able to cope with my job despite the loss of my cat. It also made me feel good to know that Jane cared enough about me to help me out in a pinch.

SERVE AS THE OFFICE PARAMEDIC

"Theresa, I have a terrible headache. I don't have time now to make a trip to the drug store for some aspirin. Could you help me out?"

"Say, Theresa, I burned my left hand this morning. Like a fool, I tried to catch the coffeepot when it slipped from my right hand. Do you have any soothing ointment in your kit?"

Theresa is neither a physician, nurse, nurse's aide, nor an ambulance medic. She is a friendly billing clerk who keeps one drawer in her desk loaded with first-aid supplies.[3] It is said that the only emergency she cannot properly handle is a snakebite. Theresa is genuine in her desire to serve other people. She glories in the role of office paramedic. But Theresa also has an ulterior motive. She explains it unashamedly:

"Helping other people in the office with their ailments has endeared me to them. I think I have more friends in the office than anyone else. Work would be a lonely place if I didn't have any friends. People have come to count on me, and that's pretty good for a billing clerk. If it weren't for my first-aid station, I think I might be just another clerk in the office."

Being the office paramedic can also pay dividends beyond those sought by Theresa. Similar to the coffee baron role, the office paramedic can be the communications hub. He or she can pick up valuable tidbits about new developments in the office. A paramedic in one office learned of a new opening while handing out a headache tablet. She was the first to apply for the position and was selected. The new job represented a $1,500 per-year salary increase for the friendly paramedic who could now upgrade the location of her office first-aid station.

IMPROVE THEIR SOCIAL LIFE

Under the right circumstances, improving the social life of one of your peers is an effective way of cultivating that person. The "right circumstances" means that the person you are trying to fix up, wants to be fixed up. Otherwise, you probably will create an enemy rather than an ally. A recommended initial gambit is, "I think a friend of mine would be interested in meeting you. Would you be interested in meeting him (or her)?" Doug is a case history of a successful application of this approach to cultivating your officemates. He describes his winning strategy:

> I'm an attorney in a large law office. A new attorney named Gary joined us as a corporate tax specialist. He was also new to town, and had been divorced for a number of years. The guy seemed so lonely that I befriended him. I realized from my own single days that the last thing a single man wants is to spend his evenings having dinner with a married couple. So I got right to the heart of the matter.
>
> I asked Gary if he were interested in meeting unattached women. He said definitely, yes. I then made up a list of all the unattached women I knew—those

I would like to date if I had the opportunity. My list contained six names. I turned over this list along with their phone numbers, to Gary. I also furnished Gary with the names of two introduction services I had used to advantage before I married my wife.

Gary was most appreciative of my friendly gesture. He became doubly appreciative when the third lead developed into a decent relationship for him. The payoff was: One, I felt wonderful at having helped out a newcomer to town. Two, Gary came to my rescue at a meeting of the professional staff. I proposed that the owner-partners give us more options on selecting a retirement plan. Gary was the first to second the motion, concurring with my proposal. After Gary spoke, several others also expressed their agreement.

AVOID BEING DESPISED AND HATED

Niccolò Machiavelli noted—approximately 475 years ago—that a prince should take steps to ensure that he is not despised and hated.[4] Machiavelli believed that so long as you did not deprive other men of their property and women, you would not be hated and despised. In today's office environment, you can be despised and hated for much less. Your peers will neither despise nor hate you so long as you are careful not to:

1. Sit on their desks.
2. Place dirty coffee containers, wads of chewing gum, or cigar butts in their ash trays.
3. Try to sell them life insurance or mutual funds.
4. Win a $1000 suggestion award, using their suggestions.
5. Sneeze over their lunches.
6. Correct their mistakes in public.
7. Borrow money without paying it back.
8. Always have your work completed on time.
9. Win more than your share of office lotteries.

10. Smugly mention that you forgot it was payday, so you will pick up your paycheck next week.

BE A STRAIGHT ARROW OR INNOCENT LAMB

Being nonpolitical can be a winning political strategy. If you develop the reputation among your peers of being a Straight Arrow or Innocent Lamb, they will trust you and support you when you need support. To develop such a reputation, you will need to avoid all devious political tactics and, in general, appear more interested in the welfare of the firm than in your personal welfare. Archie, an office politician *par excellence,* pulled one of the most clever ploys my research has uncovered. His tactic made an immediate and lasting impression on his boss and co-workers. Archie describes his coup:

As an industrial engineer, my job is to save the company money. The cost savings I suggest should far exceed my salary and benefits. If I don't provide a good return on investment for my services, I am a liability to the company, not an asset. One assignment I had 2 years ago was to design a system for decreasing the cost of paperwork in the company. I spent about 3 months studying the forms we used for internal purposes.

After completing the study, I made my recommendations to our boss and he to his boss. They were both impressed by the annualized cost savings of $15,000. It looked as though my proposal had a good chance of being implemented.

In the meantime, I had shown my report to Sybil, one of the younger engineers in the department. She had a particular interest in the flow of paperwork and she told me she liked my report very much. So such so that it sparked her thinking to piggyback on to some of my ideas. Her calculations revealed that her method would save the company about $30,000 per year. Her analysis looked accurate to me.

I requested an appointment for us to meet with my boss. I said my plan for the redesign of the paperwork flow in our company should be discarded. In its place, I proposed that we use Sybil's ideas which would save the company an *additional* $15,000 per year. My boss said, "Sounds great to me. But don't you realize that Sybil will now get the primary credit for this important system?"

I told my boss, it isn't important who gets the credit. The important issue is that our department does its very best for the good of the company. He looked at me as a father does when he has just learned the son has been accepted by a medical school. Sybil, too, was smiling. I knew I had set a good relationship for myself with two people whom I thought were well worth cultivating.

Cultivating the People Below You

Mutiny is the potential fate of the irrational and irascible ship commander. If you fail to cultivate your subordinates in the organization, you, too, may be subject to sabotage, backstabbing, stiletto throwing, badmouthing, and lack of support. To cultivate the people below you, two sensible general strategies are apparent:

One, you might use the strategies recommended earlier for cultivating your boss, higher-ups, and peers and turn them in the direction of people below you. Most of the people below you in the office hierarchy would enjoy being treated as if they outranked you or were your peer.

Two, you might read any modern book about human relations (including this one) and apply the principles contained therein to dealing with people below you in the organization.

This chapter deals with eight strategies and tactics that have particular relevance for gaining the support and respect of people below you. By featuring these eight suggestions, we do not imply that other elements of sensible office politics or sound human relations are unimportant. We merely have chosen a small number of political facts of life that the ladder-climber often neglects in his or her haste to achieve success.

FOLLOW THROUGH ON YOUR COMMITMENTS

Recently, I was playing in a club tennis tournament against Allan, a well-placed bank executive. Dusk was settling in as we finished our match, which had been delayed because of a last-minute meeting called by my opponent's boss. As we walked off the court toward the locker room, we noticed a forlorn-looking red-shirted young man seated at a table courtside. He glanced at my opponent with an air of expectation. Since his face was unfamiliar, I assumed he was my opponent's friend, or relative, who had come to watch him play. In the locker room, Allan revealed to me the man's true identity. He told me:

"I'm sorry again about being late for our match. It's been one of those crazy, mixed-up days. Would you believe it, I even have a performance appraisal scheduled for this evening? I'm late for that, too. That fellow we saw—the one in the red shirt, seated at the table—works for me. His performance review is 2 weeks overdue. He's leaving on vacation tomorrow. I told him the only way we could get together today was for him to meet me here at the club, after the match. Too bad, the fellow has been forced to wait more than an hour. I hope he's not too miffed."

Allan is not unique among executives. Conducting a performance appraisal on time and in a proper setting is an important commitment to a subordinate, yet Allan let the date slip. In the press of coping with assignments handed him by his boss, entertaining foreign bankers, and chasing his own success, Allan forgot to follow through on time with something very important to the career of one of his people. Allan's subordinate happened to be good-natured, and saw an element of humor in conducting a much-delayed performance review in a nonbusiness setting. Some bosses do not get off so easily.

Studs Plants a Stiletto.   "Walt, you told me that, after

I worked for you 6 months, my salary would be reviewed," said Studs. "Remember, I took this job at a
pay cut, but you told me the situation would be rectified within that time. With a new child and my wife
not working, I'm really hurting for cash. Will you be
able to make the salary adjustment soon? It's been 8
months since I joined the company."

"Sure, sure," replied Walt. "I'll get this matter
straightened out to your satisfaction this week. In fact,
I'll write a memo to myself right now to work on this
problem tomorrow." Walt, who had been under pressure from top management to decrease spending in his
department, was deliberately trying to back off from his
commitment to increase Studs' salary. He reasoned that
if he could delay adjusting Studs' salary for another 6
months, his budget would be close to being balanced.

Five weeks later, Walt received an unpleasant surprise. Studs resigned from the company to take a job
with a competitor at a salary that far exceeded what he
would have been making working for Walt (even if
Walt had followed through on his promise). Walt's first
reaction to Studs' resignation was relief. He could replace Studs with another individual at a lower rate of
pay, and he would not have to deal with the problem
of a dissatisfied subordinate.

Walt was wrong. His mishandling of Studs had more
reverberations than he had anticipated. Walt's boss, his
suspicions aroused because of Studs' brief stay with the
firm, requested a meeting before Studs left. Asked what
he didn't like about his job, Studs told Walt's boss:

Who said I didn't like my job? It was exciting,
challenging, and as good as advertised. It's just that
Walt lied to me. I took the job at a pay cut after
reassurances from Walt that my salary would be
properly adjusted within 6 months. I was willing to
take a temporary cut in pay for a good opportunity.
To call Walt an outright liar may be a little strong,
but he had a convenient way of forgetting about his
promises to me and, I think, to other people also.

I needed to have some visual displays made for a presentation to top management. Since the cost on these displays exceeded my authority to spend money, I needed Walt's approval. He told me he would take care of the matter, but he never did. I asked him about it twice, and he kept stalling me. Another time, we were to meet for lunch at noon. I had a 1:30 appointment, so it was important that I get back on time. I waited outside Walt's door from 12 to 12:30. Finally, I went down to the company cafeteria for a quick sandwich and returned to my office shortly before 1 P.M. Walt buzzed me at 1:15 and asked if I was ready to go to lunch. He's the most unreliable boss I've ever worked for.

DISPENSE RECOGNITION

The least expensive method—in terms of money and time—of cultivating people below you is to sprinkle them with attention, kindness, love, affection, or any appropriate form of recognition. "Show people how important you think they are," contends every primer on supervision. Similar to the omnipresent DRIVE CAREFULLY signs, many more people understand the concept than apply it to their own situations. Yet investing a small amount of time in recognizing a person of lower rank than yourself can pay large dividends in terms of cultivating a loyal follower.

Nurse Sherman Gives Flora Her Due. Militarylike, Nurse Rosemary Sherman called a floor meeting of the geriatric ward personnel. She began:

Ladies and gentlemen, the subject of today's meeting is a question of life, death, and team work. Our ward, and our very hospital, has averted disaster through the initiative and spirit displayed by one of the members of this hospital. Who performed this important act? No, it was not the chief of surgery. No, it was not the chief of medical services. No, it was not the head nurse. It was floor attendant Flora Barnes who suspected that the carafes we place on our patients' nightstands were contaminated.

Miss Barnes was correct. Our laboratory results proved that staphylococci were present in the carafes. Who knows how many of our patients would have become terminally ill if this unsanitary condition had not been caught in time? Miss Barnes, could you please tell us about your heroic act?

Blushingly, Flora said, "Thank you for making such a fuss over me. I was just doing my job. I noticed those carafes were awfully dirty. I figured somebody should be told about it. Thanks again Nurse Sherman. I'm proud to be working for such a fine woman who appreciates me."

Izzy Gets a Telegram from the Big Boss.   "We've got to work round the clock until we fix this hellish problem with our customer's pump," said the vice-president of field service. "When the pump runs for more than 2 consecutive hours, it suddenly slows down its action—too slowly to do the job. Our field service people have done the best they can, but it just isn't a repair we can make in the field. That's why the pump is back here in our factory. If we can't fix it, we'll have to replace it at a cost to us of about $20,000. Besides, it would take us about 5 months to custom make another of these monster-sized pumps. Let's put our best brains together on this project."

One week later, Izzy, a master mechanic, arrived at a tentative solution to the problem. It appeared to him that there was not enough room left for some of the intricate parts of the pump to expand as the heat reached high levels. Because of the swelling, the pump would short out. Izzy fashioned an expansion joint and sent the repaired pump on its way. Five days later, a telegram from the vice-president of field service arrived at Izzy's house. It read:

Dear Izzy: Customer problem solved. Your diagnosis and repair of problem saved us valuable customer plus $20,000. Everybody is happy. Keep up good work. Regards, Art Treadway

Scott Remembers Maurice.   Maurice, the manager of financial services, was scheduled to make a presentation to top management about the financial feasibility of launching a new product. Two days before the meeting, he said to Scott, a junior financial analyst on the staff, "Why don't you come along to the meeting with me? You collected most of the important information we needed to make the revenue and cost projections on this new product. It would make sense to me if you made at least part of the presentation. It will be a good opportunity for you."

Scott was flattered that he was asked to contribute to a presentation to the company higher-ups. Scott and Maurice performed admirably in the meeting. Their projections of a good profit for the proposed product were convincing to top management and the product proved to be a winner. Scott's reputation as a young man with potential was instantly established. Shortly thereafter, Scott received a one-step promotion to the position of senior financial analyst at another division of the company. He bade farewell to Maurice and thanked him for his contribution to his professional growth. Scott did not forget Maurice, as the latter explains:

It seems that Scott appreciated my efforts on his behalf much more than I realized. The controller in Scott's division resigned to take a position with another company shortly after Scott arrived on the scene. This immediately created an opening at the top of the financial organization—one for which Scott was not qualified. He is a rational enough person to realize that you don't jump from junior financial analyst to division controller in two steps. Instead of putting his hat in the ring for the job, Scott

recommended me for the position. He spoke glow-
ingly about how effective I was in developing
younger people and how smoothly my department
ran.

Being a member of the corporation gave me an
added edge over company outsiders and I was promoted to the controller's position. Scott was now
working for me again. Over lunch one day, I asked
Scott what was the determining factor in his nomi-
nating me as a contender for the controller's slot. He
pointed specifically to the incident about my bringing
him along to the meeting with top management so he
too could achieve some recognition.

BE SENSITIVE TO HUMAN RELATIONSHIPS

Many a manager has made a mistake in handling people while trying to be too efficient or too rational in his
or her approach to administration. If you take literally
all scientific notions about management, the result
could be so mechanistic that you could lose the support
of the people you are trying to manage. Stan, a newly
appointed manager at a branch of a chain of home improvement service centers, fell into this trap. Shortly
after arriving on the scene, he decided to reorganize
his branch office. In doing so, he broke up the old
cliques of people who had worked together as teammates on various projects. Here is what happened, as
described by one of the team leaders:

Stan thought he was an efficiency expert. He figured that we were goofing off since the members of
each team had become buddies as well as work associates. Stan hoped that by forming new teams, productivity would increase. The opposite proved to be
true. We missed the loose and easy work practices
we had had in the past. When I went out on assignment with my team, it was more like fixing up your
own house than being paid an hourly wage to fix up

somebody else's place. Now the old feeling of camaraderie was gone.

I tried to explain to Stan that his reorganization was a mistake, but he wouldn't listen. Instead, he kept mumbling something about the importance of increasing productivity and the fact that he wasn't in the happiness business. With four new teams created, many problems arose. Cooperation declined. People became huffy about which responsibility was their job versus what responsibility was someone else's. All of a sudden, people became very rigid about taking a full lunch break and leaving a job early enough to wash up from the day's grime.

Stan pleaded with us to improve productivity, and threatened us with firings if the situation didn't improve. Profits were sinking and he was looking bad in his boss's eyes. The more he urged us to get our work accomplished faster, the more we dragged our heels. Nobody was willing to help out Stan since he had ignored our requests to maintain a system that had worked well for several years.

Recognizing that breaking up the old teams and forming new ones was unworkable, Stan reorganized us back into our original teams. Something had been lost in the process. Even though the time we spent completing a job showed a spurt of improvement, we never reached the level of productivity we had before Stan arrived. He finally resigned. I think management helped him to reach that decision.

BE COURTEOUS

Asked why he was leaving his secure position in the Federal Civil Service, Dustin, a research scientist, answered, "I want to be treated like a human being. I want courtesy and respect. I'm going to work for private industry where I'll be treated differently." Scientist Dustin's hypothesis that he will be treated more courteously outside the government may prove to be incorrect. People are rude to people of lower rank than themselves, both in business and nonprofit organizations.[1] Consequently, if you show common courtesy to the people below you, you may be at a substantial advantage in gaining their respect and support. Five elementary suggestions are in order here to help you avoid the discourtesy trap.

Answer Memos and Letters. Many managers answer memos and letters according to the rank of the sender. Correspondence from the highest rank is answered promptly; correspondence from medium-ranking personnel is answered within one week; correspondence from lower-ranking people is often ignored and discarded. Answer the memos of little people promptly and you will have an advantage in cultivating their support. It generally requires only a little more time to give a quick answer to a memo than to earmark it for later action. A modern technique is to handwrite a quick response on the bottom of a typewritten memo. A photocopy is then made for your files and the original is sent back to the sender.

A curious phenomenon that exists in complex organizations is that the powerful people—those who have made it to the top—do answer correspondence. People at middle organizational levels are much less courteous. This is one reason organization outsiders often send their complaints straight to the top.

Return Telephone Calls. "I wonder what that pest from Philadelphia wants?" said Chet, the middle manager. "He's already called four times." If Chet would take 3 minutes to answer the Philadelphian's call, he might discover that it's a man from another branch of the company who wants to transfer to Chet's branch. The job-seeker also happens to be a talented individual who has a potential contribution to make to Chet's branch. If hired, he might very well become one of Chet's loyal followers—something Chet needs more than he realizes.

Failing to return telephone calls of sales representatives is a common practice in most organizations. Even if you are not interested in the message the caller has for you, saying "I'm not interested" will at least end the matter and not brand you as just another discourteous person. The message sender may prove to be someone who can someday help you.

Avoid Keeping People Waiting Outside Your Office. If you have earned the right to an office, it does not automatically grant you the privilege of keeping people waiting to see you. The man who waits until 2:15 P.M. for his 1:30 P.M. appointment may be inwardly seething with anger and humiliation, despite the fact that he is catching up on paper work while he waits for you.

A counterargument I have heard about keeping people waiting is, "Don't you have to wait to see a doctor or dentist? Isn't my work just as important as that of a doctor or dentist?" This is a specious argument. Through either natural or artificial forces, the supply of medical services is way below the demand. Thus, people recognize that all medical offices are overburdened. People tend to accept this fact of life. It is difficult to convince most people in your office that your time is in limited supply.

Acknowledge the Presence of Those Outside of Your Department. "Helen can take a flying leap over a cliff as far as I'm concerned," said Rachel. "Ever since she received her promotion, she ignores me unless she wants me to do some work for her. My boy friend and I were sitting together in a luncheonette across from our office building. In walks Helen, carrying an attaché case and looking *so* important. I asked my boy friend if he would like to meet my former boss. I beckoned to her, but she walked right past us as if I were a street beggar."

Helen's act of discourtesy—treating Rachel as if she were a non-person—is not uncommon among pretentious individuals. Such a strategy will usually backfire: As you advance in your career, you need every vote you can get. The more people you have alienated, the fewer people there are around to make positive statements about you to others. Many an individual has been denied a choice promotion because he or she developed the reputation of being unliked by people of lower rank.

Offer an Explanation for Your Actions. "Get my office painted before anybody else's," said Fred to the person in charge of maintenance. "Don't make any excuses, just get it done. I want my place looking right." The maintenance chief obliged, but he assigned his sloppiest and slowest painter to Fred's work order. In addition, Fred's office was painted blue instead of the beige he requested. When Fred complained, the maintenance man said it was an honest mistake that could not be rectified for another 3 years which was the normal interval between office paintings.

Fred might have received better service from the maintenance department if he had offered a logical explanation for the urgency of his request. Fred neglected to tell the maintenance department that he had been recently assigned responsibilities that required more customer contact. Therefore a freshly painted office would create a positive impression for the company. A small act of courtesy on Fred's part might have resulted in his getting the kind of service he needed. Few people willingly comply with orders if not given a logical explanation of why the order is given. The person who develops a reputation of giving illegitimate orders (those without proper justification) may wind up with more enemies than allies.

PUBLICIZE YOUR CONNECTIONS

People with the right connections are impressive to others, providing they publicize their connections in a tactful, nonoffensive manner. All things being equal, people in an organization prefer to befriend you if you have influential friends. (This observation applies to people above you, at your level, or below you.) People both admire others who have influential friends and also entertain the vague hope that one of your contacts will help them if you two are allies. The recommended procedure for such organizational name-dropping is to mention the influential person's name in a work context. Doing so gives the person below you the impression that the influential person relies on your advice. A person below you will be less impressed with a social mention of your connection as it may not transfer to the work environment. Many a high-placed executive has an ineffectual nephew or niece working for the company. The nephew or niece who tries to capitalize on that type of connection might come across as a weak individual.

Assuming it is not an outright lie, you might try making a few vague statements about your work-related connections, provided each statement is accompanied by the true nature of the connection. Allow the listener to interpret any way he or she desires. You may receive more respect.

- J. P. and I were discussing the problem of industrial contaminants just the other day. (You coughed continuously during a recent meeting. After the meeting, J. P. asked you if your cough stemmed from a work-related illness.)
- Murph (the president's nickname) is talking a lot about zero-based budgeting these days. I guess he has found my input useful. (Just to create the impression that you are alert, without being asked, you sent him an article on zero-based budgeting that you found in a business magazine.)
- Should Blackstone visit our department this fall as planned, I'd like to introduce you to him. (True. It is only organizational protocol for a department head to introduce subordinates to a high-ranking official when he or she pays a visit to the department.)

USE COFFEE, DOUGHNUTS, AND PASTRY
TO ADVANTAGE

A widely held belief is that if a person is being paid
more than a starvation wage, you cannot motivate him
or her with food. Experience suggests that this is a
faulty generalization, particularly because people equate
food with friendship and recognition. A remarkably
inexpensive way of cultivating little people is to find a
suitable occasion to provide them with free doughnuts,
coffee, and pastry during normal working hours. Brent,
a management consultant, explains how he used a few
bags of doughnuts to cultivate a group of foremen:[2]

My assignment was to discover the true nature of
the problems facing the manufacturing division of a
company located in a small town. Once the problems
were uncovered, we would be in a position to make
some constructive recommendations. My program
called for a series of once-a-week meetings with different groups of foremen until I had met with every
foreman in the plant twice.

The first two meetings were dreadfully dull. No
matter how much I explained my purpose in being
there, the foremen just made comments about mundane matters, such as particular machines that were
in need of replacement. One night on my way home,
I noticed a bakery shop down the corner from the
plant. On my next trip to the plant, I stopped at the
bakery to purchase a dozen assorted homemade
doughnuts.

When I entered the conference room and told the
foremen that I had brought some doughnuts, their
faces lit up like children watching seals at the zoo.
Once they had their doughnuts, they opened up to
me and began a steady stream of conversation about
the problems *really* facing the plant. Quickly the information spread through the plant that the sessions
with the consultant included fresh doughnuts. I knew

I had broken down the communications barrier with the foremen when one of the old-timers said to me that the foremen were treated like mushrooms. Perplexed, I asked for an explanation. He said, "Management keeps us in the dark and feeds us a steady diet of horse manure."

Since that experience with the foremen, I now incorporate free doughnuts into similar consulting assignments. It seems to facilitate communication and create some instant friends.

BE ESPECIALLY NICE TO SECRETARIES

Despite all that has been said about the importance of cultivating secretaries in order to win favor in the office, many insensitive people continue to alienate them. Secretaries whom you have treated unkindly and unfairly seek, and usually find, revenge. Peggy tells us how she and another secretary in her department avenged Myra's wrongdoing:

Myra was a counselor who thought she was the queen of the college counseling center. She had her eyes set on becoming the assistant head. Bit by bit, she made herself more useful to the director of the counseling center, Dr. Kilbourne, always being the first to bring forth new ideas and potential programs for the center. Whatever new fad appeared on the scene, she was there with a proposed package.

Myra's downfall was that she was a Janus. The face that looked toward the boss was smiling and pleasant. The face that looked toward the secretaries was snarling and mean. She would order us around as though she was our boss—which she wasn't. Once she overheard us talking about a weird student and proceeded to chastise us for being unprofessional.

One fact we knew about Myra that Dr. Kilbourne did not know was that she was not too well liked by the students. Students frequently complained that Myra forced herself and her programs on them. She went through the dorms, begging for people to take her workshop in women's studies. The students really took offense when she tried to develop a list of gays on campus who could be approached for a minicourse in gay rights.

Elsa, one of the other secretaries in the counseling center, and I began to drop hints to Dr. Kilbourne that Myra was kind of pushy and offensive both to us and the students. We don't know if he believed us, but soon Myra's influence began to shrink. She no longer ran workshops, but was confined to doing mostly routine things such as assisting students who wanted to change majors. If she had treated us decently, she might now be Dr. Kilbourne's assistant.

MAINTAIN OLD TIES

Willy was ecstatic about his promotion to head of the shipping department. He had worked in the department for 7 long years with the hopes of someday becoming the boss. Willy's colleagues gave a party in his honor to wish him well as the new department head. The group was happy to know that one of "their own," rather than an outsider, had received the promotion. As Willy savored his new status, the fellows in the department began to notice some substantial changes in the way he acted. Chauncey describes what happened:

Poor Willy let his little bit of power go to his head. He began by wearing fancier shirts than we did. He also wore a jacket to work and kept it on. Soon he decided to have lunch alone or with his boss. He even pulled out of his standing Thursday evening bowling date with us. It irritated us, but we figured it was just a stage he was going through. Basically, we still liked Willy.

Then he began to turn us off completely. Willy brought a spindle to the office, like the type they use in quick order restaurants. He would place orders on the spindle for us to pick up instead of speaking directly to us. Willy had forgotten who his friends were. We taught him a lesson at the company picnic. Not one person from shipping showed up except Willy. The way I heard it, Willy was very embarrassed. It made it look as though his department wasn't company-minded. We all figured, so long as Willy had forgotten us, we would forget him.

PART III

Strategies for
Gaining Power

The Information Game

One way—a modern way—of acquiring power is to make political use of information. The would-be power seeker recognizes that information is vital in every organization. If you have important information at your disposal, it enhances your status. If the only information you control is that readily gathered by others, you will be deprived of one more potential source of power. A person with trade secrets in his or her head thus is more valuable to the organization than the market researcher who reviews periodicals in search of public information. Merely recognizing the fact that information can be used for personal advantage and power grabbing is the first step in playing the information game. The 12 strategies described in this chapter, if properly applied, will help you capitalize on this subtle version of office politics.

CONTROL VITAL INFORMATION

A person who controls the significant resource—vital information—automatically becomes a more powerful individual. (Blackmail, of course, is an unethical variation of this strategy.) Many people work themselves into secure and powerful positions because they are the only ones who understand what is going on. Many an old-time salesman has coasted along in his territory, even though overpaid, because his head contains so much unrecorded information about customer relationships. In the recent past, computer scientists often held on to information that made them seemingly irreplaceable. A company that did not submit to the demands of a key computer expert risked having that person leave. Along with him or her, of course, would leave the knowledge about how to run computers on which the company had become dependent. As the field of computer science has become amply supplied with technically competent people, computer knowledge has become less esoteric. Correspondingly, few computer people control information that cannot be obtained elsewhere.

Winfred Has a Pleasant Setup. Gloria, the new personnel manager of a company that manufactured giant machinery for the aerospace industry, happened upon an inequity. Winfred, one of the field service engineers, was paid about 50 percent higher wages than anyone else in his job category. He also had a small, private office with a couch and a color television set. The other field service engineers shared one large office when they were not out in the field. Gloria demanded an explanation as to why this apparent inequity existed. She was told by the manager of field service engineering:

> The machines we make don't come cheap. The average price is about $350,000; the replacement value would be about twice as much. Although all our field engineers are highly trained technicians, it is still a whale of a problem to repair one of these machines when it breaks down. Routine repairs can be made in about 3 working days by most of our men. But the nonroutine repairs could take up to 3 weeks for the ordinary field engineer.
>
> Some repairs are seemingly impossible to make. No matter how much schooling a field engineer has, he might not be able to unravel our more complicated breakdowns. Here's where old Winfred enters

the picture. The man is a mechanical genius, and he knows it. He can uncover the source of problems that the machine designers themselves cannot figure out. Whenever we have a superproblem, we send Winfred to the site. So far, Winfred has fixed every customer problem he has tackled. We won't admit it to him, but Winfred is a bargain at his present salary. He has a certain knowhow that, as yet, we haven't been able to duplicate. When we do find one or two more people of his mechanical genius, we might start treating Winfred like everybody else.

José Gets the Law on His Side.   A psychiatrist who enjoyed the good life, José worked at a state mental hospital in Montana. He and his family liked camping, horseback riding, and the absence of the pressure of urban living. All of these pleasures were available in the small Montana town in which the hospital was located. José also enjoyed not being hurried in his psychiatric practice. He would take as much time as he pleased with his patients, despite the pleas of the administration to quicken his work pace. José was also quite rigid about the number of hours per week he was willing to devote to his job. José once refused to attend a staff meeting because it was scheduled on the first day of the hunting season. To add to the administration's annoyance with him, José was fond of telling people publicly that perhaps the patients were normal and society was sick.

Muriel, the hospital occupational therapist, asked José whether he worried about being fired from his comfortable position as hospital psychiatrist. He unabashedly told her,

Not a chance, but thanks for your concern. Anybody else who works for this hospital might have to worry if he or she behaved as independently as I do. But this hospital would be out of business if they did not have at least one full-time psychiatrist on the staff. One year before my predecessor, old Dr.

Hodges, retired, the hospital began looking for a replacement. It seems that only two people applied for the job. The other applicant was a psychiatrist from Yugoslavia, but she could scarcely speak English. They still offered her the job. She accepted another offer shortly before I applied for the job.

Whether or not the administration agrees with the way I practice medicine, I'm all they have. I'm the only person who can legally sign patients' discharge or admitting papers.

Art Becomes a Resource Person. Art worked among a group of researchers in a Washington, D.C., company whose main business was conducting research studies for the Department of Health, Education and Welfare. Within 2 years, he was elevated from research associate to vice-president. Asked how he leapfrogged ahead of so many of his colleagues, Art explained:

It started out quite informally. When my colleagues from different groups within our firm were putting together proposals for government contracts, I became a resource person on an important part of our business. I have always been intuitive about what H.E.W. wants to see in a contract proposal. My comments seemed to help the proposals. The word spread around our firm that I had a good touch for assisting with proposals. Before long, I was asked to head a proposal-making department. Any proposal that went out the door had to pass my personal inspection. As my record of hits increased, so did my stature. I was then offered a vice-presidency. What began as a casual way of helping my colleagues developed into a formal function of the firm that carried vice-presidential responsibility with it.

ACT ON ADVANCE INFORMATION

A deft political strategy is to capitalize on information that is not widely circulated. If you can react to an event before others are aware that the event has taken place, you will be at a power advantage.[1] Suppose you hear, through an informant, that your company will be actively recruiting a Mexican-American woman to fill a key job. Fortunately for you, a friend of yours—a Mexican-American woman—is currently looking for a better job. If you introduce her to your president, you will appear prophetic in your judgment. Acting properly on advance information, of course, is an advanced tactic of office politics. You need both a pipeline to the top and the resources to capitalize on such information.

Harriet Sets Up an Important New Account.   Harriet, a bank branch manager, was able to act on advance information provided by one of the members of the board of directors. In her bank, a member of the board is required to conduct an audit or trustee examination of officials at the branch locations where technical information, general procedures, and future projections are discussed in detail. The trustee who visited Harriet's bank mentioned—in passing—an item of importance: The board had indicated to the home office marketing department how important it would be to obtain the payroll account of a large local retail organization.

Without any flurry or mention, Harriet made appointments with several department stores in the community. She was able to sell the personnel executive of the largest store on the idea of having a payroll deposit account with the bank. Harriet then called the marketing department of the home office to describe her accomplishment. Within 3 days, the bank president sent Harriet a personal note, congratulating her breakthrough accomplishment. Harriet's timely response to advance information had instantly made her a more powerful branch manager.

BE AN INFORMATION HUB

An ideal way to play the information game is to set yourself up so that information passes over your desk on the way to other people in the office. Rarely will your position allow for this much control over information. However, you can move toward being an information hub by collecting as much information as your position will allow. The effectiveness of this strategy varies. How much do the people in your work environment value information? Tidbits, rumors, gossip, and other types of information are particularly valued in federal government settings. People rise to and fall from power in the District of Columbia in direct proportion to the amount of seemingly useful information they have at their disposal.

Howie Buys and Sells Information. A former political appointee, Howie, explains how he played the information game in Washington, D.C.:

> To earn my share of power, I found it necessary to cultivate fresh sources of information. Combing the newspapers and government reports was one way of bringing important information to my boss. But that wasn't good enough. I was expected to produce information that wasn't publicly available. After a while, I functioned like a gossip columnist. One source was an executive secretary; another was a barber; another was a hairdresser; another was a man who worked as a clerk in a public relations office that provided speech-writing services for key people. I paid cash for most of my bits of information. Sometimes gifts like perfume, jewelry, and hand tools were more appropriate forms of payment.
>
> I was not purchasing secret information nor engaging in character defamation. I was just plucking information before it became public knowledge or was leaked to the press. For instance, I found out 4 days early that one trade union was going to write a formal letter of protest about a new government law relating to employee safety. My boss gobbled up the information.
>
> After a while, it hit me that my job as a special

assistant was really that of an information broker. I would dig around for information, often buying it. In turn, I would figuratively sell it to my boss. The better my information, the more power I acquired. The less significant my information, the less my power.

Marty Flashes His Appointment Book.   An appropriate name for Marty, a management consultant, might be The Flasher. One method Marty uses to impress a member of a client organization is reach into his inside breast pocket, grab for his appointment book, and say, "Incidentally, is there anything you would like me to pass along to the President? It looks as though he and I have a luncheon appointment next week. Let me make a note of any thoughts you have."

Marty, of course, wants people to know that he and the president exchange information, giving him power at the top of the company.

His technique generally works well. It backfired at least once. On that particular occasion, the person Marty was trying to impress said, "Are you a consultant or a messenger service? If I have something to tell the President, I will write or phone him personally. No use something getting lost in the translation or your taking credit for my information."

BE A CONFIDANTE

Your power in an organization can increase if you create confidential information. In many instances, your power can also increase if you are *privy* to such information. A person who is in on the biggest secrets of the company develops at least a modicum of job security. Often, you have to earn the right to be a confidante.

Lester Keeps a Secret.   Baxter, the former head of the research division of a large company, was thinking of using personnel manager, Lester, as a sounding board for confidential company matters. Before trusting him, however, Baxter tested his trustworthiness. He explains how:

I liked Lester from the start. I was looking for somebody out of the mainstream of events to listen to me about personnel problems. Lester was the logical candidate. But my 30 years in the business world told me not to conclude that a person will respect confidences until you have had some solid evidence. I told Lester that I was giving some careful thought to terminating his boss, but not to tell anyone. If Lester told his boss, I knew I would hear about it. His boss was not a timid soul.

After 3 weeks, I heard nothing about the alleged firing, so I proceeded to go ahead with my plans for Lester. In the meantime, I revealed my little prank to Lester and we both had a good laugh. Next, I went over my master plan for reorganizing the company. I explained to Lester that I wanted to remove one layer of management which would involve terminating about ten middle managers. Lester and I shared impressions about the strengths and weaknesses of the whole staff.

Finally, we got down to the personnel department. If somebody was to go, the logical choice would be Lester because of his level of management. The idea shook me up. It reminded me of a gangster movie in which a criminal kingpin gives a contract to a hit man to kill another hit man the kingpin has hired to kill somebody else. It seemed like bad business to declare as surplus the man who had helped me pare down the organization. So we let somebody else in Lester's department go, and reorganized Lester's job. He wound up with a bigger job.

The lesson I learned from all this was that when you share top secrets with somebody, he has something on you. It makes it awkward, later, to make an objective business decision about the guy.

STOCKPILE A FEW IDEAS

Survivalist, Company Politician, or a Machiavelli you will probably find it morally acceptable to save some of your best ideas for a rainy day. One reason underlying this strategy is that if you are involved in creative work, you have no guarantee that you will always have a fresh idea in your desk (or in the back of your mind) waiting to be implemented. If you have the good fortune to think of a number of useful ideas over a brief time interval, it is wise strategy to save one or two for a time when your idea bank is at a low ebb. Another important reason is that sometimes the timing may not be right to receive maximum credit for a good idea.

What Have You Done for Me Lately? Energetic Sandy took a job as a fund-raiser at a college that urgently needed funds. The first year, Sandy devoted her energies to devising fund-raising campaigns for the following year, since the current year's campaign was already in operation. Sandy's third year was a blitz of activity. She tried four different fund-raising tactics including mailings, telephone calls, alumni weekends, and the sale of commemorative coins containing an etching of the oldest building on campus. Sandy's campaign achieved its goal of bringing forth $3 million in pledges. At the end of the year's campaign, Sandy's boss, the vice-president of administration, said:

"You're off to a good start. What campaign ideas do you have lined up for next year? I like your general strategy of trying out different approaches to fundraising. But I would think you would need to change your tactics each year."

Sandy was stunned. She had used up all her good ideas for her second year without giving a thought to the future. Sandy has changed her ways. She now stockpiles a few good ideas, even if she thinks she could use them all in one year.

Cash in Your Ideas when Credit is Possible. Lewis worked for Joe, a man who systematically took credit for the ideas of his subordinates, conveniently forgetting that he was not the source of the ideas. Lewis once suggested to Joe that the company should channel through ducts the heat generated by some of the largest machines on the factory floor. This otherwise-wasted heat could then be used to heat a colder, more difficult to heat, section of the factory. The suggestion worked, but Lewis's boss took about 80 percent of the credit. His boss did state, however, that Lewis provided valuable input into the problem. Recognizing that it is difficult to complain to upper management that your boss is stealing your ideas, Lewis tried another approach:

I asked Joe, if I might have an opportunity for job rotation. I explained that I enjoyed working for him, but that I felt a 6 months' assignment in another department would make me a more valuable contributor to the company. I said that I then would be happy to return to the department, if there was still an opening for me. Joe did get me assigned to a manufacturing control department which happened to be a good place to practice creativity. Basically, the department was concerned with setting standards and making sure we weren't wasting time, money, or material.

While still working for Joe, I figured that the company was using too much control in some areas. For instance, we were weighing every box of nuts and bolts or nails that came in from a supplier. That took considerable time, especially when we would repack and ship back the occasional underweight box. I recommended that we abolish weighing items like nuts, bolts and screws. It was an uneconomical procedure. I also recommended that we stop dispensing nuts and bolts to our employees as if the nuts and bolts were precious stones. Instead of having a full-time person handing these out in measured quantities, I thought it would be more economical if everybody took all the nuts and bolts he or she needed.

Two weeks after I was assigned to my new job, I followed through and made these two recommendations. Both ideas were tried and found to be money-savers for the company. I was given a special citation by the head of manufacturing. If I had launched these ideas while working for Joe, he would have gobbled up the credit.

LISTEN WITH GRACE TO GOSSIP

To properly play the information game, you need a steady source of information. When your ideas dry up, so does your idea power. Gossip often contains invalid information, but often, it also contains information that you might be able to cash in on later in your quest for power and control.[2] A good listener is quite logically the person who tends to receive the best gossip. Part of being a good listener is not to be judgmental when you hear that latest tidbit. Assume an informant tells you that the executive vice-president is declaring personal bankruptcy. Here are six of the many possible responses you might give. The first three are graceful; the last three are graceless:

1. Hmmm.
2. I appreciate your telling me.
3. I didn't know that.
4. What a laugh. He's the person who tells us how to run the business.
5. Prove what you say is true, or be silent.
6. That's the biggest scandal we've had around here in a decade.

People who supply you with gossip want you to show some small reaction. If people couldn't watch your reaction to a rumor, it would be no fun passing it along to you. However, if you overreact, it might appear that you will quickly pass along the information and identify its source.

It Is Blessed to Receive and Give Gossip. However nonjudgmental you might be in receiving gossip, you have to be an active participant in the rumor mill— unless you want your sources to dry up. If you pay for your tidbits, as did the political appointee described earlier, you may be able to get along with only receiving gossip. In other instances, you have to bring about some equitable exchange between passing along versus receiving gossip.

Arnold, the manager of a planning department, had a staff of three planners working for him. The department was concerned with collecting information that had a bearing on the future of the company—an activity that did not keep them continuously busy. Periodically, Arnold would ask his staff members questions such as, "Okay fellows, what's hot today?" or "What's the scuttlebutt?" Almost never did Arnold reciprocate by furnishing the staff with tidbits that he had collected.

One day, Tom, a planner in the department, confronted Arnold in this manner: "Arnold why don't you tell *us* something for a change. You're in a position to receive a lot more inside information than we are."

Arnold persisted in his predilection for one-way communication. Soon, his own department was no longer a source of morsels of information. He would now have to cultivate other sources if he wished to continue to derive power from his knowledge of company gossip.

DROP A FEW BUZZ WORDS

A person intent on being successful needs effective communication skills. Overloading your speech with jargon will tend to alienate you from generalists. Nevertheless, dropping a few of the latest buzz words in your organization will often help you sound more professional.

The buzz words you choose should be those used by powerful people in the organization. Avoid the jargon of the technical specialist, the clerk, or the factory hand. If an influential person uses a particular phrase in a speech, be one of the first to incorporate that phrase into your own language. Below are four pairs of statements, expressed in neutral and powerful (incorporating buzz words) organizational language:

NEUTRAL: Our department listens to complaints from dissatisfied customers.

POWERFUL: We interface with the public served by the corporation.

NEUTRAL: Our company makes many products; we have some plants scattered around the world.

POWERFUL: We are truly a multiproduct, multinational company.

NEUTRAL: We expect people to do their jobs around here.

POWERFUL: We hold every employee of this corporation accountable for his or her results.

ASK IMPRESSIVE QUESTIONS

Yet another variation of the information game is to ask questions that imply you are linked to important forces within the organization, or that you are aware of hidden realities. No matter what inference people may draw because of the questions you raise, the questioning tactic is not devious. Asking intelligent questions usually serves the good of the organization. Part of the rational decision-making process is to question every assumption you make. Asking the right questions is also part of the operating procedure of an effective manager or staff person.

Impressive questions can be broken down into two categories. One category is questions based on detailed technical or administrative information. An example would be, "How does your proposal fit into our new retrofit program for the MK-14 project?" A second category is general-purpose questions that fit many situations in many organizations. Unless you have some specific inside information, you are better advised to use general-purpose questions. Here is a starter set of ten, designed to orient you toward the habit of asking impressive questions.

1. How will (name of highest-ranking executive in organization) react to your proposal?
2. How might the board react to your proposal?
3. How cost effective is your idea?
4. What are the alternatives facing us?
5. What input from below and above did you receive before reaching your conclusion?
6. What might be some of the negative consequences if your plan were totally accepted?
7. Are you being unduly optimistic?
8. Are you being unduly pessimistic?
9. Would you like me to run your idea past a few of my contacts?
10. Is your perspective broad enough to meet the overall good of the organization?

BECOME A BEARER OF GOOD NEWS

A subtle use of information is for you to become associated with opportunities and solutions rather than problems. Every organization faces many problems, and many people are willing to focus on these problems in their contacts with peers and higher-ups. You might be able to gain advantage if you develop the reputation of being associated with good news. Artfully done, being a good-news bearer can increase your power base.

Maury Plays the Role of the Sunshine Boy. Within 3 years after he joined a small company that manufactured industrial products, Maury was appointed assistant general manager. His new appointment made

Maury the leading contender for the presidency of the company. Good-natured Maury agreed to give a talk to a group of college students enrolled in a marketing course. One of the students asked how a man as young as he, who had been with the company for such a relatively short length of time, was promoted to the assistant general manager position. Maury answered:

I owe my promotion to my philosophy of life. I try to emphasize the positive. I think that is what should be expected of a professional marketer. Too many people at Mopar Industrial Products dwelled on problems. I emphasized what *could* be done, rather than what could *not* be done. The president, who promoted me, found that to be a welcome relief. He faces enough problems without my adding to his burden. I can recall two vivid examples of my philosophy in action.

One time, the company was hit with a bombshell. We were in the process of manufacturing thousands of parts for a company that suddenly declared bankruptcy. They canceled the order too late—85 percent of the parts were ready to be shipped. It would make no sense to force the company to honor its contract because they were bankrupt. I heard that Mr. Harding, the president, was furious. He was plagued by others in the company bemoaning our fate. Instead of joining the crowd of people telling the president how bad things were, I telephoned all the companies who had a product line similar to ours. I explained our situation and asked each company if they could find any use whatsoever for our inventory.

Finally, I hit a company in Cleveland who could modify our product for their own use. All they offered to pay was 20 percent of the unit price we were to get from the bankrupt company. I asked for a conference with Mr. Harding, saying that I think I found a customer for the seemingly useless inventory. My pitch was that my prospective customer was willing to pay nearly four times the scrap value of our inventory. To add to the value of the deal, we might still be able to capture some money after the assets of the original customer were sold and bankruptcy proceedings concluded. Mr. Harding was very pleased. He thanked me for getting rid of the biggest headache in years that was facing the company.

Another time the company was faced with problem of a downturn in sales. It appeared we would have to lay off about 50 of our experienced manufacturing personnel, and also to make some cuts in the sales and administrative areas. The president did not want to take such a drastic step because he believed strongly that all the company really had to offer the world was the abilities of its people. Instead of being another gloom peddler, I developed an action plan. I told Mr. Harding that I had a plan that might be able to save our work force. He listened intently.

I proposed that we run an advertisement in several newspapers in boom areas of the country—such as Houston—indicating that we were willing to subcontract work at close to cost. Harding approved the plan and we did get enough subcontracting business to keep our work force intact. As our own business picked up again, we raised our price for subcontract work. We still do occasional work for an aerospace firm located in Houston.

When Mr. Harding promoted me, he stated clearly that every company needs somebody who can search for opportunities at times when others are mired in problems.

CULTIVATE INFORMATION LINKS

To play the information game with finesse, you need to develop sources in your organization who will provide you with useful information. Direct payments for information to people in your own organization would quickly stamp you as highly unethical. A more subtle approach is to befriend people who have a pipeline to valid and useful information. Among those individuals of lower rank likely to overhear organizational tidbits are nurses in the medical office, systems analysts (they visit other departments regularly), executive secretaries, executive dining-room waitresses, and communication specialists.

Jacques Combines Business with Pleasure. Jacques, the chief accountant of a Montreal-based company, describes his bold strategy for information gathering:

Being the chief accountant, it is within the scope of my job to have lunch with people from different departments without arousing suspicion. I tend to take my luncheon dates to places where many company executives dine. This creates the true impression that my luncheon dates are business meetings. I regularly have lunch with several executive secretaries. One of our usual topics of conversation at lunch is new developments in the company. I never interrogate, but simply act interested and curious. Among the useful bits of information I picked up that way was that an English company was trying to buy enough stock in our company for a takeover. But I never encourage a woman to make an outright statement. That way, she can never be identified as a source of information.

One of my favorite statements is "Please don't tell me anything that you are not supposed to." It works very effectively.

USE "INITIAL POWER"

One new twist to the information game in bureaucracies (both public and private) is for an executive to initial photocopies of memos and route them back to the sender.[3] For instance, you rearrange things so you receive a photocopy of all correspondence that concerns new acquisitions to the company library. When you receive your copy, you initial and return it to the sender along with the comment, "I concur. Good selection." It could be then inferred that you have some decision-making power about books selected for the company library.

If you can convince enough people to send you copies of memos, your initial-signing tactic could make you *appear* powerful. At its worst, initialing memos and returning them to their sender could create the impression that you are a pest who is looking for activities to perform. Another hazard of the initial power tactic is its instability. A current cost-cutting fad in business and nonprofit organizations is to place tight controls over the use of photocopying machines. Thus your vehicle for displaying power could be subject to the cost-cutting whims of the controller.

TAKE COUNSEL WITH CAUTION

The information game includes offense and defense. A way for a manager to prevent the erosion of power is to be very selective about accepting information in the form of advice from subordinates.[4] Asking advice sometimes results in decisions actually being made by subordinates. The strategy, "take counsel with caution," is at variance with the modern idea of allowing subordinates to participate in decision making. Nevertheless, it is helpful to recognize that, the more advice you accept, the more power you surrender.

Harold Learns the Meaning of Accountability. Harold, the head of a community action group, received a suggestion from two of his staff members that their group should organize a "sleep-in" at local merchants. The point of the demonstration was to protest the fact that very few youths from poorer sections of the city were finding employment. Harold's group noted that, in some neighborhoods, teenage unemployment ran as high as 60 percent. Sleeping in the doorways of large and small stores supposedly would dramatize the problem.

The sleep-in idea was implemented and proved to be a fiasco. Several merchants pointed out that the department stores were one of the best hopes for teenage employment. Therefore, such behavior was self-defeating. A widely quoted editorial stated that sleeping in the doorways was associated in the minds of prospective employers with sleeping on the job. The agency learned that some of its funding was not to be renewed as a direct result of its recent unfavorable publicity. Upbraided by his boss, Harold said in defense, "But don't you see, it wasn't my idea. I was just approving some plans suggested by my staff."

Harold's boss countered. "I'm going to recommend to the board that your appointment not be renewed for next year. It doesn't matter if the people who work for you are crazy. When you're the boss, you are held accountable for what they do."

Boosting Your Career

Job competence remains the most vital ingredient for moving ahead or staying on the payroll. The combination of hard work and a few breaks along the way probably will enable a competent person at any job level to earn his or her share of salary increases and promotions. Despite the validity of this observation, many hard-working, talented people to whom fate has not been unreasonable still go nowhere in their careers. Without the extra ingredient of political savvy—playing sensible office politics—an ambitious person could remain trapped in an unfavorable job situation.

The strategies of office politics presented in this chapter are aimed specifically at giving your career a boost. What has been described earlier in relation to gaining favor, also has a career-boosting impact. For instance, if you have implemented the suggested strategies for cultivating your boss and other higher-ups, you have already given your career a boost. Eighteen additional strategies for you to carefully ponder are presented next to help you maximize your career potential.

EXHIBIT ETERNAL VIRTUES

Although we do not emphasize them in this chapter Innocent Lamb and Straight Arrow tactics cannot be disregarded. It is important to set high goals, obtain a first-rate education, and carefully prepare a résumé when seeking a transfer or outside job opportunity. Any book about managing your career is replete with Innocent Lamb and Straight Arrow strategies that make good sense even for a Machiavelli. It is politically unwise to deviate too far from the image of the ideal employee. Gatekeepers give an immediate edge to the clean-cut, appreciative, well-mannered, healthy-looking, well-dressed, smiling, obedient, punctual, alert-looking, and tidy male or female.

Unless you are a person of extraordinary competence or financial influence (you own many shares in the company) appearing like a hippie (or whatever the latest name given to members of the counterculture) continues to be a liability in a bureaucracy. People in laboratories or those doing other forms of creative work sometimes are granted the freedom of choosing their own behavior and dress. But the executive suite is still occupied almost exclusively by people traditional—or shrewd—enough to exhibit these external virtues. One manager lost out on a key promotion because the vice-president making the promotion decision disliked the fact that the manager deviated from the official company office hours. The passed-over manager preferred to start late in the morning and take work home at night.

CAPITALIZE ON LUCK

Good fortune weighs heavily in most successful careers. Without one or two good breaks along the way (such as your company suddenly expanding and therefore needing people to promote into key jobs), it is difficult to go far in your career. The effective strategist manages luck to some extent by recognizing opportunities and taking advantage of them. The unlucky person is often the individual who, out of timidity, lets a good opportunity slip by. It has been said that luck is the reward of the diligent.

Neal Capitalizes Upon a Good Contact. Today, Neal, a man in his early thirties, is the national sales manager of a company that manufactures and sells a brand of plastic contact lenses. He enjoys his work and is proud of his income. Neal's story illustrates the difference between capitalizing upon luck versus letting a good opportunity get away. He tells us:

A few years ago, Julius and I were field sales representatives for one of the major manufacturers of soft contact lenses in the world. The product was doing well enough for our company to expand and for other companies to try to get into the business. Julius joined the company a year before me. His sales record was better than mine, but I was still doing quite well by company standards. After our second year with the company, a man from San Antonio contacted Julius, wanting to talk to him about a job opportunity.

The man from Texas was the president of a fledgling contact lens company that needed a sales representative in our area of the country. I suspect he wanted to speak to Julius because of his very fine sales performance. Julius terminated his discussions with the president quickly. He pointed out that he didn't care to join an unproved company when he was doing well with the leader in the field. However, he was willing to mention my name as someone else on the sales force who was doing well for the company. Julius mentioned, however, that I, too, probably would not be interested in leaving the company.

When the San Antonio executive explained his proposition to me, I was quite impressed. I liked the idea of working for a small company trying to take on established competitors. I crossed my fingers and accepted a job offer with a small starting salary but promises of big commissions. My decision proved to be sound.

The San Antonio company had an excellent couple of years. My sales record was well above average, and I also impressed the president with my ability to plan and organize. He asked me to recruit a replacement for myself. Once I did that, the newly created position of national sales manager was mine. Although Julius was asked first, I was the person who had the guts to take a chance. Today, Julius is still selling for the bigger company but his opportunities for advancement are quite limited.

BE VISIBLE

A basic strategy for boosting your career is to bring favorable attention to yourself. Any technique that brings your abilities and talents to the attention of others in (or out) of your organization can help you gain a promotion. Among the standard techniques are volunteering for project and committee assignments, getting your name in print for favorable reasons, winning a company athletic tournament, or being physically located in a position where you can be spotted by influential people. One woman accepted a position as a receptionist, hoping that she would someday be transferred to a position of more responsibility. The graceful way in which she performed her job was noticed by a company executive. The executive offered her an administrative assistant position that paid $2,500 more per year than she earned as a receptionist. She happily accepted the offer. Special assignments such as projects and committees, however, seem to be the most effective way of increasing your visibility in your place of work.

Abner Moves Ahead. Competent and industrious Abner worked as a computer technician for a large firm.[1] Although performing adequately in his job, he was intent upon attaining managerial responsibility in the data-processing field. Abner was concerned that technicians did not get sufficient exposure to higher management and that his sterling performance was going unnoticed by people who could influence his career.

Eventually, Abner's attitude began to affect his work. His productivity declined; he began to voice some of his frustration. His growing dissatisfaction led Abner to seek a managerial position by registering with an employment agency. At approximately the same time Abner began looking for a new job, he was reassigned to a different computer project. As part of his new assignment, he was appointed as a member of a committee whose responsibilities covered several company divisions. It quickly became apparent to Abner that the work of this committee would be observed by a large number of people in higher management. He therefore took steps to put himself in a position to be part of the decision-making body within the committee.

Abner volunteered to be secretary for the group. His responsibilities centered around taking notes and distributing them after meetings. Since the committee was large and a wide variety of opinions were expressed at each meeting, Abner had the chance to synthesize the various ideas into a policy which gave the committee direction. In the same way, he was able to set dates by which important decisions should be reached.

As the work of the committee progressed, members began to think of Abner as one of the committee leaders. He supplied each member with a list of problems to be resolved at each meeting. When serious questions arose in a division about a particular aspect of the committee's work, Abner would call a meeting with members of that division's management. In these brief meetings, he would resolve some of the problems prior to their being brought before the entire task force. The committee's work was completed on schedule, and Abner wrote the final report, which had to be approved by top management. When the committee received praise from management for its accomplishments, Abner was noted as being one of the key members.

As a result of this committee exposure, Abner was given additional responsibility within his own department and an opportunity to move away from the more technical (nonmanagerial) aspects of data processing. He stopped seeking new employment and began to enjoy his job. At last report, Abner was appointed supervisor of a small data-processing group within his department. He indicates he now intends to stay in his present work. Committee membership gave Abner the visibility he needed to facilitate his attaining that all-important first supervisory position.

Carmen Broadcasts His Goals.   A variation of the "be visible" strategy is to inform influential people of your goals. If this technique is overdone, you will quickly be perceived as an ingrate or a pest. Done with selectivity, broadcasting your goals can give your career a boost. Carmen explains how the broadcast technique worked for him:

I had been working for the county as a parole officer for 5 years. If you've never been a parole officer, it might be difficult for you to imagine some of the frustrations built into the job. You try hard to keep track of your parolees and make sure that they don't violate parole. But society surely doesn't cooperate. It is almost impossible for many of the parolees to find jobs or to be treated as ordinary citizens. Figuring that I had given enough of my life to being a parole officer, I began telling every county official I met that I was looking for a different kind of work.

The usual response was that I should file a formal application with the county personnel department, and explain to them that I wished to be considered for a transfer. That is such an ineffective procedure it is hardly worth the effort. Besides, it's much better to be invited to apply for a job than to ask if any openings are available. Nevertheless, I dutifully filed my application.

One night, I received a phone call from a state official whom I had met at a convention. He said he recalled our conversation about my looking for a different type of work within the state system. He told me he had an opening for a field prison inspector. The job involved visiting state prisons to check for safety and health violations. He said that if I were interested, I should apply for the job. I was interested, particularly because I felt I was well qualified for the job and I enjoy traveling on an expense account, even at the conservative per diem paid by the state.

After 6 months of waiting to hear from the state, I figured it was a dead issue. Finally, the job came through. It has proved to be exciting, and I can see it as a stepping stone to other good jobs within the state prison system.

FIND A SPONSOR

The most proven career-advancement tactic is to find a sponsor in your organization who will elevate you to a bigger (and better) job and look out for your welfare once you are there. A major goal of our strategy is to help you find a sponsor. Similarly, all the techniques described in Chapter 5 are intended to help you locate a patron who will boost your career. It is difficult to do so without at least one person of more power and influence than yourself who believes in you. A sponsor can be doubly helpful when he or she is both a personal and professional friend.

Jeff Has a Friend at the Very Top. Promotions usually are not rapid in the retail store business. Nick is an assistant store manager who has worked long and hard to achieve his status. He tells a story about Jeff that illustrates how having a friend at the top can boost your career:[2]

It's not fair how Jeff has leapfrogged ahead of everybody else. I have 13 years of experience and a master's degree in business. He has 11 years of experience and only a bachelor's degree. Now he's making 60G's in a top job, and I'm making 25G's in a much lower job. It all happened because Jeff was the best friend of Mr. O'Shea, the second highest-ranking executive in the Midwestern region.

Mr. O'Shea wanted his good friend to work a bit closer to him so he arranged for a few quick promotions. O'Shea made Jeff the store manager where I worked. Under ordinary circumstances, a store manager must stay in that position at least 2 years before his next promotion. Jeff held that post for less than 13 months. He was then promoted to the job of assistant regional manager for the Chicago region, the largest region in the country.

Jeff's salary jumped from about $30,000 per year in his previous job to about $45,000 dollars as store manager. His next jump was to a salary of $60,000 per year as assistant regional manager. All this activity took place in less than one year.

Watch Out for Backfire. Every technique of office politics has its potential disadvantages, including "Find a Sponsor." A case in point is Foster, who was a planning specialist in an international corporation based in New York.[3] At 27, he had worked himself into a key assignment as a special assistant to the vice-president of corporate planning at world headquarters, who sponsored him for a 6-months' assignment in the international division as an operations auditor. Foster's job was to investigate and oversee problems and plans with key operating personnel from various overseas subsidiaries. Upon completion of this assignment, Foster returned to headquarters. One week before his return, his sponsor was dismissed from the company.

Foster was never even asked to report on the results of his investigation. The new executive in charge of corporate planning did not require the services of a special assistant and Foster's credentials were sent to the personnel department. After a month of waiting for reassignment, he was offered an opportunity to work as a financial analyst at a company plant in Pittsburgh. Foster resigned, quite disgruntled about having lost the forward momentum in his career.

If Foster made a mistake, it was in having only one sponsor. It can be a perilous policy to be perceived as too closely aligned with one executive in the company. If he or she is forced out, you will most likely exit along with him or her. Ideally, you should cultivate sponsors from at least two different factions in an organization.

GRAB A SHOOTING STAR

A rebuttal to the Find a Sponsor technique might be that it is often difficult to cultivate a higher-up from a low vantage point in the organization. If you are typing invoices, it can be difficult to be discovered by the vice-president of finance. However, it might be possible to cultivate somebody who does have a sponsor. "Grab a Shooting Star" has also been described as "Cling to Somebody's Shirttails" or "Become a Protégé of a Protégé.[4] The trick is to find somebody who appears to be headed for big things in his or her career and to develop a good relationship with that person. As he or she climbs the organizational ladder, you will follow. Val provides an apt example:

> I work for the city. In my department, the head of the internal audit section of the finance division was the protégé of the Director of Finance. An individual in the internal audit section, because of family ties, became the protégé of the internal auditor. When the position of assistant to the Director of Finance opened up, the internal auditor's protégé was chosen over five senior members of the department. People sometimes think office politics doesn't apply to civil service jobs so a lot of people were surprised when this young man from another department was selected for the assistant position.

Dick Hooks Up with Lamont. A management development conference can be an effective place to find yourself a shooting star. After the daytime activities, you are obliged to spend a few more additional hours becoming acquainted with the other managers or staff people who attend the conference. Defenses tend to be lowered in such settings, providing you with the chance to pick up some inside information on who is going where in the organization. Dick has a relevant anecdote about how he capitalized on a contact he made at a management development conference:

The star of the show was obviously Lamont, a young man about my age who was considered a fast tracker in the company. He had received four promotions in 3 years with the company. We could see from the way he performed at the conference that Lamont had talent. He was not just a friend of the president's with limited ability. The man was a natural leader. It was rumored that he would be the vice-president of manufacturing before he was 35.

My strategy was to spend as much time as I could getting to know Lamont, without it appearing that I was trying to become an executive puppy. Although Lamont is a year younger than myself, I willingly accepted the fact that he had more potential and drive than I. Confidentially, I explained to Lamont how I wanted to get ahead in the organization but that I was not aspiring to become a vice-president. He complimented me on my realism.

About 6 months after the conference, I heard from Lamont. He was being promoted again and wanted to know if I would be interested in working for him as one of his department heads. The job was a one-step promotion and involved a relocation to Florida, a place I had always wanted to live. I'm convinced that if I had not latched on to Lamont at the management development conference, this promotion would never have come about.

DEVELOP BREADTH THROUGH MOBILITY

"Mobility at any price" was the shibboleth of the organization ladder climber of the 1960s. More recent evidence suggests that becoming a corporate gypsy may not be the optimum strategy for boosting your career.

Managers who stay with one company for a relatively long period of time wind up with more responsibility and more higher incomes than their job-hopping counterparts. However, there are many exceptions. The underlying principle is that your value to an organization increases to the extent that you acquire broad experiences. Ideally, this is best achieved by performing different kinds of work for the same organization. Project and committee assignments rank favorably as broadening experiences. To achieve the necessary breadth, you sometimes have to take the matter into your own hands. Timidity can be a serious detriment to your career.

Biff Fails to Practice Self-nomination. Biff, a general foreman in a heavy equipment manufacturing company, held high hopes for broader and more responsible management experience.[5] He had been a general foreman for approximately 5 years when he heard of the general manager's plan to create a new position—manager, planning and control. He strongly desired to be considered for the position; however, he believed it would be presumptuous of him to express his desires to his superior. He was afraid to have others believe he was overstepping his bounds. He rationalized that both his superior and the general manager knew him well and that undoubtedly the administrative and planning ability he had shown on projects over the past years would be recognized by them. Consequently, he did nothing to convey his desires to management.

Unknown to Biff, the general manager, in answer to the question, "Had you thought of this man as a prospect for the promotion?" said, "Heavens, no. I wouldn't think of it. Biff's strength is in line operations. We'll be expanding his operation within the next 3 years, and he's looking forward to the added responsibility our expansion plans entail."

CHOOSE THE RIGHT PATH TO THE TOP

Corporate superstars—those who make it to general manager or presidential positions—rise to the top from a number of paths. Many top corporate officials were formerly marketing, financial, manufacturing, or engineering managers. Other company presidents are former legal advisors. The key point is that for different industries—and different companies within those industries—the most likely path to the top is not the same path. If we assume that a person is a highly talented executive (still the number one reason somebody becomes a president of most public firms), he or she is best advised to seek out a company that seems favorably disposed toward his or her discipline.

Bernie Outpsyches the Competition. Clinical psychologist Bernie had impeccable credentials for his position as chief psychologist in a large hospital. In addition, his administrative skills were solid; he was well liked by superiors, subordinates, and colleagues; and patients thought he was doing a good job. One day, Bernie announced his resignation, stating that he was accepting a position as the chief psyschologist in a community mental health center at a 15 percent cut in pay. Asked if the bizarre behavior exhibited by some of his patients had become contagious, Bernie replied:

> Not at all. Mine is a well-thought-through, rational decision. My basic reason for leaving my fine job at the hospital is that I want a chance to rise to the top. In this hospital—or any other hospital—no psychologist will ever get the top job. Top executive positions in hospitals are occupied exclusively by physicians. No psychologist, even if he or she won a Nobel prize, would become the hospital chief.
>
> In a community mental health center, the cards are not stacked against psychologists. Many such centers are headed by psychologists. I'm not going to work any place for the rest of my life where I'm guaranteed second-class status.

Bernie's plan worked although it took him one more step to reach his goal. After 2 years of administrative experience in one community mental health setting,

Bernie moved to another health center as director. By the age of 41, he had achieved his goal of reaching what he considered a top position in his field.

DOCUMENT YOUR ACCOMPLISHMENTS

The track record of his common-sense political strategy is very good. If you want to impress people above you with your accomplishments, documentation will strengthen your case. The more objective the data, the better it will serve your purpose. An ideal form of documentation would be one that translates your accomplishments into financial terms. Evidence, that you saved your organization a specific dollar amount or that an idea of yours increased sales by so many dollars, is impressive. Subjective documentation, however, is still better than no documentation.

Harvey Produces a Few Testimonial Letters. Commercial insurance sales representative, Harvey, had established a good sales record. For 5 consecutive years, he had met his quota, but his boss was not satisfied. Harvey asked his boss how he could be criticized if his sales continued to be at an acceptable level to the company. The latter replied:

"Harvey, we all know that you are doing a decent job of keeping your sales volume high. What I'm concerned about is your service record. I get the impression that you are letting the servicing of your policies slide. I think you make too few appearances at your clients' places of business. If you visited them more frequently and answered their questions, you might find a lot of new business waiting for you. If you don't do a better job of servicing your accounts, you may start to lose some of them to the competition."

Harvey did not passively accept the criticism leveled by his boss. He replied, "That may be your opinion, but I think I might be able to produce some evidence to the contrary." Harvey then telephoned his five best clients and asked them to write a letter to his boss, indicating the extent to which they were receiving good service. All complied, and Harvey's boss was pleasantly surprised by the letters of testimony. (In fairness to Harvey's boss, the insured and the insurance company may not agree on what constitutes good service. Many insurance customers only want to talk to their insurance representatives when they have a claim to file. The company prefers a frequent review of the customer's insurance package.)

Brenda Cashes in on Some Scrap.   Observant Brenda worked in the advertising department of a textile company, reviewing plans and programs with advertising agencies used by the company.[6] Her habit of arriving later than most employees necessitated that she park in the rear of the company parking lot adjacent to the company loading and refuse dock. Brenda noted that the wooden boxes being discarded probably had some scrap value. A careful checking of waste dealers uncovered one who would pay the company a tidy sum each year for the rights to the company's waste boxes and cloth.

Brenda did not overlook this opportunity to capitalize on her savings to the company. She wrote a memo to her boss, detailing how much the annual savings would probably be, and included a suggestion that the company look further for such sources of revenue. Brenda thus had a tangible reminder of her alert thinking in her personnel file. Such items are very useful when one is being considered for a promotion.

ANALYZE THE COMPETITION

An important strategy for boosting your career is to compete in an environment in which you have an edge over the competition. Age can sometimes work to your advantage. If you are middle-aged, you might have a competitive edge over a group of very young people in a department. Your lengthy experience might be associated with wisdom and psychological maturity. However, being a younger person in a department where most are considered too old to be promotable can also work to your advantage. You might be chosen for a key promotion. Many a young executive has sought a new job in an organization where most of the top executives are close to retirement. Among the most important relevant factors for analyzing the competition are the capabilities and aspirations of the other people trying to get ahead in your organization.

Phil's Brashness Pays Off. The company consultant asked Phil his primary reason for wanting to join the company. Phil confidently said, "Bartow Industries is ideal for an ambitious and well-trained manager like myself. Like cream, I will rise to the top. The financial boys tell me Bartow is a company with great potential but immature management. If Bartow doesn't get some capable management soon, they may not be able to capitalize on the opportunities facing them. I've been looking for a chance to prove myself in a company that needs me."

Phil's brashness irritated the consultant, but he saw more than an element of truth to his pronouncements. Bartow did need to recruit a goodly number of ambitious and confident young managers. Five years later, Phil, the brash young job candidate was a manufacturing vice-president at Bartow. His analysis of the competition in relation to his capabilities proved to be devastatingly accurate.

SWIM AGAINST THE TIDE

The college placement director said to 24-year-old Sharon, "My records indicate that a woman with a master's degree in business administration is in demand in many large corporations. Major banks like Chase Manhattan hire hundreds of MBAs. It would make sense to apply to institutions such as those if you want to maximize your chances for finding a job."

"Mr. Prichard," replied Sharon, "I don't want to

work for an organization in which I'll be doing the same thing as everyone else. I'm afraid I'll get lost in the crowd if I join a bank that already has 800 MBAs on board. I want to try something a little different. Do you have any request from a meat-packing plant or a foundry for a woman MBA?"

Adventuresome Sharon was intuitively choosing a nonconventional path to career success. Often, if you do not follow the same path as do other people with your background, you will be at a career advantage. Following this logic, an outgoing, personable young man or woman should enter accounting or engineering, *not* sales. Assuming he or she can make the grade as an accountant or engineer, his or her chances of rising to the management level are quite good. Personable and outgoing accountants and engineers have a good shot at managerial positions. Conversely, if you are highly analytical and reflective, but you still get along with people, sales might be your path to success, since marketing and sales departments are usually in search of such people to promote into managerial assignments.

Glenn Finds Civil Service Honorable. Young CPA Glenn explains how he successfully swam against the tide:[7]

> Many people of my age have become disillusioned with federal, state, and local governments. You hear talk of all the budget-cutting in government, the uncertainty of many jobs, and the stigma attached to "bureaucrat." Because of these negative reactions to government work, there are good opportunities for young professionals in government. Less competition seems to exist for jobs today than, I'm told, existed in the past. A person who wants to work for the government, particularly at the local level, can earn himself a responsible job early in his career.
>
> I left a public accounting firm at the age of 26 to take a job with the city as a senior accountant. At 27, I was the director of accounting. By 28, I was

promoted to internal auditor. One year later, I left the city to become manager in one of the "Big Eight" public accounting firms in Washington, D.C. Altogether, I doubled my salary in 3 years. The people in the accounting firm where I began my career certainly did not make that kind of progress.

Barney Drowns Swimming Against the Tide. Barney was a successful middle manager in a large corporation and a onetime semiprofessional baseball player. Much of his emotional energy was devoted to baseball. An opportunity came along for Barney to become the general manager of a minor league baseball team at a modest salary. Despite the pay cut, Barney welcomed the chance to apply his professional management skills to something he loved. Few people with Barney's big company background could be found managing a minor league baseball team. After 1 year, he found himself at the start of a tedious job search because his contract was not renewed. As Barney saw the situation:

I made a bad mistake. The owners of the minor league team told me they wanted some professional management, but they were only paying lip service to the idea. They second-guessed every move I made. If I made a decision that went counter to their beliefs or the coach's, it was they who got their way. Before I arrived on the scene, every business decision was made on the basis of intuition. Apparently, the owners and the coach wanted to continue along those lines. After I left, they brought the former general manager out of retirement.

Barney's situation indicates what can go wrong with the strategy "Swim Against the Tide." You may place yourself in an environment where the uniqueness of your background is not welcomed and you are not accepted. Before jumping into a situation, try to discover if the cards are stacked against you.

TOOT YOUR OWN HORN (SOFTLY)

"Buck, you're too nice a guy," said his wife. "You're a harder worker and much better qualified than some of the other people in the office who have been promoted more rapidly than you. When are you going to get out there and sell yourself a little better?"

The advice offered to Buck is regularly repeated by managers' spouses who believe actions speak louder than words. Ideally, good performance should be recognized. The most competent people in any organization should be offered the most responsible jobs. Since most organizations are not pure meritocracies, it is important for the career-minded person to find a subtle way of tooting his or her own horn. If your tune is too loud, you will give an earache to influential people, thus losing your audience. Documenting your accomplishment, as described earlier, is one method of self-merchandising or tooting your own horn. Another effective method is to request a formal audience for your best ideas. If you present your best suggestions in offhand comments made in the parking lot or elevators, they are less likely to be sold. If sold, the source of the ideas may be easily forgotten.

Henry the Flip Chart Artist. Buried 12 levels from the top of his company, Henry aspired toward bigger responsibility and higher status. Since so many of his colleagues had similar aspirations, Henry sought a way of bringing attention to himself and his ideas. He describes his solution:

I'm in the distribution field which, in a nutshell, means getting our company's products where they are needed, when they are needed. I'm very interested in distribution. It's like one mammoth chess game. To impress the people above me that I'm serious about my job, I used to write them memos outlining my suggestions for improving our operations. Typically, I would receive a reply thanking me for thinking about the company.

To add a sense of drama, I next asked permission to have a 10-minute audience with my boss for a new idea that I wanted to present to the company. I explained that a memo describing the idea would be unduly lengthy. At my presentation, I used a flip-chart with the pages prepared beforehand. The reaction to my first presentation was so positive that I now use the flip-chart method whenever I have something important to present to my boss. I also use flip charts in describing new programs to my subordinates.

I have no way of knowing for sure the rate at which I would have advanced without my flip-chart technique. But I do know that my career in the company has been moving at a more than satisfactory clip since I began making formal presentations—aided by flipcharts—to management. It helped me gain recognition for my ideas. Nobody else was going to sell them for me.

LOOK SUCCESSFUL

No book on office politics or career management would be comprehensive without at least passing mention of the importance of projecting a successful image. Your clothing, your desk and/or office, your speech, and your attitudes toward money should project the image of a successful but not necessarily flamboyant person—at least in most organizations. Your standard of dress—and other accoutrements of success—should be appropriate to your particular career stage. Many observers of company politics contend that you may do harm to your career if it appears you are trying to upstage your boss. If your boss purchases an $8,000 car and you purchase one for $10,000, you may be seen as overstepping your bounds.

Conventional suggestions about wearing freshly polished shoes, neatly pressed clothing, dressing stylishly, and appearing physically fit are generally career boosters. A necessary addition to this list is to appear confident and not overly concerned about being wrong or failing. Appearing to be cheap can also hurt.

Oliver's Penny Pinching Behavior Proves Costly.
Young attorney Oliver came up the hard way. He attended both college and law school at night, scrimping and saving at every turn. Among the tricks Oliver and his wife used to save money during his law school days were collecting food coupons from neighbors and rounding up returnable bottles. Unfortunately for Oliver, he could not leave all of his penny-pinching behavior behind. Mr. Strawbridge, the senior partner in Oliver's firm, explained to him why the firm was concerned about his future in the firm:

> Oliver, we like your keen legal mind and your hard work. Your point of view and perspective at times seems to be that of a rather miserly individual. Your wardrobe is sparse; your attaché case appears to be cardboard. You have recommended that every attorney in the firm donate 4 hours per week of free legal services to poor people. Your supervisor informs me that, while dining with a client, you urged him to not leave such a large tip for the waitress. Perhaps you would find greater happiness working for the Legal Aid Society than for our firm. We're just thinking about your long-range personal happiness.

Despite the image he projected, Oliver did enjoy working for an affluent law firm. He was indeed societally minded, but he did not think such attitudes were incompatible with a successful law career. Oliver could change his behavior and hope that Mr. Strawbridge would notice the changes. Or Oliver can seek employment in another law firm—not an easy task considering the present oversupply of young lawyers (particularly if the young lawyer is not aligned with influential forces within the community).

AVOID HIGH-RISK JOBS

A defensive career-boosting tactic is to avoid jobs where the probability of failure—or looking bad—is high. An inherent disadvantage of this strategy, however, is that high-risk jobs (those where the probability of looking good is small) usually carry high rewards. Safer jobs have smaller potential rewards. The offshore oil driller may someday strike it rich, while the first-line supervisor in an oil refinery will be safe but secure in his or her career. The latter has avoided high risk but has also avoided the possibility of high reward.

Harry's Lament.   Thirty-seven-year-old Harry is wondering what his next assignment will be. His company management is understanding enough not to fire Harry from his present job, but neither has he accumulated any glory. Harry sees it this way:

About 3 years ago, I was offered the position of new product manager. I was to supervise the group with direct responsibility for developing new product ideas. A raw idea, of course, is not enough. It has, ultimately, to wind up as a successful product in the field. Sometimes, I think getting a new product idea accepted by people outside your department is more difficult than getting it accepted by customers. However, I do not want to give you the impression that I was not eager to tackle this new position. It seemed like the best possible opportunity for me in the company.

The agony proved to be that no new products were forthcoming from my group. Our score was zilch after 2½ years. We came up with nothing that would have been worth the investment required to launch it. Now I am faced with the gruesome reality of being reassigned because I failed. My prospects right now do not look good.

BE DISPENSABLE

"Why wasn't I considered for the administrative engineer position in the department?" exclaimed Maurice to his boss. "I was looking for a promotion and you knew about it. Don't you think I have enough talent to be promoted?"

"Frankly Maurice," said the boss, "you have too much talent to be promoted. We need you right where you are. There is nobody else in this department who has an equally good inventive mind. If we had put you in the administrative slot, the department would have lost its best engineering talent."

So goes one of the oldest saws in management. If you become indispensable, or very difficult to replace, it can ruin your chances for promotion. Most managers are reluctant to part with a star individual performer. The situation is analogous to a movie studio being reluctant to promote a top-drawing actor into an executive position. Solid technical talent is difficult to replace in any field. So is administrative talent. Many a branch manager has been secretly by-passed for promotion because he or she is doing such an outstanding job for the company. Top management is often unwilling to break up a winning combination. By being effective, yet dispensable, you increase your chances of being eligible for promotion.

Audrey Trains a Replacement. Audrey was the manager of the municipal bond department of a substantial-sized bank. During one of her discussions with her superior about advancement opportunities, Audrey heard a familiar refrain, "But Audrey, municipal bonds is a specialized business. You know more about that operation than anybody else. We need you where you are. You're too valuable to transfer right now." Having heard these same attitudes expressed a year earlier, Audrey had prepared her rebuttal. She explained to her boss:

I agree that the field of municipal bonds is a specialized business, and I agree that I have accumulated considerable knowledge about it. Recognizing these facts, I have shared all my knowledge with two subordinates, George and Kathy. George is ready, right now, to take over my job. Kathy should be ready in about 6 months. I have given each one of them a turn at running the department while I was out of the office on vacation or a business trip. I could be transferred or resign tomorrow, and the department would run very smoothly.

The management of Audrey's bank became aware of its oversight. Three months later Audrey became manager of correspondent banking at her bank (relationships with affiliated banks). George was moved up into her slot, and Kathy took over George's job. Her new position gave Kathy additional breadth and a high salary.

HELP YOUR BOSS GET PROMOTED

An indirect, difficult-to-apply career-boosting tactic is to help your boss get promoted in your own organization. (Getting your boss promoted will only be of direct benefit to you if *you* are the logical successor.) A variation of the same strategy is to help your boss be recruited away to an outside company. The latter strategy is appropriate for a Machiavelli or Company Politician since it serves to weaken your own organization by removing a presumably competent manager. The straightforward strategy of "Help Your Boss Succeed" is the most effective way of getting your boss promoted. Under the right circumstances, a more focused approach can be used to vacate your boss's job.

Mike Sings the Praises of His Boss. Mike attended a management development conference at a hotel. Seated at a poolside luncheon, he chatted with his table mates, one of whom was the vice-president of human resources. The conversation turned to the plant in Colorado that would be opening in a year. Mike said to the vice-president, "I know these things are confidential, but I'll bet I know who will be chosen to head up the Colorado operation. Bill Grimsly (Mike's boss) would seem to be the logical choice. He's the best plant manager I've worked for. I would say Bill could successfully run any operation in this company."

The vice-president of human resources dutifully scurried back to the home office with this valuable input from Mike. Bill was, in fact, one of the contenders for the plum position in Colorado. Mike's unsolicited endorsement helped influence the decision in Bill's favor. The company then began screening internal and external candidates as a replacement for Bill. Mike was one of the contenders, but an outsider was chosen. Mike was disheartened, but only temporarily. One month later, the outsider decided not to join the organization, and Mike was selected as Bill's replacement.

VOLUNTEER FOR AN UNDESIRABLE TOUR OF DUTY

If you are a particularly patient person, it might be worth your while to volunteer for an undesirable position to later on obtain a desirable one. A long-range perspective is required to successfully implement this strategy. You also have to be placed in the relatively unusual situation where there is an undesirable assignment to volunteer for that is not also a dead end.

Crandall Sweats it Out.   Zoology professor Crandall worked in a small zoology department where the chairmanship of the department was lowly regarded. Professors were generally rotated through the job. The position paid a $1,000-per-year premium over a person's regular salary, and offered only a one-third reduction in teaching load. Yet the time demands of the job were quite heavy in comparison to other faculty positions. Crandall told the administration that he would like the opportunity to serve as department head. He noted that his long-term desires were in the direction of becoming a college administrator, not a professor and researcher. Crandall recounts his experiences:

> It was 4 years of hard work, modest pay, and very little gratitude. I set up course offerings and schedules, listened to hundreds of complaints from students and faculty alike, acted as an intermediary between the faculty and the administration. I even taught freshman zoology. My hours were long, and, at times, I wondered if I had made a mistake. Finally, my judgment was vindicated. Four years after volunteering to become the head of the zoology department, I was chosen as dean of the College of Biological Sciences. I was where I wanted to be after 4 years of sacrifice.

REFUSE A PROMOTION FOR THE GOOD OF THE COMPANY

A delicate political maneuver is to refuse a promotion because, in your judgment, the overall good of the organization could best be served by your staying where you are. The payoff is that your superiors will be struck by your loyalty and unselfishness. It is wisest to refuse a promotion to a position that you believe might not be highly beneficial to your career. Thus your sacrifice is smaller than it appears on the surface.

Jack Thinks First of the Good of the Store. Store department head Jack describes why he refused a promotion:[8]

> Last fall, my store manager, Merv, told me of an upcoming division manager's job for which I was qualified. The job would mean more money for me. I told Merv that I would be glad to take the new job if that was what top management wanted, but

this was a bad time to change jobs. I explained that the Christmas season was fast approaching, that the toy department needed to be set up. Not enough time was available to train a replacement.

Merv accepted my reasoning, and dropped the idea of promoting me to the division manager's job. Sure, I was interested in the good of the store, but I also had another reason for turning down the promotion. I knew that Merv was becoming disenchanted with his job as store manager and might quit at any time. Because of my experience and good record, I was in line for his job. In our company, a store manager outranks a division manager.

HITCH YOUR WAGON TO YOURSELF

The ultimate career-boosting strategy is to have faith in what you are doing and persist in doing it well. If you hitch your wagon to yourself, you will not be bothered by your detractors. Eventually, your contributions will be recognized because what you are doing is worthwhile and of value to the world. Hitching your wagon to yourself is your career foundation. Other strategies of office politics are designed to supplement this basic strategy. If you lack technical, clerical, or administrative skills and ideas of your own, you are lacking the basis for a successful career. As noted by one observer of power and politics in organizations:[9]

"While dramatically illustrated by Galileo and Pasteur who persisted in their experiments despite the criticism of their associates, the technique * has been used by countless other people who have faith in what they are doing and put their efforts into doing it well."

* Keep on Sawing Wood or By Their Works Ye Shall Know Them.

Power Grabbing at Lower Levels

Power is like money. Not everybody is obsessed with power or money, but few people would refuse more of either if it were offered to them. Without attaining power, you run the risk of early dismissal in times of a business recession or when political infighting becomes intensified. It is not uncommon for a person in a high position (formal power) to make an early exit from the organization because he or she was unable to acquire a solid power base. You also need a modicum of power at lower levels in the organization in order to qualify for more responsibility or your share of the budget.

Techniques and strategies for gaining and keeping power can be roughly divided into those used at lower levels in the organizations versus those used at the top. Judicious use of the techniques to be described in this chapter will help you move far enough up in the organization so you will be in a position to apply some of the techniques described in the next chapter. If you think plotting and scheming to acquire power is distasteful (many an Innocent Lamb feels this way), it will, nevertheless, help you to acquaint yourself with power-grabbing techniques other people might be using to take away what little power you have.

BE DISTINCTIVE AND FORMIDABLE

A first step in acquiring power is to stand out favorably from the crowd. If you have charisma, grace, or charm, it helps you exert influence over other people. *Personal power* is the technical term given to this idea. Although it is difficult to mold a bland personality into one of distinction and uniqueness, sometimes an ordinary characteristic suddenly becomes unique. Having a German accent will not add to your uniqueness in Germany, but it can be impressive in the United States. One of the world's best-known management consultants speaks with a German accent although he has been bilingual since early childhood and has lived in the United States for 40 years.

Terry Finds a Way to Be Distinctive. Government employee Terry faced a problem shared by thousands of individuals who aspire to occupy a big job in a vast bureaucracy—how to distinguish himself from other people with similar ambitions. As an economist, his work did not lend itself to theatrics and Terry had no unusual physical features that would make him particularly easy to remember. However, he did develop a social skill that helped him gain recognition. Terry explains it this way:

> For several months, I wrestled with the problem of how to become distinctive. Browsing through a D.C. bookstore, I happened upon a book about remembering people's names and faces. It dawned on me that such a skill would be very helpful working for a mammoth, impersonal organization. I already had some talent in this area. I had always been better than average in recalling a person's name after having met him or her only once.
>
> Remembering the names of the many people I came in contact with in my job became an intriguing game. Gradually, a number of people commented on my facility for remembering names and faces. My

skill helped me phase into assignments that inter-
faced with key people outside my department. My
outside contacts led to a position with a much
higher GS rating than that carried by the job of a
junior economist. My career with the government
had been launched because I finally found a way to
stand out from the crowd.

SEEK LINE RESPONSIBILITY

In almost every organization, those people whose work
is tied in directly with the mission of the organization
(line personnel) have more power than service groups
and advisors (staff personnel). Many staff people do
become powerful people. A vice-president of personnel
or the head company lawyer usually has considerable
power, but not as much power as their counterparts in
line units (such as sales or manufacturing). If you
spend your entire career in staff jobs, you may never
have as much power or make as much money as people
in line positions. An executive secretary who works for
the head of manufacturing (a line function) is usually
paid more than the executive secretary who reports to
the head of maintenance (a staff function).

The nature of the work you are performing is not
the crucial factor in determining whether you are line
or staff. What is significant is how vital that function is
to your employer. A photographer is a staff person
when he works in the photo department of U.S. Steel.
When he works for a photo studio, he is performing a
line function.

Mannie Finds Himself a More Powerful Job. Working as a market researcher in a consumer products
company, Mannie received some disheartening news
one Monday morning. "Sorry, Mannie," said his boss,
"you won't be invited along to the sales conference at
the Towering Pines. Because business conditions aren't
that great, we can only afford to send people to the
conference this year who are directly involved in cus-

tomer contact. Maybe next year we'll be able to send along some staff people."

Mannie had no choice but to accept the company decision and silently suffer this blow to his dignity. He vowed to himself that he would not face such an insult again. Mannie's solution was to find himself a line position—one where his particular discipline would be considered crucial to the success or failure of the organization. As Mannie notes:

> It didn't take long for a man of my background to find a position with a market research firm that provides services to a number of important companies. Now when I work on a client's account, I may be a staff function to them, but I'm a line function in my own firm. A market research firm cannot exist without market researchers. My job may not be as secure as my industrial job, but I feel more appreciated. I'm also treated with more respect and I feel more powerful. I have an equal chance of rising to the top of my firm.

BE STREET WISE

Earlier, we talked about the importance of sizing up the climate before jumping into the political fray. Such action is imperative when you are trying to grab power for yourself. A streetwise individual understands how to influence decision making in his or her own organization.[1] The term *maze brightness* refers to the same phenomenon. The streetwise or maze-bright individual learns who makes the big decisions and who influences the big decision makers. A discrepancy usually exists between the way decisions are supposed to be made and the way they are actually made (the formal versus the informal organization).

Pam Conducts Her Periodic Campaign.   Claims Pam:

> As a product manager, I don't have much formal authority. The box I occupy on the organization

chart is a small one at the bottom of the hierarchy. For me to gain clout, I have to do a lot of politicking. If I don't sell a few influential people on my ideas, my product will wind up getting short shift. Early in my career as product manager, I was responsible for a new cologne that was packaged in a sexually suggestive container. I was naive enough to simply present my case on its own merits. The product died in the field for lack of support from my company.

My tactics have since changed. When I want to ensure that my recommendation is going to be improved, I campaign for supporters. I try not to beat the drums too hard, for fear of arousing suspicion. I also have to be careful that the influential people I contact do not feel that I'm using them. But I do make sure that anybody who could possibly influence the decision has a clear understanding of my position and the benefits of the recommendation I'm about to propose. I get in touch with executives, key sales representatives, and financial people. I have to be as thorough as any political lobbyist.

MAKE A QUICK SHOWING

Staff groups are forever scheming about ways in which they can increase their power. A standard technique is for the staff group to prove its mettle by taking care of a minor problem, thus gaining the confidence of the line department. Having demonstrated merit on the minor problem, the staff group is in a strategic position to take on more major, and thus more powerful, problems. "Make a Quick Showing" can be used as a stepping stone to building an empire.[2]

Chad Pushes Forth the Frontiers of Management Science. As the manager of management science in his company, Chad found himself with an empire consisting of one full-time assistant and the part-time help of a secretary shared with another department. Chad's thirst for power was far from quenched. He describes his path to glory:

> I should point out first that I was sadly disillusioned by the respect paid to management scientists in our company. I thought my little department would be deluged with requests to solve important corporate problems. No such luck. We were creating work for ourselves. One day, I finally received a request to work on a true operating problem. An executive in the marketing department wanted to compare our growth to the industry as a whole.
>
> My assistant and I gleefully took on the problem. We had an accurate answer back to the executive in 3 days. He was quite happy with our analysis. Capitalizing on the good relationship we had begun, I asked if we might help the marketing department with its sales forecasting. He agreed, and before long, we had two marketing researchers assigned to my staff. Manufacturing asked us to work on a small problem concerning machine obsolescence. We solved that problem; soon, we were conducting analyses to tell manufacturing how many spare parts should be stored in inventory. We took over one of their inventory control specialists. Aside from seeing my staff jump from one to five in 1 year, plus our own full-time secretary, we were performing more interesting work. A good situation all around.

PLAY CAMEL'S HEAD IN THE TENT

This is another technique for gradually accumulating power.[3] Just as the camel works his way into the tent inch by inch (beginning with his nose), you might grab power in a step-by-step manner until you acquire the amount of power and responsibility you are seeking. "Camel's Head" has become a widely practiced technique in big organizations, where large numbers of people are engaged in trying to enlarge their empires.

Cappy Engulfs His Neighbors. Cappy was hired as the sales manager of a camera and audio visual products company. Nat, the company president, was interested in the customer aspect of the camera and audiovisual business. Because of this interest, the sales, customer service, advertising, and marketing research departments all reported to Nat. Cappy regarded the arrangement as unusual, but welcomed the opportunity to work as sales manager for this small but prosperous company. Inherent in this arrangement seemed to be an opportunity for Cappy to increase his power.

Cappy's first power-grabbing maneuver took place when the manager of customer service suddenly resigned. He suggested to Nat that he would be willing to serve as acting manager of customer service until a suitable replacement could be found. Although Cappy had to work extra-long hours, his temporary takeover of customer service proved to be a winning power-grabbing strategy. After a new manager of customer service was appointed, Nat approved Cappy's request that customer service now permanently report to the sales department.

Cappy next took after the marketing research department. His strategy was to have his sales department begin to conduct some of their own market research. Cappy then explained to Nat that since market research was already being conducted by the sales department, why not have the marketing research department report to sales? It made sense to Nat, particularly as Cappy continued to turn in a fine performance for the company.

At last report, Cappy had submitted a proposal to Nat suggesting that a marketing vice-president be appointed. Reporting to the marketing VP would be sales, customer service, market research, and advertising. A new sales manager would need to be appointed, because Cappy has recommended himself as the vice-president of marketing. Should Cappy pull off this coup, he will no longer be grabbing for power at lower levels. He will have graduated to become a top-level power player.

PLAY I TOLD YOU SO

Gloria, the company training director, was convinced that the office supervisors were critically in need of a human relations training program. She believed that many of the supervisors were insensitive to the problems faced by the clerical and secretarial help. When Gloria broached the topic to her boss, she received an icy reception. She describes what happened next:

I knew that if we didn't have a training program soon, the morale of the office staff would become lower and lower. When you have a situation whereby employees think they have received no sympathy from management, you are inviting unionization. At that time, the office personnel at one of our competitors were represented by labor union. If our supervisors didn't do a better job of responding to the problems of our office personnel, it was likely that a labor union would be able to make inroads into our company. The purpose of the training program was to improve the quality of supervision, which, hopefully, would lead to improved morale.

As time went by, conditions deteriorated. Rumbles of unionization were heard throughout the office. One union began to circulate petitions in the parking lot. Now my boss listened to me. He and the president agreed that a supervisory training program might improve the situation. I was given the go-ahead for my training program. In addition, management made more concessions to the office staff, such as cost-of-living adjustments and longer coffee breaks. When a formal vote was taken, the union was narrowly defeated. I guess I have to thank the union for dramatizing to management the importance of good supervision.

CREATE YOUR OWN JOB

A highly ethical method of power acquisition is to do something so important for the organization, that it is justified in expanding your activities into a department. Many a company division or government department began with a project handled by one individual. As that project gained in importance and value, it necessitated the employment of an increasing number of people. (The meat inspection activities of the Veterinary Corps of the United States Army had its origins when one army veterinarian was ordered to inspect the meat served to the troops.)

Marshall Becomes Manager of the Office Furniture Department. Marshall was a sales representative for a supplier of typewriter and office equipment. He waited on customers who entered the store and made periodic visits to local businessmen to stimulate sales. Marshall noticed that an opportunity existed to sell office desks, chairs, and file cabinets to some of his customers. At first, he did this on an informal basis by ordering merchandise from a wholesaler when a customer requested a specific item.

Marshall then convinced the store manager to stock a small selection of low-priced office furniture. Business grew at a steady clip and the profit margin on this line of merchandise was better than for office equipment. The store owners then agreed to expand the store in order to create an office furniture department headed by Marshall. Sales of office furniture now account for about 25 percent of the store's business, and Marshall is negotiating with the owners to become a partner in the business.

PLANT A SELF-FULFILLING RUMOR

People sometimes react—on the basis of a rumor—as if it were a suggestion for action. For instance, when people hear a rumor that a particular product is in short supply, they will often buy ahead, thus decreasing the supply currently available. The rumor has become true because the product is now in short supply. An advanced player of office politics also might be able to plant a rumor about his or her power base increasing so that the rumor eventually becomes the truth.

Keenan Lets People Know What He Would Like to Happen.   Manufacturing head Keenan began to worry about his shrinking empire. Because overhead costs had risen steadily in his company, a decision had been made at the top (several years ago) to subcontract a number of machine parts to other companies. This type of subcontracting arrangement was not unusual in Keenan's industry. During a 2-year period four supervisors were transferred out of Keenan's department, reflecting the fact that subcontractors were performing work formerly done by the department. Keenan planned to make an elaborate presentation to management about the problems associated with subcontractors, but he was concerned that such a maneuver would appear to be motivated by self-interest.

Keenan developed an alternate plan. He mentioned to three different people that he had overheard a conversation revealing that the company was going to severely curtail the subcontracting program because of many flaws found in the subcontractor's work. As the rumor ran through the plant and office, top executives began to ponder the merits of the rumor. A study was made of the subcontracting program. It was concluded that the company had moved too far in the direction of farming out work to smaller companies. Gradually, the company once again did most of its own work. Within 1 year, Keenan's department added 100 new people, including five supervisors. Keenan had more than regained the amount of power and influence he had lost in recent years.

CONTROL ACCESS TO KEY PEOPLE

A standard approach to garnering power for yourself is to occupy a position whereby people have to go through you to conduct business with a key person.[4] People tend to be nice to you, including granting you favors, when you control their access to powerful figures. To see the chief executive, frequently the appointment has to be cleared through an administrative assistant. Unless that administrative assistant thinks you have an important reason for seeing the chief, or likes you personally, he or she may reject your request without even checking with the chief.

Tessie Explains How Power Helps Her. Tessie functioned as both an administrative assistant and an executive secretary to Mr. Gray, the vice-president of finance of a major corporation. All major and some minor expenditures had to be personally approved by Mr. Gray. His phone rang constantly from 8:30 A.M. until about 6 P.M. Very few people were directly connected with Mr. Gray. Tessie frequently made comments such as "Mr. Gray will not be returning any phone calls until later this week. Even the president is waiting to see him. Perhaps you can call again next week."

When Mr. Gray was legitimately busy in top-level matters, he would often ask Tessie which appointments ahead were the most expendable. Tessie would exert her power by canceling the appointments of those people she thought had the least justifiable reason for conferring with her executive boss. Asked what fringe benefits she derives from her position, Tessie explained:

> I guess you could say I'm in a powerful spot. I see myself as performing a very valuable service for Mr. Gray and the corporation. Top executive talent is one of the company's most precious resources. My job is to see that people don't squander one

particular resource, John Gray. Knowing the service I perform, people treat me with much respect. I am no longer one of the girls, nor am I treated like a typist in the steno pool. People smile at me, open doors for me, and send me nice gifts. I have an important job in the corporation and I enjoy every minute of it. Twenty years ago, I began as a file clerk in this company. I felt like a nobody. Today, I am somebody."

CONTROL THE FUTURE

Rightly or wrongly, many people believe that personnel specialists have a great deal of influence over who gets which future assignments.[5] Because of this belief, some people go along with the requests of personnel staffers to stay on their good side. A personnel specialist—or anyone else whose job deals with future assignments—can gain a moderate degree of power because of this perceived control over the future. However, a person who influences future assignments must move cautiously in exercising this power. It can backfire.

Milt Oversteps His Bounds. Milt was a human resources planner, a job that included filling personnel requirements for future job openings. During one 2-year period, he was particularly active in staffing a new company plant to be located in the South and spent much time busily processing recommendations from managers for transferring people to this new plant. Another part of Milt's job was his responsibility as manager of his own personnel department. Five people reported to Milt. One day, he approached Cal, a manufacturing manager, with this proposition:

"I'm in the process of developing my own staff. One of my people, Jeff, needs some direct manufacturing experience. Will you please accept him as a first-line supervisor in your department? I'd like him to have a 1-year tour of duty. That will give him the hands-on manufacturing experience he needs to move up in my department. Could he start next month?"

"Hold on, Milt. Right now, I don't have the room for you to move an untried supervisor into my department. It would mean bumping somebody else to give your man what amounts to a training program. By the way, since when do you have the authority to arbitrarily assign people to my department?"

"Cal, let's lay the cards on the table," said Milt. "What we're talking about here is a little reciprocity. I get good assignments for your people, especially with that new plant location. All I'm asking for is a little cooperation in return."

Cal replied, "Milt, you're not doing me any favors. It's your job to help staff the organization. Because the payroll department gets my people their paycheck, it doesn't mean that I owe them a favor."

Cal did not let the incident drop. He brought it to the attention of the vice-president of personnel who agreed that Milt was abusing his power. Milt received a verbal reprimand. His error was in being so blatant about his demands. If people wanted to grant him favors because of his influence over future assignments, Milt should have let such favors emerge naturally.

COLLECT AND USE IOUs

Another way of looking at Milt's error was that he was trying to cash an IOU while the other person felt that he really owed Milt nothing. Properly handled, IOUs can be used to bargain for favors, favorable assignments, and even raises and promotions.[6] After you have done somebody of higher rank an important favor, he or she then owes you a favor—the equivalent of gaining some power for yourself.

Johanna Covers for Her Boss.   Johanna worked for Roy, a man with a penchant for being out of the office when an important person needed his assistance. Without being specifically asked by her boss, Johanna had developed a variety of effective excuses to cover for him. Among her favorites were:

Roy is on his way to an interdepartmental meeting. Perhaps I can get your message to him.

I know Roy said something about meeting with the internal auditors. I'm sure he'll get back to you later this afternoon.

Roy just phoned me. He said the meeting he is attending is running late.

Roy usually did get back—in a reasonable time—to the people who sought his assistance. He welcomed the smooth manner in which Johanna kept suspicions to a minimum as to his true whereabouts. He hoped that he could someday reciprocate. His opportunity came sooner than he anticipated. Johanna made the following request:

"Roy, I have a ticklish request to make. My daughter has started nursery school, and I don't have a ride for her three mornings a week. This means I will have to do the driving, and I will have to begin work about 30 minutes late on Mondays, Wednesdays, and Fridays. Of course, I'll eat my lunch at my desk to make up for the lost time. I know this is asking for a lot."

"Johanna, let's keep this request within the department. I think I can answer my own phone for such short periods, without making this a formal request. I'll make a mental note of the change, and nobody else need be informed. You've given me extra-good service so you deserve a concession now and then."

ACQUIRE SENIORITY

The most low-key method of gaining power is to acquire seniority.[7] In our society, longevity in a work organization still commands respect and privilege. Labor unions have long emphasized the rights of seniority. Although seniority alone will not prevent you from being ousted from your company or guarantee you more power, it helps. The compulsive job-hopper always works against the implicit threat of "last in, first out" in managerial and individual performer jobs. Acquiring seniority in *one particular job* can be as important as acquiring seniority in one particular organization.

Hector Gets Bumped. High-school science teacher Hector wanted to get involved more directly in helping students with their personal problems. His solution was first to work for master's degrees in guidance and then to apply for a job as a guidance counselor in his own school. Three years later, Hector did get his master's degree, and he did get a job in the high-school guidance department. With 8 years of classroom teaching experience behind him and a sincere interest in students, Hector performed well as a guidance counselor.

One year, Hector's high school went on its first austerity budget in a decade. As part of the budget-cutting process, three elementary school counselors in the district were laid off. Two weeks later Hector was called into the principal's office. The latter had an unfortunate message for Hector:

"It looks like you're going to be bumped. One of the elementary school counselors that was let go has more seniority than you. She will be entering our department. Since you have the least seniority on the staff, you will be laid off. And we have no more room for another science teacher."

Hector retorted, "But what about my 8 years of seniority as a member of the school system? Doesn't that count?"

"Sorry, Hector, it's your seniority as a guidance counselor that counts. You should have thought of the possibilities of a layoff when you left teaching. Good luck in finding a job."

Last seen, 29-year-old Hector was looking for a job where his background in biology and counseling would be an asset. The first four employment agencies he spoke with did not even have a warm job lead for him.

LET SOMEONE ELSE DO YOUR BIDDING

Another modest way of gaining power is to win favor for your position or point of view. It is doubly impressive when a neutral third party makes the pitch for your program as the one with the most merit. This takes you out of the realm of being accused of acting in self-interest. The more credible the outsider, the more impressive it is if he or she agrees with your point of view.

Lloyd's Stainless Steel Wins Out Over Plastic. Product designer Lloyd recommended that his company's new automatic coffee maker be constructed with a stainless steel housing. The manufacturing department noted that a plastic housing would be much more economical and look better after wear. But Lloyd, believing that the distinctiveness gained by a stainless steel coffee maker would lead to a higher sales volume than that possible with a plastic one, recommended that a design consultant be called in to settle the issue.

Lloyd also suggested that the executive involved in negotiating the dispute call in any design consultant he wished. (Lloyd realized that relatively few industrial design consultants existed and that most of them disliked products made of plastic.) Jacques Borzoff, a design consultant, was called into the company. After studying the relative merits of a stainless steel versus plastic housing, he concluded, "I will have to side with the concept of a stainless steel coffee maker. It is so sleek and glistens when properly cleaned. It will add to the distinctiveness of any kitchen."

Lloyd was pleased with the recommendation, the product was successfully launched, and Lloyd was a more influential person in the company because he was associated with a successful new product.

BE A NAME-DROPPER

Dropping the names of powerful people, if artfully done, can provide you with a small amount of power in the form of cooperation from others, who if convinced that you influence influential people, tend to go along with some of your requests. Even if they are not convinced that your name dropping is of consequence, they may take the conservative course and give you their cooperation.

A modern variation of name-dropping is to mention that a powerful person will be upset if your recommended course of action is not followed. The implication is that the Big Boss will exercise a sanction if things are not done the way you recommend they be done. Of course, the person from whom you are trying to gain cooperation must believe that the Big Boss has sent you as his or her personal messenger.

Bert Staffs His Project. Project manager Bert, who deserves at least a Company Politician rating on our scale, was in charge of an important project to develop a prototype for a sports car. The project was given the backing of top management but was not necessarily more important than several other projects being conducted simultaneously at this particular auto maker. Nevertheless, the chief operating officer of the company mentioned to Bert at a luncheon conference that he would be very happy to see the sports car project launched successfully.

In the process of staffing his project, Bert encountered a few difficulties, one being that the engineering executive did not want to part with one of his most creative body designers. As the executive in question presented excuses as to why the design engineer could not be spared, Bert interrupted with the comment, "If it were just my decision, I would not ask for your very best talent on this project. But the chief operating officer is going to be very unhappy if this project fails. I wouldn't want to give him the excuse that the reason we failed is that the right engineering talent couldn't be spared. Won't you reconsider?"

The engineering executive did reconsider, and Bert picked up the talent he needed. The ultimate success of the sports car project placed Bert in a more powerful position in the corporation. Although Bert was a name-dropper, he was not an outright liar.

PLAY THE MONEY GAME

Modern organizations—both profit and nonprofit—are strongly money-conscious. Almost all decisions are related to their financial consequences. Even acts of social good such as funding a public museum may be gauged in terms of their write-off contribution and the free advertising they provide. You can gain more power for yourself by tying your proposal to financial gain than by ignoring its financial consequences. Making money and saving money are equally blessed virtues. Many more people are in a position to save money for the organization than to make money. Unless you are directly involved with the product or service offered by your organization, it is difficult to categorize your contribution as money-making.

Avery Sells Himself to the Company. Branch sales manager Avery enjoyed his work and his company, but he wanted a job where he could tackle bigger problems. A possibility came to mind. He envisioned a solution to the problems facing the marketing force. Avery thought that the company needed a field sales manager who would spend full time recruiting and training new sales representatives. He brought forth his proposal to the marketing vice-president, only to have his request turned down as "a luxury we can't afford right now." The phrase *we can't afford right now* gave Avery an idea. He later came back to the vice-president with a more reasoned pitch:

I have a plan that should provide the company more than a 100 percent return on investment and, at the same time, help resolve one of our most embarrassing customer problems. Last year, 25 sales representatives, who worked for us less than a year, left the company. If you figure that it costs the company about $8,000 for each representative who leaves in less than one year, that's a grand total of $200,000.

If we created the position of field sales manager, we should be able to reduce turnover at least 50 percent, and that's a conservative estimate. The field sales manager, as I see it, would provide assistance to the branch managers in recruiting, selecting, and training the sales reps. If we did a better job of selecting and training the field force, fewer would leave.

If I were appointed field sales manager, the total annual cost to the company would be about $50,000, including my salary, benefits, travel expenses, and secretarial help. By cutting turnover in half, we would be saving $100,000 per year. In other words, if the company invests about 50 grand, it gets back 100 grand. Aside from a good investment, we would eliminate some of the embarrassment caused by high turnover.

USE THE HOME COURT TO ADVANTAGE

A power tactic for the individual who wants to gain advantage at every turn is to try to conduct business negotiations in your own office, seated at your own desk. (If you don't have an office, then negotiate in a restaurant, library, on a park bench, or other neutral ground.) When a person enters your office, you are home team and he or she is the visitor. A successful life insurance representative explains how the home court advantage works for him:

It's not an easy trick to pull off, but I always give my prospect a choice of discussing an insurance program in my office or his. Most people are accustomed to insurance people visiting them. When a person does consent to visit my office, it automatically becomes a situation whereby he is coming to me for advice. Also he cannot retreat from our conversation by answering a telephone call. It's a bit like going to a bank to ask for a loan. The loan officer seems to have the backing of the whole bank and you sit there virtually begging them to take your business. My biggest sales have come from situations whereby we closed the contract on my premises.

THINK, ACT, AND LOOK POWERFUL

If you have reached the top of your field and you control vast resources, it may no longer be necessary to think, act, and look powerful. People already know who you are and how much you can influence their lives. On the way up, there is something to be said for acting the role of a powerful person. If you act the part, people will treat you as a powerful person or will grant you power. Many a power seeker has rented a limousine, airplane, yacht, or private secretary for a particular occasion in which he wanted to play the power game. Insisting on paying the check when dining with a person of higher rank is another gesture toward appearing powerful.

Troy Overplays the Power Look.   Financial executive Troy was particularly power-conscious. A student of nonverbal language, he studied his actions to ensure that he was perceived by others to be a powerful person. To emphasize a point, he would half-sit on a desk and point at an individual with his arm cocked and his index finger pointed directly at his listener. He looked people straight in the eye and outsqueezed the hand of every person with whom he shook hands. On one business trip to a newly acquired subsidiary in Arkansas, Troy attempted to convince the president of the firm to use some of the home office financial systems. Mr. Perkins, the president, interrupted Troy in the middle of one of his persuasive appeals with the comment:

"Hold on, young fellow, I think I've heard and seen enough for one afternoon. Why don't you go back to your motel and change from your costume into some suitable clothing? We don't wear pin-striped, vested suits in the office of an Arkansas refinery. And don't point your finger at me like it's a gun. If you want to challenge me to a duel let me know. One more thing. I think you should learn to respect your elders."

TITLE YOUR WAY TO POWER

Uncomplicated job titles are among the most powerful. People respect your power when your job title reads, "president," "chairman of the board," "chief engineer," "head coach," or "ambassador." Titles such as these are granted to a clearly defined organizational role. Your discretion for giving yourself a more powerful title, and, therefore, being thought of as having power, is limited; however, with perceptiveness on your part, you can sometimes grant yourself an unofficial title to gain power. Under the best of circumstances, your unofficial title will become official.

Zeke Finds Some Hidden Power in Pest Control. Laboratory technician Zeke was assigned the laborious task of writing a pest-control manual for a food plant.[8] Following the dictates of Zeke's manual could prevent embarrassing problems such as a customer's finding rat pellets in a can of stewed tomatoes. A wide range of other annoying sanitary problems could also be prevented. Despite the importance of this mission, the only official recognition Zeke received was to affix his signature and job title to the manual.

To increase the chances that people would take his manual seriously, Zeke upgraded his job title from laboratory technician to "plant sanitarian." Within 2 weeks, people began to phone Zeke with questions about pest control and other health problems. Zeke's supervisor noticed some of the memos addressed to the plant sanitarian. The supervisor conferred with his superior, and both agreed that Zeke deserved the formal job of plant sanitarian. He would now spend about 80 percent of his time as a laboratory technician and 20 percent of his time dealing with pest-control problems. Other people's pesky problems had now become a source of power for Zeke, the newly crowned plant sanitarian.

Power Plays at the Top

People at the top of the organization have already tasted power. Instead of being satiated, frequently their appetite for power intensifies. Thus, the offensive thrust for power continues. Simultaneously, the person who has worked himself or herself into a powerful position must now practice several defensive strategies to remain in power. Techniques of gaining favor and grabbing power used at lower levels are not necessarily discarded when an individual becomes one of high rank. Many forms of office politics, such as cultivating influential people, are applicable at all job levels. As a career-minded person reaches close to the summit (or the actual summit) he or she may need to practice a few additional strategies of office politics particularly suited to high-level players and situations.

WIN BIG IF YOU WANT TO BE ACCEPTED

Cliff, the corporate vice-president of manufacturing, was younger than most of his colleagues and subordinates. Despite the short length of time he had held his position, Cliff was well accepted. When he visited a plant, the key manufacturing people generally gave him their full cooperation. As a consequence, Cliff felt confident and powerful in his new position.

Ralph, the corporate vice-president of engineering was about the same age as his colleagues and older than most of his subordinates. During the short period of time in which he held his position, he had received no positive indication that people were going to accept him. When he visited company plants and laboratories, the cooperation he received was really a form of minimal compliance. His administrative and engineering suggestions were countered with explations as to why they would not work locally. Ralph felt uneasy and unsure of the power he really held as a corporate vice-president.

Personality and ability could conceivably account for the difference in the acceptance received by Cliff and Ralph. A more important difference is that when Cliff was appointed to his position over the competition, he won big. When Ralph was appointed, he won small. Cliff was considered the outstanding plant manager in the company. He had established himself as a golden boy—a person who operated at a level a full notch above his competitors. Ralph was an unpopular choice for the top manufacturing job. He was a plant manager at a plant plagued by labor disputes and associated with an unglamorous, marginally profitable product. People begrudgingly accepted the authority of a man they considered no better, if not worse, than themselves.[1]

MAINTAIN A MYSTIQUE ABOUT YOUR JOB

The most powerful executives have an element of mystery about them. Somewhat by intuition and somewhat by design, powerful people are not entirely "up front" people. Although they are not necessarily devious, they sparingly let others know of their plans. If not done to the point of appearing paranoid, maintaining a mystique about your job can add to your aura of power. A typical way in which people in powerful positions cultivate this mystique is by alluding to impressive negotiations in the offing which cannot be fully disclosed at the present time.

Vivian, the Mystery Woman. Vivian Ballantine appeared on campus with the job title, Director of Development, reporting directly to the president. The news release announcing her arrival talked in glowing terms about many other affiliations. Her credits included membership on the boards of two businesses and three community organizations. The announcement of her appointment included a statement by the college president indicating what an important impact Vivian was expected to have on the college community.

At a luncheon meeting given in her honor, Vivian made a statement to the public about how much she hoped to facilitate communications between the college and the community. She waxed ecstatic about the chance this job would give her to become better acquainted with members of the college and business community. An assistant professor of political science, who was attending the luncheon, stood up and fired this salvo:

"Okay, Vivian, we have heard those fine platitudes expressed and we all wish you luck in carrying out your mission. But will you please tell us what your mission is? Are you a good-will ambassador at an embarrassingly high salary? Are you a fund raiser? Let us know what services you actually intend to perform for the college."

"Professor, thank you for your concern about my contribution to our college. I wish I could pin it down as neatly as you would like. I hope to make my biggest impact in terms of directing funds from the business sector to the educational sector."

"Thank you for your answer, Ms. Ballantine," responded the young professor. "Now, could you tell us exactly how you intend to raise funds for the college?"

"It is premature to divulge all my plans now. However, rest assured that I have a few major projects in the mill. You will all hear the details, once the project has entered the implementation stage."

The professor left the luncheon in anger but Vivian stayed on. In fact, she stayed with the college for 3 years and did raise a surprisingly large sum of money, although her exact function and the manner in which she carried it out seemed unclear. The next power spot Vivian occupied was a key mental health post with the state.

WORK ON KEY PROBLEMS

In large business organizations, the people who occupy the most powerful positions are often those who have been identified with the solution to pressing organizational problems. Similarly, those people who were associated with breakthrough developments in the company tend to become the most powerful executives. This method of power acquisition is most apparent in the automotive industry where individuals can be associated with particular car models of legendary success such as the Ford Mustang or the Pontiac Firebird.

Percy Gets the Law on His Side. Young attorney Percy worked for an industrial company whose product line included a variety of commercial pumps. The company developed a pump to be used in the manufacture of trucks and trains that held promise of being highly successful. Percy's contribution to the pump project was to establish an elaborate set of patents to prevent other companies from making a copy of the pump. After extensive negotiations with the patent office in Washington, D.C., a 15-year protection agreement was formulated for the company's line of pumps. High demand for the product combined with the patent protection engineered by Percy led the company to unprecedented profits. As the company was carried along by the pump, so too was the young attorney's career. He became a corporate vice-president and a member of the board. Percy ultimately left business for local politics as a happy, wealthy, and powerful person. His contribution on one key project had turned around his career and his life-style.

PLAY THE POWER GAME

The person who plays the power game makes decisions in favor of the option that gives him or her more power.[2] (Power in this sense means that the individual has control over people and situations and that other people comply with the power seeker's wishes). If you want to obtain something from a person who plays the power game, your best bet is to cater to that person's quest for power. You get what you want (and acquire more power in the process) by giving the other person a chance to gain more control. Since power brokers are found mostly at the top of organizations, playing the power game can be best played at the top.

Sloan Needs More Space. General manager Sloan was happy to learn that the demand for his company's line of decorative telephones was enjoying a seemingly endless boom. His biggest problem was to find more manufacturing space since corporate headquarters had already ruled out any new construction for the next 2 years. One alternative facing him was to use the manufacturing space of another division in the company that was willing to grant such a request. Sloan describes his solution to the problem:

> The only suitable space belonged to one of our oldest divisions, located some 40 miles from our division. Dan, the head of that division, was hardly a cooperative person. He gloried the days of his past when his was the biggest, most profitable division. I knew it would hurt him to see my division become even bigger and more powerful by taking over some of his space. Yet Dan had more space than he needed for his division's manufacturing requirements.
>
> Knowing that Dan likes to control things, I cooked up a deal I thought might attract him. I explained to him that our division could use about

10,000 square feet of his manufacturing floor. What I would do in exchange would be to have mostly his employees work on our product. We would be using his factory, but his work force could be expanded. In this way, we would both enhance the stature of our divisions.

When Dan realized that the deal would make him more powerful, he jumped at the opportunity. He talked to other people about the deal as if he were making a big concession in order to save my division from embarrassment. The truth, of course, is that we were helping him take care of his biggest problem— unused plant capacity. Dan is always happiest when he thinks he's in control of the situation.

KEEP YOUR COMMUNICATION CHANNELS UNCLOGGED

An astute manager keeps informed about the problems brewing in his or her department. A manager who is out of touch with the feelings and opinions of subordinates is vulnerable to a palace revolt. Such revolts typically are found at the top of organizations but can also take place at lower levels. A sound defensive strategy is to take care of problems before they reach an uncontrollable size.

One self-confident manager I know asks at an occasional staff meeting, "Folks, is there anything I'm doing that interferes with your doing your job as you would like to do it?" By acting on suggestions (such as "be more specific about what you want us to accomplish"), he is able to prevent a minor annoyance from becoming a revolution.

Don Loses His Power in a Palace Revolt. Corporate executive Don was recently deposed by one of his vice-presidents, much to his surprise and dismay. Several of the subordinate executives became disenchanted with his style of management. They felt Don had become too detached from people and the real problems of the business. As one insider explained to a company out-sider:

> The man had become obsessed with paperwork and controls. He never visited with us any longer. Don simply read computer reports and made pro-nouncements about what we were doing wrong on the basis of the computer findings. I don't think Don had ever seen some of our products; he made only two personal visits to plant locations. We finally met secretly with the board of directors and suggested that they axe Don. Instead, he was given a staff job as vice-president of special projects.

GROOM PRINCES AND PRINCESSES

An indirect, long-range, but often successful high-level power play is for an executive to become known as a person who grooms successful managers for the organi-zation. Managers who are adept at developing younger managers are in short supply. If you have both the patience and talent for such work, you might be at a power advantage. Princes and princesses of the organi-zation may remember your contribution to their de-velopment when you need their backing.

Debbie Remembers Her Benefactor. At age 33, Debbie had become Equal Employment Opportunity manager at the home office of her company. Her job focused on encouraging managers throughout the cor-poration to promote women and minorities into re-sponsible, highpaying jobs, and at times it was necessary for Debbie and her small staff to apply pressure to recalcitrant managers. Debbie felt that her being young, black, and female made it difficult for her to establish a good working relationship with some of the older plant managers in the corporation. She thought she needed a troubleshooter who could work closely with some of the more traditional plant and personnel man-agers in dealing with some of her more sensitive problems. The troubleshooter would spend as much time as necessary at plant locations where the plant managers and personnel specialists were having difficulty implementing EEO programs.

Jack, the man who gave Debbie her start in the organization, came to mind as an ideal candidate for the troubleshooter assignment. He was compassionate, intelligent, and well accepted by older management personnel. Debbie asked Jack if he would be interested in trying such an assignment. He replied:

"Debbie, how thoughtful of you. My job as labor relations manager for the division is folding up. Top management thinks this is a job for an attorney, which I am not. So you could say I've just begun to explore possibilities for myself in the corporation. I'd be very interested in looking into that troubleshooter assignment with you. I enjoyed having you work for me before. I think our relationship would be just as good if we switched sides of the table."

CONDUCT A MASS, CONCENTRATED OFFENSIVE

A power holder must occasionally carry out activities that both he and the people affected find distasteful. To minimize lingering animosity toward the power holder, it is often best to get the distasteful task accomplished in as short a period of time as possible.[3] Under such circumstances, people may forget the reprehensible act after the initial sting has worn off. Layoffs represent the best case in point. Executives who are forced to lay off a substantial number of the work force usually try to do it all at once, rather than dismiss people in small groups over a period of time.

The Hatred for Preston Turns to Admiration.   Preston recounts what happened to him when he took over as president of a large commercial printing plant and was forced to take some drastic personnel actions:

One month after I arrived as president, the owners of the parent corporation told me I would have to trim down the size of the executive group. According to their analysis, seven people in top jobs within the company were not needed. This was half the management team above the first-line supervisory level. However, I agreed that the analysis was essentially correct. The company was top-heavy.

After negotiating with my bosses for a couple of weeks, it was agreed that five managers and two supervisors would be laid off. We anticipated two problems. First of all, a layoff of these oldtimers might create morale problems within the company. Second, the company was located in a small town, so we figured there might be a negative community reaction.

Concerned though I was, one Friday afternoon I announced the termination of all seven people at once. Each person was briefed individually the morning before the announcement was made. By Monday, the whole company was buzzing about the incident. My wife told me that she heard some pretty negative things said about me in the supermarket. People in the office stared at me as if I had done something terribly wrong.

The company began to operate more efficiently than at any time in the past. Both sales and profits picked up and people received bigger salary increases than they had ever received before. After 1 year, people were complimenting me on having improved the company. If I was ever a villain in their eyes, it was apparently all forgotten.

TRY A COUNTERINVASION

If somebody tries to encroach on your territory, it is sometimes helpful to conduct a counterinvasion. You will both fight for a piece of each other's territory but if you put up no defense, you will, most likely, be gobbled up by your adversary. Your counter-ploy may not get you a piece of the adversary's territory, but the confrontation could force the problem to a logical solution.

Hy Gets Invaded. Sales training director Hy was well regarded by most people who knew of his work. His job was to help train sales representatives for the company's largest division. Hy describes how he became involved in a bitter power struggle with Lance, the corporate director of organization development:

> Lance invited himself to spend a day visiting my operation. While there, he and one of his staff asked a number of people lots of questions about what we do and why we do it. It was hard for me to figure out if he was conducting some kind of an audit for the corporation. Whatever he was doing, it didn't phase me because we were performing very necessary work for our division.
>
> About 3 weeks after Lance's visit, I received a large envelope—sent by his office—in the mail. It contained a master plan for reorganizing organization development and training in the corporation. Lance wanted all training in the corporation to report to his office. I would report to him, as would other training directors in the other divisions. It didn't make sense to me because we deal with a product line peculiar to our own division.
>
> Not to be outdone by Lance, I also came up with a suggested plan of reorganization. My plan called for a small organization development department reporting to sales training. My reasoning was that our division was unique—enough so to warrant its own services; that the corporate division was too far removed from us to appreciate our unique problems.
>
> The upshot was that the president, who had received copies of both our suggested plans for reorganization, ordered an outside consultant to study the problem. After 1 week of study, the consultant recommended that we keep the organization as it

existed. One exception was that we should add one organization development specialist to our staff. The president took that person from Lance's group and gave her to us. Lance was upset but not totally surprised. Before long, he'll try more fancy footwork.

KEEP YOUR DEPARTMENT LEAN

Without a job, you have no organizational power. A defensive power tactic is to take whatever steps are necessary to ensure that you will not be taken away from your empire.[4] One common-sense approach is to keep your department lean and, therefore, a less likely candidate for a reduction in force than a department where too many people are handling too little work. In the past, a simple solution to an overstaffed department was to dismiss a few clerks or administrative assistants. The trend now is to cut from the top.

Casey is Excised.   Department manager Casey thought he had a sound method of protecting the size of the department he controlled, even during hard times. Casey would intentionally overstaff. When a reduction in force was called for (as is often done in 4-year cycles), Casey would eliminate those people in the department he considered least competent. Casey could then weather cutbacks without a loss in department efficiency. Unexpectedly, the company decided to play organizational musical chairs. Top management moved everybody in the department up one notch in responsibility. Casey was one exception. He was moved out of the department and into the street.

BE FEARED RATHER THAN LOVED

In 1515 (or there about), Niccolò Machiavelli suggested that a prince is better off being feared than loved. His reasoning was: It is nice to be both feared and loved, but it is easier to maintain control when you are feared.[5] Here are five techniques that are particularly useful if you want to be feared:

1. Give subordinates frequent reminders of how dispensable they are.
2. Announce that expense account reports will be carefully audited at unpredictable intervals.
3. Place people over the age of 55 on early retirement when they openly disagree with company policy or philosophy.
4. Threaten to have every department justify its function at the start of each fiscal year.
5. Mention you are using an executive color chart. Each subordinate will be given one of three ratings: green for promotable, amber for "wait and see," and red for not promotable.

GIVE PROOF OF PROWESS

The top-level power seeker of today might also heed Machiavelli's advice that you provide people an outstanding example of your greatness.[6] If you are not great, it is difficult to provide such an example: Here are five possible ways of exhibiting greatness:

1. Have a newly announced company policy rescinded for your area of responsibility because you believe it disregards local circumstances.
2. Obtain the highest raises possible in the organization for your subordinates.
3. Suggest to people that they set their own working hours because they are so mature and intelligent.
4. Become a member of the board of directors of a large bank.
5. Serve pastries, doughnuts, and freshly brewed coffee at a staff meeting.

BUILD A MONUMENT

The most powerful people in organizations frequently have something tangible by which they will be remembered.[7] Such a monument is a testimonial to your greatness. Only the most powerful people can create such a monument during their working years. Slightly less tangible, but still monumental, is to create a new organization structure for the firm or for a significant portion of it.

Al Invents the Bowditch Process. Al worked in a managerial position for a manufacturer of aluminum alloys. Since the company had a staff of about ten managers and 100 mill workers, the managers in the company performed a variety of functions. One of the primary functions of the company was to recycle old aluminum products. The scarcity of aluminum, combined with its high demand, almost guaranteed a good future for Al's company.

In search of a way to make a big impact on the firm, Al happened upon a good idea on an overseas trip. A Japanese competitor had an inexpensive process of recycling aluminum from light appliances that Al thought could be used by his firm. As soon as Al introduced the process into his company, he called it the Bowditch process. Following Al's instructions, his secretary was careful to use the term Bowditch process on every piece of correspondence that mentioned salvaging aluminum with this new Japanese process. Al's stature in the firm rose as people began to associate his name with the most important refining process used by the company. Al Bowditch had made his mark.

BUILD AN OUTSIDE REPUTATION

In an earlier chapter, mention was made of getting your name in print to impress influential people at your place of work. The same principle of getting *outside* recognition applies in the executive suite. Developing a national reputation in your field could help you to be treated with the respect usually afforded a powerful individual. Powerful business executives are frequently appointed to federal- or state-level commissions and special task forces. Conversely, being appointed to a national- or state-level commission or task force can add to your base of power in the company. Serving as a high-level consultant (paid or unpaid) to the government can also enhance your status. Many variations of this theme (of developing an outside reputation) exist to enhance your status and power within your own organization.

Will Becomes President of a Trade Society. Will had been devoted to paper-making all of his professional life. Ever since he received a Ph.D. in chemistry, Will had conducted research in or given advice about paper-making. At the age of 47, Will was working as a top manager of a large management consulting firm and felt that he had reached a career plateau. He enjoyed consulting but had not quite made it to the top of his firm. In his quest for a more fulfilling professional role, Will became more active in a trade association of paper manufacturers. His active participation was welcomed by the many members of the association who gave only perfunctory effort to the organization. Suddenly things began to click for Will. He tells us what happened:

One of the members suggested that I run for president of the association. At first, I laughed at the idea; then, I recognized that here was a big opportunity. My campaign consisted of writing an honest letter to every member, explaining what I would do if I became president of the association. Above all, I stressed the fact that I would be willing to take care of the many administrative chores imposed upon the president. It felt good when I was elected president by a wide majority.

Out of courtesy—and common sense—I sent the president of my consulting firm a photocopy of the trade-paper announcement—noting that I had been elected president of the association. Immediately, things began to happen. The president of my firm invited me to lunch to personally congratulate me on my appointment. I was invited into more important meetings. I think the firm believed that my new position would lead to substantial new business for the firm. Whatever the reason, I enjoyed my elevated status. One year after becoming president of the trade association, I became a vice-president in my firm; my office décor improved; and I became responsible for more important clients. The size of my staff also increased.

SELECT A COMPLIANT BOARD OF DIRECTORS

If career advancement strategies, talent, and luck have enabled you to become a chief executive, you may be able to capitalize on the ploy of selecting a board of directors who comply with your most important requests. Without a cooperative board, it is difficult for a company president to expand his or her power.[8] Chief executives attempting to use the board for aggrandizing their power opt for as many inside board members as possible. If you report to the president, it is awkward to cross swords with him or her in a board meeting. The president of an insurance company helped pack the board of directors with people who were aligned with his thinking. His tactic was to casually recommend new members of the board as old ones retired or resigned. People recommended, of course, were individuals whom the president knew were compatible with his thinking.

OBTAIN AN EMPLOYMENT CONTRACT

A powerful executive creates conditions whereby rules are bent to satisfy his or her demands. The top-level manager who obtains an employment contract as a precondition of employment immediately establishes himself or herself as an aggressive, forceful, and powerful individual. Management expert Robert N. McMurry notes that it is particularly important for the newly appointed executive to obtain a contract when his primary assignment is to salvage and rehabilitate a sick or failing operation or to pioneer a radically different field of activity that no one in the business knows much about.[9] If dismissed from such high-risk assignments, the contract gives the executive a financial cushion against the hardships of finding a new position.

Aldo Has Things Under Control.   With some trepidation, Aldo left behind his successful career with a big corporation to take over the presidency of a medium-sized electronics company. He described the position as an unusually good opportunity to prove what he could do when given total responsibility for an operation. A friend asked Aldo why he insisted on an employment contract if the opportunity was so good. Aldo replied:

> I wanted to be treated with the same respect they give a baseball coach. If the team gets off to a slow start and the owners want to blame it on the coach, they may decide to fire him at midseason. But they are obliged to pay him full salary for the entire term of the contract. On the business scene, if the board gets a little impatient for results, they are more likely to let the manager with a contract follow through on some of his ideas and plans. If would be wasting money to fire a president with 9 months to go on a contract unless he was ruining the company. More important, when you have a contract, you're in control. And that's where I want to be.

PART IV

Misfortune, Mistakes, and Misdeeds

Coping with Defeat

Playing it cool and rolling with the punches when adversity strikes is part of playing sensible office politics.[1] The manager who rants, raves, pounds his or her chest, or throws a temper tantrum when things don't go his or her way is paving the way for harder times ahead. Nobody always wins in the game of office politics. At one time or another, you will be passed over for promotion, demoted, fired, chastised, criticized, sent to a corporate Siberia, abandoned by a favorite subordinate, or ridiculed in public. More than one public politician who has been jeered, mocked, and literally spat upon has moved on to a higher office. It might be worth your while to think in advance of how you will handle the next downside episode in your career.

WELCOME THAT ROCK BOTTOM FEELING

Small company president Winfred turned to his secretary, Mary, and noted with a tone of optimism. "Cheer up, Mary. It looks like we have finally hit the bottom of the barrel. From now on, things are going to get better. We have laid off half our work force, our business has shrunk 45 percent this year, and our new computerized order system has caused us endless problems. The future looks better. Business conditions are improving, and the people still in the company are mostly our better employees. It's a good feeling to know that things won't get any worse."

Winfred is doing more than wishful thinking. He is developing a mental set of attitudes that is almost indispensable in bouncing back from defeat. When you are truly convinced that your problems have bottomed out, you are preparing yourself emotionally for a recovery. That "nothing-else-can-go-wrong feeling" helps you mobilize your energy to begin your counterattack. Another way of using this strategy is to initiate your counterattack only after your opponent has used up all of his or her ammunition.

Shelly Gets Shelled.　Sales promotion manager Shelly had just spent $10,000 promoting a new line of skis. Despite his efforts, the skis did not sell at a volume high enough to cover costs. Shelly's boss, Jerry, called Shelly into his office for a chewing-out session: "Why did you spend $10,000 on a promotion that did no good? What kind of lousy judgment is that? Are you a sales promotion manager or some kind of a hack that throws company money around? I thought you had some business sense."

Shelly surprised Jerry with the comment, "What else have I been doing wrong lately?"

"I'll tell you what, you've been counting too heavily on standard types of promotions. You ought to be more creative, that's what. If you were more creative, you could think up a campaign to get our new line of skis off the ground."

"Tell me one more thing, Jerry," said Shelly. "In the 5 years that I've worked for you, have I made any contributions to the company?"

"Of course Shelly. I'm just upset with how slowly the new line of skis is moving. Try to do a better job along those lines."

Shelly's ability to absorb all Jerry's blows helped put Jerry's criticisms in proper perspective. Before the end of the chewing-out session, Jerry admittedly recognized that Shelly had performed generally well in his job. Had Shelly tried to retaliate before Jerry had vented all of his anger, he might have intensified Jerry's current negative attitude toward him. Shelly's tactic turned a negative situation into a neutral, perhaps even positive attitude.

TAKE CRITICISM GRACEFULLY

In the situation just described, Shelly was really using two tactics to cope with defeat. Aside from absorbing all the blows his boss had to offer, he gracefully accepted criticism. A Survivalist, Company Politician, or a Machiavellian learns to handle criticism, because doing so makes you appear unflappable—a highly desirable characteristic of a winner in any field. A Machiavelli, it must be cautioned, may take criticism gracefully but is probably plotting revenge (while appearing to be graceful).

Totally or partially agreeing with the criticism made of you is generally the most effective way of appearing graceful when under assault. Part of a criticizer's fun is to watch you squirm and become angry when under attack. Take away that fun and the criticizer feels ineffective. Another advantage of agreeing with criticism is that it may appear that you have nothing about which to feel guilty or defensive. Some specific examples:

CRITIC: You didn't even listen to what our client was saying. If you don't listen to clients, how can we ever keep their business?

YOU: You're right. I could do a better job of listening to clients. I'll keep that in mind next time I speak to a client.

CRITIC: I notice your expense account shows a charge to the company for a double-occupancy rate at the Sheraton. Do you expect the company to pay for your sleeping with another person while on a business trip?

YOU: I did charge the company the double-occupancy rate. It's very restful when you're away on a trip to bring along company. Would you like me to write you a check for the difference in price between a single and a double room?

CRITIC: A finance company called today saying you were 3 months behind in your car payments. How do you explain that?

YOU: They are probably right. I think I owe them for May, June, and July. I'm thinking of making a big 4-month payment in August.

DISCOVER THE FACTS BEHIND YOUR DEFEAT

When you are demoted, fired, passed over, or suffer any other significant defeat, you owe it to yourself to find out why.[2] Getting a true answer may not always be easy, but the facts could help you avoid a similar defeat at a later date. Despite all that has been preached in recent years about the importance of honesty and openness in management, you may still have to probe to get an authentic answer as to why you were defeated.

Gary Vows to Curb His Rudeness. "How can I tell my wife," Gary thought to himself. "It's the third time that I have been passed over for a regional managership. Each time, the company told me that I would be warmly considered for the next promotion." Gary's reflection was followed by sullenness and then finally by action. He demanded a conference with his boss, Elmer, to discuss why he was again passed over. With some hesitation, Elmer did agree to review the reasons why Gary was not selected for the position of regional manager.

"Your work performance has been fine," began Elmer. "It's just a few little things that made us decide to give somebody else a chance this time around. It's not too much to worry about."

"Elmer, that is precisely why I came to see you. It *is* something I worry about. Is there something holding me back in this company? I must know. Maybe it's something I can correct. What are these little things you refer to?"

"Gary, this may hurt, but you asked for it. My boss and I think you are rude to top management. It's this rudeness that's keeping you back."

"I don't recall being rude to anybody. Could you give me a couple of examples?"

"The best example I can think of is when Mr. Finney, the executive vice-president, joined us for lunch. When we were returning from lunch, you barged through the revolving door ahead of him. During his presentation, you clipped your nails. Just like you do in other meetings, you interrupted him before he had a chance to finish what he was saying. Do you get the point? We think you need more polish."

Gary felt the company was being needlessly picayune, but now he had a clear understanding of what aspects of his behavior where holding him back. Gary could quit in a huff or conform to what the company thought constituted good manners in dealing with the higher-ups. By taking the latter course of action, Gary's hopes of becoming a regional manager were re-ignited. At no sacrifice to his sense of morality, Gary did become more deferent toward higher-ranking executives and he did stop clipping his nails at meetings. Fourteen months later, a new region was formed and Gary was selected to become regional manager.

CONDUCT BUSINESS AS USUAL

Maggie lost out in her power struggle for a window office close to the vice-president. After the floor planner's dust had settled, Maggie was assigned to a cubicle-like office without a window, located some 15 feet from the men's rest room. Jane, her rival, who did get the more choice office, gleefully dropped by Maggie's new office 2 days after the new office assignments were made. Her fond expectation was to find Maggie either in a fit of anger or sulking about her second-class status. Instead, looking well rested and energetic, Maggie said, "Jane, nice of you to drop by. I should have my half of the figures analyzed on the Buyrite account. Could we get together at 4 this afternoon to merge our figures?"

Maggie showed herself to be unflappable in this incident. She was not going to let her status battle over the physical location of her office interfere with her appearance of being cool and efficient. By sulking over her loss, as Jane wanted her to do, Maggie only would have been compounding her losses.

Blair Burns His Bridges. Blair was unceremoniously fired from his job as chief engineer—an action he thought unjust. Blair's boss patiently explained that he was being let go because the company wanted fresh blood at the top of the department; Blair had run dry of innovative technical ideas. Blair would not accept his firing. He wrote angry letters to the president, chairman of the board, and board of directors. He cried foul and said he might take up the matter with his lawyer. A friend in the marketing department urged Blair to control his rage, but Blair felt he was justified in creating a stir. His last step in proving himself right and the company wrong was to submit a list of the names of ten people who agreed that he was a creative engineer.

Fourteen months later, Blair was still looking for new employment. He had several good leads, but mysteriously, once Blair's references were checked, a candidate other than he received the nod. One perspective employer leveled with Blair about the reference from his last employer: "The reading we get is that you used to be a stable person but that recently you've become very excitable and stubborn. Those aren't the qualities we are looking for in a chief engineer."

SWING INTO CONSTRUCTIVE ACTION

After a reversal, the person with a capacity to bounce back takes almost immediate constructive action about his or her problem. The person fired because he or she was caught in a political squeeze play should start looking for a new job within a week after being fired. Inaction leads to further inaction, often resulting in a hard-to-shake lethargy. A simple procedure such as a phone call to a friend or an employment agency may be an important first step in finding another suitable position. However grim the problem, there is almost always some kind of constructive action that can be taken to begin the process of recouping your losses. Bouncing back from defeat is mental-health sustaining, while sitting in a corner licking your wounds usually detracts from your mental health.

Elroy Prospers in the Boondocks.   A big-city person, Elroy was stunned by his assignment to manage the South Dakota refinery of his company for he had been a golden boy several years previously. He had boasted to many that he would be the corporate vice-president of manufacturing before the age of 40. However, Elroy's abrasiveness rubbed a couple of key executives the wrong way. As a form of corporate punishment, Elroy was sent from the home office to the South Dakota assignment—70 miles from the nearest city and the refinery had been losing money for 4 years. His friends thought that Elroy was end-played, but Elroy had different plans for himself. His recollections of the South Dakota experience included these comments:

> My first reaction was one of shock. I thought I had been sent to a corporate Siberia from which I would never return. I was the *enfant terrible* of the company, and this was my fate. I was smart enough not to quit. My track record at the company had

been too good for a stunt like that. Instead, like a good soldier, I packed my bags and, along with my wife and two children, went off to that little South Dakota town.

Shortly after arriving, I developed a better understanding of why the refinery had gone so far downhill. Almost no new blood has been infused into the refinery in years. The previous manager had made all the decisions. People below him were treated like peons. He behaved as if customers did not exist. Housekeeping in the refinery had gone to pot. Many of the production processes were antiquated.

Immediately, I gave laid down plans for improving as many things as I could, giving people more responsibility and asking them to make suggestions for improving refinery operations. I hired a few new technical people. Within 1 year, we were close to breaking even; within 2, we were making a profit. Morale had improved more than I would have imagined possible when I took over the job.

By close to the third year, the refinery was doing so well that it was regarded as a moneymaker for the corporation. My performance at South Dakota now endeared me to the same management that had sent me there as a punishment. I was offered a promotion back to headquarters. It was with some regret that my family and I left the small refinery town. We had gotten to like the austere life-style even though we didn't want to stay there for the rest of our lives.

COOPERATE WITH THE VICTOR

A political street fighter will not quickly throw in the towel, but once he or she is defeated, the victor will get his or her full cooperation. To do otherwise is foolish. Holding a grudge against a boss or peer who has won (over you) in a political fray can only worsen your situation. One of the most damaging labels to be tagged with in an organization is *uncooperative*. An equally bad reputation to acquire is one of being *difficult to supervise*.

Gail Digs a Bigger Hole for Herself. Faith and Gail both wanted to become department manager Hal's administrative assistant. Gail was selected for the position, a decision that upset Faith. She told a friend from another department in the company, "Gail got the position because she's forever playing up to Hal's male ego. She laughs at his worst jokes, serves him coffee, and compliments him on his creative ability. She is not nearly as efficient as I, but because of politics, she was given the job."

After Faith was promoted, a slight reorganization took place within the department. All secretaries, typists, and clerks now reported to Faith. Gail seethed in anger. She expressed her anger by dragging her heels when Faith gave her assignments. In contrast, if she thought an assignment came directly from the department manager or a supervisor in the department, Gail was her usual efficient self. Faith reported Gail's poor cooperation to Hal.

Hal counseled Gail about the importance of cooperation, but she responded with stoney-faced silence. After 2 more months of negative attitudes on Gail's part (but not substandard work), a four-way conference was called among Gail, the personnel manager, Faith, and Hal. Gail protested that she wanted to become an administrative assistant and that her attitude would improve if given such an assignment. The personnel manager retorted that only a highly cooperative secretary could be recommended for promotion to an administrative assistant.

Gail suddenly recognized the folly of her ways. She had become embroiled in a departmental feud so big that the personnel department had to intervene. She had done permanent damage to her reputation in her own department and her own company. By giving Faith her full support, Gail perhaps would have been next in line for an administrative assistant position.

MOVE OUT OF THE GRAVEYARD
AS SOON AS POSSIBLE

Elroy, mentioned above, was able to turn an unprofitable and demoralized operation into a winning situation. Not everyone sent to an undesirable assignment has the talent—or good fortune—to emerge so victoriously. A generally sound strategy is to earnestly try to be transferred away from an unfavorable assignment after you have made a sincere effort for a reasonable period of time to improve the situation. A large corporation established a salvaging department staffed mainly by people with emotional physical disabilities (such as people with cardiac problems who had been advised to avoid stress). From the outset, the department became known throughout the corporation as The Graveyard. Managers in the department were generally considered unpromotable.

Fifty-five-year-old Judd was appointed under protest to a middle-manager position in The Graveyard. A friend in personnel gave Judd her honest opinion about the situation: "Judd, you've just about been put out to pasture. The only way you'll ever get out of this department is through retirement. But if you like that kind of work, your future is assured with the company. Besides, the people working there are stable and appreciative. You might feel like you're doing some good for them."

A vigorous man, Judd did not wish to see himself placed in a terminal position; however, he did enjoy the challenge of a salvage operation. He decided he would stay in his graveyard position until he acquired enough knowledge about salvage operations to enter business for himself. Two years later, Judd, his brother-in-law, and a close friend established a small scrap metal business. His career was anew with excitement. Judd had escaped the graveyard.

RECOGNIZE WHEN YOU ARE BEING DUMPED

Large organizations have subtle ways of removing from the mainstream people whose contributions are no longer valued but who are yet considered immune from firing. Humanitarian reasons may mitigate against a long-term contributor being axed. Political factors, such as that person's tie with the influential people, may also prevent a person from being dismissed from the organization. Valuable contributors, too, are sometimes shunted to the side rather than fired. The valuable contributor may get dumped because he or she was the victim of an internal power struggle. Whether a particular assignment is a dumping ground depends on the organization and the specific circumstances.

One aggressive young manager was assigned to an important project simply because his manager no longer wanted a troublemaker in the department. The project itself was important, but one manager used it as a dumping ground. In organizations with large corporate staffs, it is not uncommon to place an out-of-power manager into an internal consulting role. His salary and job title may be impressive, but requests for consultation with him are infrequent. In other instances, an internal consultant may make an important contribution to the corporate welfare. In short, you have to recognize whether your new assignment means you are beeing groomed for even bigger responsibilities or simply cast aside.

Welby Glories in His Elevated Status. Public relations manager Welby was the son of the largest stockholder in his company. His boss, the president, was displeased with Welby's performance but unwilling to undertake the delicate task of asking a person of his financial weight to resign. According to Welby's boss, he is deficient in this manner:

Welby is a difficult person to have on your staff. The only public relations people who stay working

for him very long are docile, uncreative types. Anybody with a little spirit or talent quits after about a
year. They claim he tries to make all the decisions
and rejects any idea that departs from the ordinary.
On the other hand, we get a lot of muted complaints
from the public relations firm that supplements the
efforts of our internal staff. The owner once told me
that Welby rejects all their good ideas. They figure
that they cannot serve our corporation well if they
are not treated as professionals.

Welby's boss found a temporary solution to his problem. Welby was appointed to a task force that would
study the future of the corporation. It would attempt to
answer such questions as "What products and services
should we be offering in the next two decades?" "What
demands will be made on us by the public?" "What
government regulations will be influencing us the
most?" Because of the importance of his project, Welby
was released from his responsibilities as public relations
manager.

When asked if Welby could make a contribution to
such an important assignment, his boss responded:
"No problem. I just want him to coordinate activities
and collate the opinions and information that the committee digs up. He'll be more of a recording secretary
and historian than somebody who provides input to the
project. His tendency to veto ideas won't hurt us on
this effort."

Welby's attitude toward his new role was positive: "I
welcome the opportunity to serve the corporation in
this important capacity. I envision the job as integrat-
ing information from a wide variety of sources. We will
leave no stone unturned in uncovering information that
will help us adapt to the demands of the future."

BE PREPARED TO DESERT A PATRON

Another form of defeat is when the power of your
patron erodes. If his or her influence begins to wane,

you will have to find a new patron or join your patron in a lesser role. In extreme circumstances, you may even be asked to leave the organization along with your patron. You will know your patron is losing power when he or she is dumped or when his or her empire is fragmented into smaller units. Another indicator is when he or she is transferred to a lesser job. A management development specialist from England offers whimsical but cogent advice on coping with the situation of a patron who is losing power:[3]

"As soon as the vultures start to gather, it is time to nail your colors to some other mast. Discreetly, you will begin to air your 'reservations' about your patron's policies. You will stay silent at meetings when he is expecting your support. And during casual conversation with his most bitter opponents, you will confess to a growing disenchantment."

LOOK FOR SIGNALS OF GOOD NEWS

A curious, almost mystical, way of bouncing back from defeat is to receive subtle signals from the environment. If you keep your mind finely tuned to the world around you, you will be able to notice these signals. Once they appear, you can face your rivals with renewed confidence and realize that your turn at good times is imminent. Just as a bird chirping signals the end of a violent rainstorm, the world of work offers its own indicators of good times ahead. Not everybody gets the same signals, but here are a few that could mean the turning point in your particular funk:

- You have been trying to see a key executive for over a week. One morning, his secretary phones you and says, "Mr. Blank will be able to see you at 11:00 this morning."
- A manager whom you insulted in a meeting last week smiles at you with forgiveness and invites you to join her for lunch.
- A substantial-sized customer prospect returns your

phone call, asking to learn more about your product.

- You learn from the personnel department that you will not be cut in the next layoff.
- The new annual report includes a photo essay of employees at work. You are one of the employees pictured.
- Your request for additional clerical help is approved.
- Your rival for promotion resigns.

13

Organizational Taboos

An important part of winning at office politics is knowing which actions to avoid. The sensible office politician practices offense, defense, copes with defeat, and also senses what actions will lead him or her into disfavor. Most of the positive strategies mentioned so far in this book have hinted at what kind of behavior is taboo. If you conduct yourself in a manner opposite to most of the major strategies of office politics you are committing an organizational taboo. For instance, your actions would be taboo if they were disloyal to associates or if you alienated higher-ups instead of cultivating them. Here, we will concentrate on 13 actions (so far mentioned only in passing or not at all) that, unless avoided, could prove unlucky for the person carrying them out.

DISPLAYING A LOOSE TONGUE

A quick way to fall into disfavor in an oraganization is to pass along to other people information that should be kept secret. One negative consequence of having a loose tongue is that you may lose the trust of people who count in your career. Another problem with being a blabbermouth is that you may place others in embarrassing situations. A good rule of thumb is: There are almost no secrets at work. Whatever you tell someone else will be passed on to at least one other person. If you want a piece of information kept secret, tell nobody. Our advice does not imply that there are no situations in which candor is beneficial. If you tell a colleague that his performance is substandard, negative repercussions are unlikely (if he tells others of your evaluation). However, if you tell that same person that your *boss* is incompetent, that message *may* be relayed back to your boss, causing you trouble.

Priscilla Blabs About Her Perks. A talented computer programmer, Priscilla worked for a small company that provided computer services to organizations without computers—or those lacking sufficient computer capacity to handle all of their information-processing requirements—since its origin some 8 years ago. On the birth of her second child, Priscilla decided that she needed to spend more time being physically present in her house. She made this pitch to her boss:

"Over the last couple of years, I have been doing an increasing amount of programming at home, particularly during rush periods. At this point, I can keep one eye on my children and one eye on the computer terminal I have installed in my office. What I would like to do is spend Wednesday, Thursday, and Friday afternoons working out of my house. Since my work can be measured quite specifically, you would be able to tell if working out at home was interfering with my productivity."

Ted, Priscilla's boss, agreed to the plan, but cautioned her that the arrangement was an informal one and should not be interpreted to mean that this constituted a permanent arrangement. Priscilla expressed her gratitude for the flexibility Ted showed her. Ted described what happened next:

About 2 months later, two more programmers on my staff came to me with similar requests for working out of their house. One was a woman with a small child, the other was a man who had a particularly long commute to work. I turned both down, but they both countered with the argument that Priscilla was being granted the privilege of doing some of her programming at home. I asked how they knew that to be the case. Each one replied that Priscilla had bragged to them about her new hours. I was so angry with Priscilla that I wanted to fire her. Instead, I passed an edict that all employees were required to work in the office during normal working hours.

Priscilla's loose talk ruined a good thing for herself and placed her boss in a compromising position. He did not wish to be seen as a manager who treated his subordinates unequally. Nothing was gained by Priscilla's sharing her good news with her colleagues.

DISPLAYING AN ACID TONGUE

"How do you enjoy working for our firm so far," said the founder of the CPA firm to Norbert, a young accountant who had recently joined the firm. "To tell you the truth," said Norbert, "I like everything around here except for some of the management attitudes."

"Could you elaborate on that, Norbert," requested the founder.

I'm glad to have the opportunity to give you some idea of how I see the firm. I get the feeling that the firm is suffering from hardening of the arteries. Some of the policies around here are right out of the Dark Ages. It looks as though an accountant would have to work 4 years before he was given any independent assignments. Another problem is wages. We're about 5 years behind the times with respect to the wages paid young accountants. With some new blood in top management, I think this firm would be just fine.

Norbert's acid comments went beyond the requirements of good sense. He was being too pointed in criticizing polices that obviously the founder of the firm had been instrumental in developing. Norbert's insensitive display created conditions whereby he was unlikely to become a person with enough power in the firm to change the conditions he thought needed changing. Later that day, the founding partner in the firm said to Norbert's supervisor, "I think that your new accountant, Norbert, bears watching. He seems rather impulsive in his judgment and hypercritical. We wouldn't want him to act like that in front of clients."

An acid tongue is much less taboo when directed against outside competition or rival factions within the firm. Yet venom released against a rival may come back to haunt you. With reshuffling of people and responsibilities so common in modern organizations, your internal rival today may become your boss tomorrow.

Fran Attacks His Rival. Product manager Fran was upset because Dave, another product manager in the company, had put together a strong product team. In a private confrontation, Fran tore into Dave. "You've been hogging all the good talent for your own team. You took the best package designer in the firm to work full time for your product. Then you cajoled the president into believing that your product needed a bigger budget then anybody else's. Unfortunately, the president couldn't see through your empire building. You want your product to look good at the expense of other products."

Dave politely told Fran that he misperceived the situation and that he should be careful about making unfounded accusations. One year later, Dave was promoted to vice-president of marketing. One of his major responsibilities as the head of marketing was to assign products to the various product managers. Dave reshuffled some of the assignments to the satisfaction of everybody but Fran. The latter's reaction was shock and disbelief to the news that he would now be responsible for three of the company's lowest volume products, all of which had yet to contribute a profit.

Despite Fran's pleas, Dave would not reconsider his decision.

UPSTAGING YOUR BOSS

The most elementary principle of human relations suggests that one should never publicly criticize a subordinate. The same principle can be extended to relationships with your boss: Never criticize or show up your boss in front of others, however irresistible the temptation. Upstaging is interpreted by many people as a form of criticism. A wise office politician avoids upstaging the boss at work or in a social setting.

Mack Craves for Recognition. Ray, the executive director of the Boy Scouts in his area, was making a presentation to the Community Chest to review the developments of the recent year. (In his area, the Boy Scouts are eligibile for a small share of Community Chest Funds.) Toward the end of his overview of the year's event, Ray commented:

"Ordinarily, I do not like to brag of my personal achievements, but an aluminum recycling drive that I personally organized netted us $275 this year. It shows how we help ourselves raise funds."

Mack, an administrator who worked on Ray's staff, raised his hand at this point and said to the Community Chest members:

I agree that Ray's recycling operation was worthwhile for the Scouts. But it is an inefficient way of raising money in comparison to the project I have completed. I have information that I have not yet reported even to Ray. A group of scouts under my supervision were actively involved in a yard-care program last summer. The final results are just in. We have $550 to contribute to the Boy Scout fund, and it took us about one-third the time required by the aluminum operation.

After the meeting, Ray upbraided Mack. His most cutting comment was that a person who had personalized the Scout philosophy of life would never try to upstage his boss. Furthermore, Ray told Mack, in the future, he would have to clear with Ray any information he intended to present to outsiders. Unknown to Mack, Ray gave him a negative recommendation for promotion to executive director of another region.

BEING A PEST

In an era where being assertive about your demands is considered a virtue, many people are overzealous in making childlike demands upon management. The individual who insists on always being granted every possible benefit or advantage legally coming his or her way often winds up being seen as a pest. For instance, if you are on the exempt payroll (which means exempt from overtime pay), it would still be possible to receive some premium pay if you worked overtime on a systematic basis. However, if you made a plea for overtime pay after working two Saturday mornings, the damage you would do to your reputation would outweigh your few small dollars of gain. Another form of organizational peskiness is chronic complaining about work-related matters such as the amount of snow accumulation in the company parking lot, the quality of food served in the company cafeteria, or the caliber of top management.

Mickey Demands His Way. Industrial engineer Mickey was happy to be working for a small company. He believed that his competence and hard work would be noticed by top management, giving him a good chance to work his way up the organizational ladder. Mickey's first important misstep occurred when his manager was 2 months late in formally reviewing Mickey's work performance. He told his boss that by delaying his performance review, his salary increase would automatically be delayed and he was, therefore, being underpaid for the period of time in which his review was delayed.

Once, Mickey put in a request for a mileage allowance to cover his expenses for the few days per month that he worked at another company plant, located in town. Mickey reasoned that any work assignment not at his regular office must be categorized as authorized travel and compensated for by the company. Mickey's boss recalls the incident that finally branded Mickey as too small-minded to be considered management timber:

> One day in July, I received a call from Mickey while he was on vacation. He told me that he had taken ill and it seemed that his illness would last 2 days. He wanted to know if it would be all right to extend his vacation time to make up for the 2 days of illness in which he could not take advantage of his vacation. Mickey said that his previous company had had such a policy. I explained to Mickey that our small company was not General Motors or IBM. He became adamant about extending his vacation but did consent to return to work on time. Still, he did not let the matter drop. He wrote a memo to the personnel department protesting my decision.

Mickey has a keen legal mind in terms of attempting to squeeze from management everything coming to him. In contrast, his political sensitivity is that of a dullard. The few small advantages he might gain for himself with his demands will not compensate for the blocked opportunities (such as promotions) attributable to his peskiness.

Alec Likes to Complain. Audio-visual specialist Alec had a fun job.[1] Working for a large corporation, he was a member of a film production team that produced a variety of movies dealing with company products or company training. Producing a film required that the audio-visual production group visit various departments in the company to gather ideas or to actually shoot pictures. Alec habitually used people he met in these field visits as sounding board; for his complaints about the company. His complaints centered around the theme that the company did not provide the film group with proper equipment. One day, Alec's boss called him into his office for a leveling session:

"Alec, they tell me you don't think too much of the equipment the company gives you to work with. I admit it's not exactly up to the standards used by Paramount Pictures, but we are an industrial filmmaking department not a Hollywood studio. Since it gives our department a bad image to have a representative making these public complaints, I'm reassigning you for an indefinite period. Your new job is that of darkroom technician. Complain all you want to the other darkroom technician."

THROWING TEMPER TANTRUMS

Baseball and football coaches throw temper tantrums as part of their act. It is probably politically unwise for a coach never to throw a towel to the air, stomp on the ground, or raise a clenched fist at an umpire. Chefs, artists, and movie stars are also allowed their temper tantrums during working hours. Unless he or she is the company founder, the large organization employee must guard against more than one or two tantrums in a career. One company president planfully goes through a table-thumping, fist-pounding episode during labor negotiations. He never really loses control; therefore he does not arouse suspicion about his emotional stability.

The more an organization resembles a total bureaucracy (such as AT&T or the Pentagon), the more important it is for a person lower down the line not to break out into uncontrolled rage. (People at the very top of an organization are allowed more excesses than those in the middle.) A bureaucracy prefers to think of itself as a smooth-running machine where everything fits into place. Instead of getting emotional, the ideal bureaucrat points to a rule book to prove his or her point.

Charlotte Returns from Primal Therapy.   Looking for personal growth, office supervisor Charlotte attended a 3-day primal therapy session. She learned all about screaming out her feelings to uncover past hurts. During the session, she beat into a pillow and screamed at her father for all the wrongs he had done her in childhood. She ranted and raved at the therapist because she reminded her of her mother. Charlotte felt emotionally unblocked and invigorated upon her return from primal therapy. She explains what happened when she tried to transfer this emotional learning from the primal therapy sessions to the job:

> One thought that surfaced during the group therapy sessions was that I was too constricted in my emotional responses. I was told by the other group members that people at work would probably accept me better if I gave freer rein to my emotions. The therapist, too, encouraged me to let loose some more, just as I had done in the group. Back at the job, I decided to give emotional looseness a try. During a closed-door session with my boss, I really let loose about how the company was pushing too hard for productivity, that I just couldn't squeeze anymore productivity out of my people. Tears came to my eyes as I described how punitive and unrealistic the company had become.
>
> Instead of being complimented on my emotional honesty, I was lambasted. My boss said he sent a note to the company medical department, recording the incident. He also told me that he was going to recommend that I receive no assignments that call for customer contact if I was capable of acting like that on the job. My company won't tolerate full emotional expression. Never again will I let go like that on the job.

CHISELING ON THE EXPENSE ACCOUNT

Manipulating expense accounts to personal advantage has become so common a practice that the topic is no longer secretive. One maneuver is so widespread that many people no longer consider it dishonest: A person charges the organization the price of a full dinner, perhaps $11, eats at a diner or fast-food restaurant for $3, thus making an $8 "profit." Many male business travelers regularly eat at McDonald's to subsidize their trips to massage parlors and the like with such profits.

Sensible office politics suggests that you do not jeopardize your career for the sake of pocketing a few unearned expense-account dollars. Governmental agencies—both at the federal and state level—and some large business firms have reduced such temptations by granting people a standard per diem for travel.

Lucien Travels One Block by Cab. A middle manager with big hopes, Lucien severely damaged his reputation in his company. His boss tells us what happened:

Lucien attended a 5-day trade show in Chicago on company business. He seemed to have profited from the experience because he brought back a few tentative orders and much useful information about new developments in our line of business. One of my chores is to approve the expense-account reports of my subordinates. Usually, the process is quite routine. Unless something is way out of line, I approve it without question.

In this particular case something struck me as curious. I noticed that Lucien made an entry for 5 days of cab fare back and forth from the hotel to the convention center. I used to work in downtown Chicago and I know that the hotel was only one block from the convention headquarters. I faced Lucien with this discrepancy. He said to remove his request for reimbursement, that it must have been a mistake.

Ever since that incident, I have never fully trusted Lucien. It made me wonder if this petty gyping of the company was only the top of the iceberg. What was to stop him from being dishonest on a larger scale? Lucien resigned from the company about 1 year after the incident. I think he somehow realized that I no longer had full confidence in his judgment.

COMPLAINING ABOUT A FORMER BOSS

A taboo of moderate intensity is to make frequent complaints about your former boss. Needless complaining about a former superior might be interpreted an act of disloyalty. It also suggests that, when you move on to another department, you will make similar complaints about your present boss. Complaining about your former boss is also a poor idea when you are trying to gain entrance into an organization. Ron, a financial manager, tells of an interesting experience along these lines:

I spent 6 months looking for a new job. I needed a job because I worked for an impossible manager. He did about everything a manager could do wrong. He was tyranical, dishonest, and played favorites. I couldn't take the pressure any longer.

When I went for a job interview, inevitably, they asked me why I was looking for a job. I explained the situation about my incredibly bad boss. They seemed to show some sympathy, but I received no job offers. It dawned on me that I should stop complaining about my situation. I changed my strategy. I told prospective employers that everything was wonderful at my company, that I was learning a lot from my boss but that I wanted more responsibility. I received two good job offers within 2 weeks after I changed my tune. The lesson I learned is that people are afraid of bringing a complainer into their organization.

DEVIATING TOO FAR FROM CUSTOM

Rigid conformity is no longer a virtue in most successful organizations. The intellectual maverick often forges ahead because of his or her innovativeness and enthusiasm. Despite the merit of this generalization, it is still taboo to deviate too far from accepted customs dealing with dress, speech, or courtesy. "Custom" also includes such things as carrying your lunch to work versus having it served to you in a restaurant. Either practice may reflect current custom. Some organizations are more picky than others with respect to following custom. In one bank, a junior officer was sent home to change clothing because he appeared at work in a turtleneck shirt under his jacket. The price one pays for violating custom is to be branded "difficult to get along with," "immature," or "stubborn"—all labels that are potentially damaging to your career.

Bitsy Expresses His Independence. By 1977, leisure suits for males were considered so "out" that fashionable dressers would not even wear them washing cars. Bitsy, a lower-level manager in a vast bureaucracy, maintained his independence. The first time his manager cautioned him against wearing leisure suits to the office (the year was 1977), Bitsy had this comment:

"So what if a few men's clothing designers have now decided that leisure suits are now inappropriate for business? I think they are still the best compromise between a three-piece suit and blue jeans. I feel comfortable in my leisure suits. I have two left and I'll continue to wear them until they are worn out. If anybody can show me a clause in the employee handbook that forbids the wearing of leisure suits, maybe I'll reconsider."

Bitsy won the battle of the leisure suit but at a great hidden cost. His manager placed in Bitsy's personnel folder a statement that can lead to one's demise in a bureaucracy. It read, "Bitsy refuses to cooperate about wearing appropriate business attire. He frequently shows up to work in clothing unbecoming to a junior executive, despite my counseling that he should do otherwise. This behavior bears watching because it may reflect a spirit of not wanting to follow company rules."

CHALLENGING FOND BELIEFS

Most organizations, profit or nonprofit, have certain fond beliefs that are implicit rather than stated. Within several months of employment in an organization, you should be able to ferret out the nature of these beliefs, possibly from a friendly old-timer. People who are blindly loyal to the organization will rarely admit that they exist; yet, their comments on the subject suggest that these beliefs are cherished. If you make public statements challenging the folklore of the organization, you may be branded as disloyal or unappreciative. Six of these fond beliefs contribute to the folklore of many organizations, large and small.

1. *We are the best in our field.* Many a hapless organization finds some rationalization to delude itself into believing that it is the best in its field. A marketing manager might show his belief in this statement by a comment such as "True, our model KFG is priced higher than that of the competition, but the quality-conscious buyer will always choose it. It is the best in the field in the minds of the sophisticated buyer." The president of a mediocre college will often state, "Our graduates are welcomed by employers across the country. We have developed an enviable reputation for the practical-mindedness and solid values of our graduates."

2. *People at the top of our organization are wiser and stronger than people at the bottom.* A fascinating children's toy is a closed cylinder containing four sets of marbles—each with a different color. When the toy is inverted the marbles pass through a series of multi-

holed shelves. The holes for each layer are of slightly different size. Within 3 minutes, the blue marbles lie on the first shelf, the red on third, and the white on top. Each shelf then consists of marbles homogeneous in color and size. Most organizations lead you to believe that their hierarchy is arranged in such a manner: The wisest and most talented people are at the very top, followed by a group of the second-most talented and wise people at the next level, and so on down to the bottom. You are supposed to speak of people of highest rank with awe, indicating that you believe only those people of superior talent, ambition, and moral character rise to the higher levels. In short, hold dear to the belief that your organization is a pure meritocracy.[2] Only an Innocent Lamb would be iconoclastic about the myth of the meritocracy.

3. *Administrative ability is more valuable than technical skill.* A man who is now president of one of the ten largest industrial companies in the world once commented to me, "I wish I knew what to do with all the programmers we have in our company. They are like carpenters. When you need some carpentry done, they are very useful. But if you don't need any carpentry done, what do you do with them?" Business and governmental organizations fondly hold the belief that administrative skill is more valuable than technical skill. In universities and scientific laboratories, this belief is much more tenuous. An eminent researcher in these two types of organizations might become better known and earn a higher income than an administrator. In a bureaucracy, one way to slight a rival is to say he or she "is a good technician."

4. *The founder of our firm was (or is) a genius.* Speak with a tone of reverence when you refer to the founder of your firm (whether your firm is a bank, law office, branch of the government, or junkyard). Revere that oil painting in the lobby or the president's office depicting the founder in a noble pose. The *true* founder of a firm is often the founder's father who left him with $300,000 in cash with which to start a business. The

struggling young entrepreneur—with barely enough money for groceries—thus bought a fledgling company and turned it into a great one. Despite the truth, it can serve you no good to challenge any old-timer's belief that the founder was (or is) a genius. Never make the young bureaucrat's impulsive mistake of saying, "If we got the old man to retire, this place would make some real progress." Reserve such impulsiveness for an exit interview, after you have already secured employment elsewhere.

5. *Most people who leave our organization are people whom we prefer would leave.* The implication of this statement is that the most competent people stay and the least competent people leave. Once an organization passes its rapid-growth phase and enters a plateau, the opposite is more nearly correct. Highly competent and ambitious people, when they feel their opportunities for advancement are limited, have a tendency to leave an organization. In one well-known glamour company, three vice-presidents left in a 2-year period to become presidents of major business corporations. Even if you are objective enough to praise the virtues of the person who voluntarily leaves the organization, never imply that those who remain are of lesser caliber. One manager in a mammoth corporation was reprimanded by his boss for stating at a management development conference that "most of the people with guts and talent left us long ago."

6. *Other organizations in our line of work who do things differently are faddists. The fads they have embraced will soon disappear.* Carried to extreme, this belief destroys an organization. If you are concerned about the progress of your firm, you may have to inform the traditionalists (delicately) around you of new developments by your competitors that bear watching. Never rub against the grain of this belief by making the inference that your firm is weak because it ignored the competition. A marketing manager in a bank took notice that a competitive bank was establishing mini-branches in two supermarkets. Aside from making bank

services more convenient to shoppers, subletting space from a supermarket was less costly than establishing a full branch.

When the marketing manager brought this new development to the attention of management, he abrasively said his own bank was falling behind the times. They countered with the idea that bank outlets in supermarkets were a fad that would soon fade. Three years later, the bank finally had to join the "fad." Had the marketing manager been more diplomatic about criticizing his own bank when trying to sell a competitor's approach to his bank, he might have emerged a hero. Instead, his bank was slow to participate in this new method of customer service.

VIOLATING THE CHAIN OF COMMAND

Protocol is highly valued in multilayered organizations. Avoid making an end run around your boss to communicate with his or her boss unless you are sure this behavior is acceptable. An important exception is when you are faced with an emergency situation such as working for a highly incompetent or unreasonable boss. Under those circumstances, a gentle confrontation with your boss's boss about his or her problems might be appropriate. A general principle is that going around your boss (or over the boss's head) is taboo, but may be necessary when you get no satisfaction from speaking directly to him or her. Asking your boss for permission to speak to a higher-up is another workable alternative. A sneak play will often backfire.

Henry is Castigated.   Sales order clerk Henry wanted to work as an outside sales representative. He took his request to his boss who replied, "That doesn't sound too unreasonable, but I think you should spend another 6 months on the sales desk before we give serious consideration to your request. This way you can learn a lot more about our product line."

Henry did not like what he heard. He was concerned

that his boss was engaging in stalling tactics. Henry waited for Len, the branch sales manager, to drop by his department before further pursuing his transfer request. Henry casually asked Len if he might speak to him for a few moments. Len obliged, and Henry informed him, "My boss won't let me out of the department, and I want to become an outside salesman. How do I get past the guy?" Predictably, Len simply reported the conversation back to Henry's boss. His boss, in turn, called Henry into his office and delivered a straightforward message:

> Len tells me you think I've locked you up in this department and won't let you out. It so happens that every sales representative in this company has served at least 1 year on the sales order desk before being let out into the field. In your case, we think you need a little extra seasoning. Len and I agree that you need a lot of improvement before you are ready for outside selling. Bring up the matter again next year if you are still interested.

DUMPING A PERSON WITH CONNECTIONS

"John, I'm sorry," said his boss, Rudy, "I've given you four warnings so far. I've told you that if your attendance and punctuality did not improve, I would have to recommend that you be dismissed. What good is a draftsman who isn't around when we need him? I will recommend to the personnel department that they give you 30 day's severance pay. If you prefer, I will accept your resignation. Let me hear from you by noon tomorrow."

At 10:00 the next morning, John said politely to Rudy that he decided that he liked his job too much to resign. Rudy, in turn, sent a letter to the personnel department recommending that John be fired. One week later, the personnel department had still not acted on Rudy's request. During that week, John was absent once and late three times. Furious, Rudy went to personnel demanding an explanation. The personnel director told him, "You've created quite a problem for us. We've had to turn down your request, but the news leaked to the chairman and he's on our back to get on your back."

"Why?" asked Rudy, "Doesn't an engineering manager have the power to recommend that we get rid of a loafer? We're not running a welfare department."

"We may not be running a welfare department, Rudy," answered the personnel manager, "but neither do we try and fire the nephew of the chairman of the board without first getting his permission."

FLAUNTING CHANGES FROM TRADITIONAL SEX ROLES

A modern taboo of moderate consequence is to flaunt deviations from traditional sex roles. The push for women's rights in the last decade has led to more flexible attitudes about appropriate roles for both males and females. Yet many people, who are not blatantly sexist in their attitudes and behaviors, still become upset when somebody goes out of his or her way to demonstrate that the traditional concepts of how males and females should behave are no longer valid. A truly liberated person does not have to go out of his or her way to prove that the world has changed.

Jane Squelches a Polite Gesture. Staff assistant Jane was appointed to a committee on which she was the only woman. The males in attendance made no particular mention of the fact that she was female. During the first half hour of the meeting, not even one mild sexist comment was made. Jane then took a cigarette from her handbag. Rob, seated to her left, almost reflexively took out his cigarette lighter and gestured that he would light Jane's cigarette. She said abruptly, "No, thank you. I'm perfectly capable of lighting my own cigarette." Rob replied, "Your choice."

As the meeting ended, the committee chairman held

the conference room door open for Jane. She commented, "Please don't hold the door open for me unless you intend to hold it open for the other members of the committee. My hands and arms are well enough coordinated to open doors. Or didn't you know that about women?"

Jane, in her efforts not to be treated in a sexist manner, had become oversensitive to the meaning behind normal social amenities. The committee chairman developed a negative reaction to Jane. He now prejudged her to be touchy and difficult to work with. Other members of the committee would now be self-conscious in their dealings with Jane because of her insistence on equal treatment in two trivial incidents.

Cecil Sports the Latest Fashion. At the height of the tax season, tax advisor Cecil strolled into the downtown Internal Revenue Service office wearing a shoulder bag. He kept his shoulder bag dangling from his chair while advising citizens about their tax problems. At the coffee break and at lunchtime, Cecil walked across the room in public view displaying his shoulder bag.

Joe, the supervising agent, was concerned that an agent wearing a shoulder bag would look inappropriate in an IRS office. He also realized that the federal government should be the least likely organization to infringe upon somebody's civil rights. No IRS code touched upon the topic of appropriate attire (for males or females). Joe made the decision he thought best, and approached Cecil with these comments:

Cecil, I have a delicate topic to talk about. It's your constitutional right to wear whatever clothing and accessories you want to the office. But let's use common sense. Our office is in Pittsburgh, not Los Angeles, San Francisco, or New York. If a male agent wears a purse in our office, he looks like some kind of kook. Perhaps you have noticed some of the snickers on the faces of the taxpayers when you walk across the room. Would you consider not wearing your shoulder bag to the office?

Cecil pondered and then said, "I will consider no such thing. Until the time that carrying the latest in men's fashions interferes with the caliber of tax service I offer the public."

Case closed? Not at all, as far as Joe was concerned. Cecil's performance review was very positive in terms of actual work accomplished but low on cooperation. From the standpoint of individual freedom, Cecil was justified in disregarding Joe's suggestions to refrain from wearing a shoulder bag to the office. Yet at the time and place, wearing a shoulder bag deviated so far from stereotyped expectations of male dress that it constituted a politically unwise act.

SAYING NO TO TOP MANAGEMENT

Consider yourself fortunate when top management makes a request of you individually or as a manager of a group. The surest way to get recognition is to perform well under the scrutiny of a higher-up. Yet, there are times when you or your department is already so over-burdened with work that more responsibility would test your breaking point. A simple resolution to the problem can sometimes be found to avoid saying no to top management when saying yes might result in an insufferable burden.

Jason Hedges His Way to Victory. Frank, the executive vice-president of a manufacturing company, was spearheading a move to relocate company facilities. One day, he approached Jason, the manager of facilities planning and one of the busiest people in the company. Frank had a request:

Jason, I know your group is already overloaded, but we need to do a quick feasibility study of taking over an old macaroni factory in the center of town.

I know the place doesn't look like much, but if we did move some manufacturing down there, we would be able to hire a number of people from the inner city who badly need jobs in their own neighborhood. If we don't make a decision within 30 days, I think the building will be demolished and converted into a parking lot. What can you do about the situation?

Jason's first impulse was to scream that if he asked his people to take on one more project they would quit in protest and he, personally, would suffer a nervous breakdown. In lieu of such histrionics, quick-thinking Jason thought of a more politically astute response. "Of course, our group would be more than willing to take on the assignment. It's just a question of a crushing work load at this time. Do you think we could get authorization to subcontract some of our more routine work to an outside consulting engineering firm, so that we might tackle the macaroni factory project?"

"You're the professional in this area, Jason. You have my backing to do whatever you want to get this study done. Anybody who gives you a hard time will have to answer directly to me." By saying yes to the macaroni factory feasibility study, Jason had created a strong bond between himself and an influential member of management. Had Jason rejected the recommended feasibility study, he would have violated the taboo of saying no to top management.

14

Devious Tactics

To an Innocent Lamb, almost all forms of office politics are dishonest, dirty, or devious. Labeling a given tactic as honest or devious is a question of values. To a Machiavelli, any maneuver that helps you gain advantage without getting you into legal trouble is fair game. Thirty-eight tactics uncovered in our research would probably be considered dirty politics by most people who work in an office. Some of the tactics are well known and have been practiced for centuries; others are less well known and more recent in origin.

The person who practices devious political tactics does so at considerable risk to his or her career. Practicing dirty office politics may lead to your being unwanted, unloved, and fired. You might be sued for libel, punched in the nose, or perhaps sent to jail.

DIVIDE AND RULE

The age-old strategy of encouraging your subordinates to scrap among themselves so they will not form alliances against you is still with us. Ned, a division manager, felt that his acceptance was on the decline. His solution was to try to get his three key department heads feuding among themselves. Ned told each department head that his department would be given top priority for moving into a new building currently under construction. Predictably, the three department heads did bicker about who would be relocating. What Ned did not realize is that the department heads also discussed how they knew they would be relocating. When the truth was uncovered, the three men pressed Ned to explain the misunderstanding. Ned blamed the error on a question of interpretation. He told them he meant to communicate the fact that their needs for additional space was a top priority for all three departments. The amount of respect Ned commanded eroded further after this incident.

SHOOT TO KILL

Also entitled "Embrace or Demolish," this ancient strategy suggests that you remove from the premises rivals who suffered past hurts through your efforts. Those wounded rivals might retaliate at a vulnerable moment. The origin of this strategy is found in Machiavelli's advice regarding the conquest of smaller nations:[1]

"Upon this, one has to remark that men ought either to be well-treated or crushed, because they can avenge themselves of lighter injuries, of more serious ones they cannot; therefore the injury that is done to a man ought to be of such a kind that one does not stand in fear of revenge."

Owen, a vice-president of finance, bitterly opposed the takeover of his firm by an outside company. Despite his protests, the merger took place. The president of the acquiring company learned of Owen's displeasure about the acquisition. One month after the merger, Owen was fired. Owen's boss was forced to give him the bad news. He told Owen, "They are forcing me to put one of their people in the top financial spot in our company. It's a question of somebody experienced in their way of looking at finances."

DISCREDIT YOUR RIVAL

A transparent, devious tactic is to discredit your rival by direct accusation or innuendo. Only a naïve boss will accept a damaging statement made by one peer about another without additional confirmation of the adverse information. For the record, here are a few discrediting statements made by people desperate to gain advantage:

Plumber talking to his boss about another plumber: "I wonder if, on my next assignment, I could work with somebody other than Jack. I've tried working with him, but he just doesn't seem to be any good with his hands."

Subordinate talking to boss about fellow worker: "I think we're really going to miss Vince. I saw him filling out an application blank to join the CIA."

Subordinate talking to boss after she returns from convention: "I couldn't find Ginny at any of the meetings. Was she called back early? I hope she didn't take ill."

Boss talking to his boss about ambitious subordinate: "When he's around, Marty is a terrific worker. But he's hard to find. I guess he's usually in some other office, politicking to find a good job for himself."

BACK-STAB

Back-stabbing is similar to Discredit Your Rival except that you pretend to be nice all the while planning someone's demise. A safeguard against being stabbed in the back is to ask yourself why a particular person is trying to befriend you. If the reason seems legitimate, forget your suspicions. Tracy, a systems analyst, explains how she was stabbed in the back:

Yvonne, another analyst in my department, made a special effort to cultivate my friendship. As we got to know each other better, the conversation naturally turned to the competence of various people in the department. I mentioned a couple of times that our boss was a much better administrator than a technician. Which really isn't an insult.

Yvonne then tried to use this information against me. She knew that Bill and I had a good working relationship. It was generally thought in the department that I was next in line as department manager. Yvonne went to Bill and told him that I didn't respect his technical competence. Being an up-front guy, Bill confronted me with what Yvonne had said. I told Bill my version of the story; he laughed at the incident. He told me that he wanted to be seen as a better manager than a technician. I let the matter drop, but I completely avoided Yvonne from that point on.

RAISE QUESTIONS ABOUT YOUR COMPETITION

A mild form of discrediting your opposition is to simply raise questions about his or her capabilities. Raising questions is an effective technique because it allows the other person to make his or her own decisions. If you say outright that your rival is incompetent, the boss may resent your implying that he or she has made a serious error in judgment. Among the penetrating questions that might be asked about a rival are these:

1. Is he or she irreplaceable? Has he or she trained a replacement to take over the job should he or she receive a promotion? (It is usually difficult to demonstrate that you have a ready replacement.)
2. Is he or she overloaded? (In other words, could your rival possibly take on any more responsibility without risk to efficiency, physical health, or mental health?'
3. Is he or she more of a specialist than a generalist? (A good criticism to make about any technically competent person. Most people become good generalists after much experience as specialists.)

COVER UP THE TRUTH

Lying might be the most frequently practiced devious tactic people use to look good. "Bury the truth" is the gambit of the dishonest office and public politician.

"Your check is in the mail" and "your order has already been shipped" are such common lies in business that few people become upset when the mails, rails, airplanes, or trucks are mysteriously a few days late.

THE SETUP

One way to get rid of the opposition is to set them in a situation where they are likely to look bad or fail completely. The setup often involves the cooperation of several people in the plot. Donna, a Black woman, describes how she was set up to fail by her employer:

I had been an assistant manager at the bank for 4 years. My boss told me that I was doing a good job. According to both merit and seniority, I was overdue for a promotion since most assistant managers are promoted to manager within 3 years. The next opening for a branch manager in the bank was at a branch located in an affluent, white, upper-middle-class suburb. I think the bank didn't want to give me this assignment because I am black. It has been a kind of unwritten policy of the bank to match managers with the social and economic climate of the branch locale. Usually, a Black manager is placed in a branch located in a lower-class city neighborhood.

It seemed as though the bank was plotting to make me look bad so I wouldn't be eligible for the suburban branch opening. My manager was sent on special assignment outside of the office leaving me to take care of the branch alone. Instead of providing me with an experienced employee to cover my duties, I was given a newly hired trainee. At the same time, the bank was introducing a new form of checking account which, by itself, created a good deal of confusion.

I was faced with the challenge of running the branch, training a new worker, and instructing the office staff in the new checking account service. That first month, two tellers quit giving me 3 and 8 days' notice, respectively. The bank told me that no replacements were available, which I found hard to swallow. A friend of mine was working at another branch and asked to be transferred to mine. She was told I had no openings in my branch.

The bank then conducted an unannounced audit of my office and found it to be in very bad shape. All the chaos was blamed on my poor management. My manager was then ordered to immediately return to my branch to clean up the mess I had created. I had been set up to fail. My only option for defending myself was to bring charges of discrimination against the bank. I decided not to take on the bank.

TAKE UNDUE CREDIT

A devious political tactic and a devastatingly poor management practice is to take credit for work performed by others.[2] A manager who uses this tactic often takes full credit for the successes of his subordinates, but disclaims any responsibility for their failures. The same technique as practiced by Sam, can be used with peers, who worked in a computer printing department.[3]

For each job that was processed, the operator had to log the start and stop time of the job. This list was used to check for responsibility of printing quality and, to some extent, as a measure of job performance. As each job was set up, Sam would log his operator number even if the job was not processed by him. However, when he observed that the print quality did not measure up to standards, he would change the operator log number to that used by one of his co-workers. He did not, however, adjust the printing machine to produce the proper print quality.

TRADE ON SEX FOR POLITICAL ADVANTAGE

A woman can be accused of trading sex for advantage only if she has sex with a person of higher rank who would not otherwise promote or grant her other favors. A woman who genuinely cares about a man—dates him, has sexual relations with him, and then is promoted because of their personal relationship—is not really trading sex for advantage. The key element here is that the man is promoting a friend—a frequent political arrangement.

Aside from moral reservations about the tactic, most people are opposed to trading sex for advantage because it is unfair competition. Assume the person in power is a young heterosexual male. The only people in the department eligible to participate in exchanging sexual favors for organizational favors are young females who have no moral compunction about using sex to get ahead. The 60-year-old male supervisor and the hard-working grandmother in the department must use other tactics to get ahead.

An investigation of classroom politics reveals another reason why trading sex for advantage is considered unfair and devious. Robin, a college senior, told one of my researchers:

> What gets me so upset about students who go to bed with their professors to get good grades is that it penalizes other students. Let's say the professor grades on a curve. That means that he gives only a fixed number of A's. If one student in the class is going to bed with him, and she would have received a D honestly, two things happen. One, she gets an A, depriving a deserving student of that A. Two, some poor fool gets her D because if the professor grades on a curve, so many people have to get D's as well as A's.

WORK IN A CRISIS MODE

A criticism sometimes levied against staff people is that they create crises so they may be assigned the job of resolving the crises they create. A quality control staff member might tell management that there are an unusually high number of customer complaints about the poor performance of the product. Top management then worries and gives the quality control department full support for studying the problem further and recommending solutions. A variation on this theme is to exaggerate the magnitude of a problem and then receive credit for a major accomplishment when actually very little was done.

Considerable selectivity has to be used in creating a crisis for your personal resolution. A maintenance man dares not be caught damaging delicate parts of a machine to emerge a hero when he repairs the baffling problem. Luke, a drugstore manager, explains how he looked good by solving a fabricated crisis:

> It seemed to me that the locations of our checkout counters were poor. When the store was very busy, such as on a Sunday morning, people trying to get out of the store were crowding people trying to get into the store. I told management what a major problem this was and how we were losing business because of it. Whether we were losing business was a matter of conjecture on my part. The storeowners agreed that the problem was significant and asked me if I would work on the problem. My suggestions resulted in a partial remodeling of the store. The final result was so attractive that I received compliments from management for taking such bold and important action. It definitely helped me get promoted to a bigger store 7 months later.

BLACKMAIL

Extortion has been a long-standing criminal activity. It has also been used by company politicians to gain power and favor, or even boost their careers. A curious aspect of company blackmail is that one deviant person threatens to make public the deviant behavior of another, unless the former makes certain concessions to the latter. Blackmailers, however, lead a hazardous existence.

Dan, an accountant, noticed a few major irregularities in the expense account submitted by an executive in his firm. One abnormality he noticed was that the executive's daily expenses were higher than those of others taking similar trips. A more pronounced problem, Dan discovered, were two hotel receipts with smudged-in areas over the dates. In addition, the hotels seemed unusually far from any company location. Dan called these hotels to verify the receipts submitted by the executive. Dan's hunch was correct. The executive was submitting phony hotel receipts that he had collected while on private travel. He had apparently stayed with friends in place of using a public hotel. Dan even suspected that the executive might be submitting expenses for phantom trips.

Dan confronted the executive with his findings. He demanded a promotion into his department and threatened to disclose the expense-account irregularities if his demands were not met. Dan did receive a promotion to a supervisory position. Four months later, he and the executive were both fired. The executive was caught receiving a bribe from a company supplier. On his way out, he revealed Dan's act of extortion.

CREDIT AND REMOVE THE OPPOSITION

Earlier, we discussed the career-boosting strategy of helping your boss get promoted by singing his or her praises to other people in the organization. When you carry this strategy one step further—finding a way to get him or her hired by another organization—you are using a devious tactic. Assuming your rival is effective, you are weakening your own organization by facilitating that person's leaving the organization. Maggie explains how a rival used this tactic to get her out of the way:

Vivian and I worked for the same company as first-line supervisors. We were both eager to be promoted but our company had very limited advancement opportunities at the time. Vivian invited me to a cocktail party at her house. During the evening, she introduced me to Barry, a personnel manager from a local company. Barry mentioned to me that Vivian had told him very impressive things about me. He handed me his business card and asked me to call him to discuss an exciting job opportunity.

Barry was truthful. His company had an exciting opportunity—an open requisition for a female manager in a key spot in the company. It seems that Barry's company was underrepresented by females in management and they wanted to correct the situation. I wound up taking the job. It dawned on me that Vivian had set me up so she would have a better chance at being promoted. I guess Vivian didn't want to risk leaving the company herself or she might have applied for the job in Barry's company. I think Vivian pulled a dirty trick, but I proved to be the winner since the meeting with Barry did give my career a shot in the arm.

EXCLUDE THE COMPETITION

A not-uncommon, underhanded maneuver is to keep the competition away from important meetings without actually using physical restraint. Let's assume you know your rival is scheduled to be on vacation or out of town on a business trip on a particular date. You schedule a meeting on that date, knowing it would be important for him or her to attend. Danny explains how excluding the competition can advance your own cause:

Our place is such a political jungle, people are afraid to go away on vacation. You don't know what you're going to miss while away. The purpose of keeping the competition away from important meetings is so you will look good in the eyes of important people who attend the meeting. Your rival, of

course, will not be noticed because he isn't there. A
former boss of mine set up a budget meeting during
the time I was sent out of town to audit a branch
operation.

I was told that, at the meeting, he presented the
figures from the department and did not mention
that I was the person who really assembled them.
He received the compliment for having done a good
job while I did all the work. It was a missed opportunity for me.

THE SMOKESCREEN

"Say, Craig, have you and your wife tried Dante's, that
little Italian restaurant near Lake Avenue?" asked
George. "It seems like they have ten different Italian
dishes. Linguini is their best pasta dish. You need reservations, but it's worth it. Did you know the boss
wants us to stop giving discounts to small-volume buyers? When you're at Dante's you should order their
spumoni. I hear it's the best in the city."

George is not deficient in communication skills. He
knows that an important message from the boss should
not be sandwiched between linguini and spumoni.
George is using the smokescreen on his rival.[4] Later,
when Craig continues his policy of offering discounts
to small buyers, he will be criticized by his boss for not
following orders. Craig will contend that he never heard
about the policy. George will insist that he carefully
mentioned the new policy to Craig. "Don't you recall?
We were also having a discussion about Dante's restaurant."

SHAM SUPPORT

A manager is often caught in a squeeze between a
superior and subordinate. Your boss wants your support of a particular program but your subordinates are
strongly opposed to the program or policy. The solution for many devious office politicians is to pretend

they are supporting the boss to his or her face and then to behave in the opposite manner in front of subordinates. Chuck provides an example of sham support that illustrates how it can backfire.

The regional manager of our bank informed us of a new policy. When cashing a check for any customer, we would ask for a computer reading on their present balance. We were not to cash checks in excess of anyone's present balance. Tellers hated this policy because they were the ones who bore the brunt of the angry, established customer who considered the process an insult. A new customer can accept checking out their balance as a reasonable business practice. Well-known customers who are also large depositors object very strongly to the policy. The problem gets particularly sticky when a good customer doesn't have a balance large enough to cover the check he wants to cash.

Terry, our boss, openly agreed with the regional manager that such a policy was long overdue and that he and his staff would learn to live with the policy. When one of the tellers would complain to Terry that the new policy was creating problems, he would wink and say "Do what you think is best." In a short period of time, very few computer checks of balances were made in our branch.

The regional manager was much less naïve than Terry thought. He had a couple of bank employees from the main office enter the bank to conduct some minor transactions. While there, they observed what was going on. When the regional manager learned of Chuck's disregard of the policy, he was very upset. Chuck was transferred to a bank in a rough section of town.

THE DOUBLE CROSS

The idea here is to feed incorrect, or partially correct, information to a rival to lead him or her into mistakes.

One market researcher, who wanted his rival to look bad, volunteered to take a number of questionnaires dealing with preferences for different types of bread along with him on a vacation. He contended that the bread preferences of campers would contribute to the scope of the sample. The campers he chose to complete the questionnaires were people who were more concerned about guzzling beer than accurately recording their impressions or teen-agers who wanted to have some fun. Enough of these almost invalid questionnaires were collected to contaminate the results of the rival market researcher's study. The study proved to be valueless, much to the satisfaction of the friendly vacationer.

LET YOUR COMPETITION HANG

The old adage, "give them enough rope and they will hang themselves," is put to good use in organizational warfare. Specifically, it takes the form of failing to point out a person's errors, to facilitate his or her failing. Rick, a personnel specialist, was hoping that Fred, his boss, would fade away. His dirty trick was to let Fred make a fool of himself in front of top management. Tricky Rick explains how:

Fred went through a dry run with me of his upcoming presentation to management about the problems of management obsolescence in the company. Our company was suffering from too many managers who were over the hill. In his trial run, Fred kept saying managerial "adolescence." My first reaction was to laugh at his malapropism, but instead, I decided to say nothing. After all, was it my job to correct my boss? I attended Fred's presentation. He made a royal fool of himself in front of management. When Fred mentioned the term managerial adolescence the second time, the people in attendance roared with laughter. The company president said it was better than a problem of managerial senility.

ABOLISH THEIR JOBS

A new way of squashing people you dislike is not to fire them, but to eliminate their jobs. In this way, they can be sacrificed even if they are outstanding performers. Vera explains how her job was abolished because of a personality clash between herself and her boss:

> My boss had three computer programmers and one systems analyst reporting to him. The analyst quit, so one of the programmers was promoted to that job. My boss then phased out one of the programmer positions, saying it was no longer needed. I was let go. The department still accomplished all of its work because the person who was promoted to systems analyst really spent most of his time programming. There really wasn't enough work for a full-time systems analyst. If the systems analyst's job had been eliminated, my boss would not have been able to dump me.

TRIGGER A RIVAL'S FLARE-UP

As explained earlier, temper tantrums are taboo in most places of work. You can score against your rival if you don't mind the sight of emotional bloodshed. The trick is to provoke your antagonist into a public outburst of anger or rage so the rest of the office group can appreciate the extent of his or her emotional immaturity. Before pulling off this devious stunt, you have to be aware of your rival's most sensitive areas. An incident of this nature took place in a departmental engineering meeting, the purpose of which was to reorganize the department.

Keith, one of the contenders for more responsibility in the department's reorganization, knew that Fritz was under consideration. Fritz was a self-made engineer with very little formal technical training. (He had taken some mechanical engineering courses in Germany but did not have an engineering degree.) Keith knew that Fritz became indignant anytime the subject of importance of formal education for an engineer was discussed. As the group conversation turned to the nature of the changes that would be made, Keith said to Fritz, "Could you tell us something about your background? Some people here may not be familiar with your past experience."

Visibly irritated, Fritz went into a rage. He sputtered and said, "What business is it of anyone's what my background is? When I want people to know about my background, I'll be the first to tell them. Anybody who thinks he is a better engineer than I, please step forward. I learned enginering the hard way. I'm qualified and that is all there is to it."

Fritz looked so weak to the group on the basis of his tirade, that he could not be seriously considered for an administrative assignment in the department's reorganization.

FRONTAL ASSAULT

One vice-president in an international company personally disliked one of his most talented subordinates. Since the vice-president controlled communications back to the home office, he shaded everything about his disliked subordinate in a negative tone. To make life even more miserable for him, the vice-president conducted a relentless assault. The subordinate describes his version of what happened:[5]

The conflict affected our personal life as well. He controlled my living conditions and my expenditures. Company executives abroad get an overseas package which includes housing and living expense, furniture allowance, sometimes a car and other benefits. If you really want to hurt someone, you can make his home life miserable by delaying his car or not approving housing expenditures and so on, which is exactly what this man did to me and my family. For

14 months, he moved my wife, our son, our dog and cat from city to city, hotel to hotel. He never allowed us to stay in one place long enough to settle down and rent a house. And since I was traveling 28 days out of 30, my wife was always alone.

The manager's subordinate succeeded in telling his version of the story to top management, but soon thereafter did leave the company. He had created too much ill will in the process of defending his reputation..

FAKING SUCCESS

To look good, you can, under some circumstances, pretend to have achieved an objective. Faking success is not always a highly devious tactic. An engineer describes the successful application of this technique in his company:

Each engineering project in our company has a set of major milestones established which often becomes almost as important as the project itself. For instance, we always attach great importance to the first time we can talk through a new telephone system. One engineering manager was assigned a major development program that was to last 3 years.

About halfway through the program, he was to make his first call through the new system. As the critical day approached, it became evident that the system would not be ready. Undaunted, he proceeded to rig the system to demonstrate that his project was on schedule. After the demonstration, he recovered the slipped schedule through a combination of overtime and tighter supervision. The upshot was that the project completed on time and a profitable product was marketed. Had the manager not faked success, he would have probably faced so much harassment from higher management that the total project would have been off target.

UNDERESTIMATE THE COSTS FOR YOUR PROJECT

Many appliance and automobile dealers have been accused, and some convicted, of bait-and-switch tactics.
In essence, this technique is also used for gaining power
within organizations. It takes the form of underestimating the true cost of a project you wish to undertake.[6]
The organizational bait-and-switch schemer hopes that,
once the company likes the project, it will agree to go
along with the added cost. Underestimating costs should
be done infrequently and selectively; otherwise, you
will lose your credibility. An amusing incident is reported by an engineer who worked for a lowball cost
estimator. "The first time he submitted a cost estimate
to his vice-president, he was asked, "Is this a true
estimate or is it a W.H. (his supervisor's initials)
estimate?"

KEEP A BLUNDER FILE

A dastardly maneuver is to keep a blunder file on
everyone in your office. Assuming you are a Machiavelli at heart, you never know when the moment will
be propitious to discredit someone in your work sur-
roundings. Almost everybody commits a blunder once
in a while. In one company, a group of managers had
a background and credit report run on a newly joined
manager. Although nothing derogatory turned up, the
older managers were looking for a way to depose the
new manager should he prove to be a menace to their
cause. Here are a few specific items found in a blunder
file:

- On July 18, Betty Lou turned in her department
  budget 3 days late. It contained several inaccura-
  cies and vague projections.
- On August 8, Mannie came back from lunch at
  3 P.M. He appeared red-eyed and had difficulty

walking. A secretary from another department was with him.

- On May 20, at Sea Island, Georgia, Glenn made a presentation to the sales force on forecasts for the upcoming year. He was so nervous that it took him 4 minutes to get past the first sentence.

GET HIGH WITH YOUR BOSS

At lower levels in some organizations, it is not an uncommon practice for some people to try to ingratiate themselves by getting high with their boss. The jovial mood found among drinking or pot-smoking buddies creates a bond that is difficult to break once back on the job. As one young man, formerly a box packer, said, "The reason we got high with Gus at night was so he would be easy on us the next day. It was easy to tell the guys who went along with Gus's wine-drinking and pot-smoking parties. They were the ones who were allowed to goof off." In short, getting high with your boss is geared to the office politician who is playing for very small stakes such as work shirking or being liked by a person of narrow outlook.

TELL THEM WHAT THEY WANT TO HEAR

A cheap and unprofessional political stunt is to tell management what they want to hear despite some reliable data to the contrary. The bearer of good news thus avoids a confrontation with management over matters of judgment. In the long range, such a fearful approach to your job will be self-limiting. Since you are seen as a person who only confirms what management already knows, you will not stand out as a person who brings important new ideas to the organization.

Telling them what they want to hear works in this manner:[7]

Garth, a man in charge of a small sales forecasting department, was informed by one of his subordinates that the sales forecast for a particular product was

$1.3 million for the next fiscal year. He took this information and changed the final to $1.1 million. When his subordinate asked why Garth shaved the figure, the latter replied, "Management predicted sales of $1 miillion. Why make them look bad?"

HOLD A GUN TO MANAGEMENT'S HEAD

A heavy-handed, thuglike approach to boosting your income or advancing your career is to force management into submitting to your demands by threatening to quit at a key stage in a project. Lloyd, an engineering manager who worked for an aerospace firm, was assigned to a project with a tight deadline since the customer was the United States Air Force. A penalty clause was attached to the contract whereby the company would be fined $1,000 for each day the completed project was overdue.

As the project approached its most critical stage, Lloyd asked his boss for a promotion and a $2,000 salary increase. He threatened to quit if his demands were not met. The company reluctantly met his demands but handed him a termination notice 24 hours after the project was complete.

DEATH ON THE VINE

In some circumstances, an executive finds it wise to agree with a plan or program he or she really does not want to implement, only because disagreeing would precipitate too much of a harangue. So the executive engages in the devious maneuver of saying he or she will go ahead with the controversial plan or program, then plays a stalling game.[8] The executive is always in the process of making the agreed-on changes, but nothing really ever happens.

Jerome, a company president, received a petition from an employee representative that demanded a modern cafeteria in place of the substandard lunchroom currently available for employees. Jerome realized the gripe was legitimate but he felt his company was not in a position at the time to assume such a large capital expenditure. Concurrent with the employee demand for a better cafeteria was a demand from the board of directors to improve profits. Jerome agreed that a cafeteria should be built. He assigned a committee to study the problem and suggest several different types of cafeterias. Whenever approached about the status of the project, Jerome would point out that roadblocks were being encountered, that many complications had arisen. Two years later, ground was actually broken for the cafeteria at a time when the company's financial situation could absorb the costs of such an improvement. Jerome's devious tactics had created considerable ill will, but he was able to keep peace with the board of directors and prevent an employee insurrection.

THREAT OF NEGATIVE REFERENCES

One way to force a political enemy to resign is to promise him or her a favorable reference if he or she does resign. Conversely, if he or she does not resign, a strong negative employment reference is promised. According to the *Federal Political Personnel Manual* used during the Nixon Administration, there are three key steps in using a frontal assault on an employee victim:

First, you promise him that he will leave with honor and with highly favorable recommendations. A farewell luncheon is advisable, perhaps coupled with a department award.

Second, you indicate that should he or she not accept your offer, and that he or she is "forced to resign or retire through regular process or on his own volition"; that his, references from the department will be much different than if he or she cooperated.

Third, there should be no witnesses in the room when you make your offer. A caution is offered to the government official: "This technique should only be used for the timid at heart with a giant ego. This is an extremely dangerous technique and the very fact of your conversation can be used against the department in any subsequent adverse action proceedings."

NEW ACTIVITY TECHNIQUE

A high-level power play at the expense of taxpayers or stockholders is to transfer an opponent, or a whole department, into an activity that seems meaningful but is essentially meaningless. Ultimately, some of the victims of this technique will be sufficiently frustrated to resign at their own accord.[10] Burt, a former big company executive, describes how he and his small department were transferred into a meaningless new activity:

> My job had been as manager of long-range planning. I had a small staff, and we were engaged in helping to plan the future of the corporation. When people listened to us, we had a real contribution to make. A new president, who thought very little of our activity, was appointed. He transferred our small department to another building and gave us the new title of Quality Review department. We were to audit the quality standards in every department. It quickly became apparent to us that everybody felt that he was already doing a good job of meeting quality standards. We felt awkward and uncomfortable. My three subordinates all requested a transfer to more solid jobs. I finally resigned because I couldn't take the insult to my pride of not having a real job. Things did work out for the better. I obtained a job with a management consulting firm that was doing a long-range planning for some clients.

SHIFTING RESPONSIBILITIES AND ISOLATION TECHNIQUE

Although this technique was formalized for governmental use,[11] it has also been tried in industry. The underlying assumption here is that an entire bureau or agency can be isolated and by-passed by making it superfluous. A parallel agency or bureau is set up that will take over the work being performed by the now-obsolete agency. As the department members discover they have no legitimate work to perform, many of them seek productive employment. Soon, the obsolete department withers away. Only in a large complex organization can this technique be used. Chet explains how his department was eradicated by this approach:

I was the director of management development. I was part of the corporate staff—an arrangement that the new executive-vice president did not like. He thought management development should be a divisional responsibility. I discovered later that he and the general manager of our largest division worked out a plan for my company demise. The division set up its own management development department without even consulting me. Since about 90 percent of the people who participated in our programs came from that division, we were left in an embarrassing spot. We had a fine staff and good programs, but very few clients.

It didn't take us long to get the message. A few of my people transferred to the new department, and I found a good job in the corporate personnel department. My first thoughts were to plot some kind of revenge against the executive vice-president, but I realized that would be immature on my part. Besides, he has twice my clout.

THE TRAVELING SALES REPRESENTATIVE ROUTINE

Part of the frontal assault applied to a victim described earlier in this chapter was to keep him traveling. One application of this technique in government is to send the victim on a prolonged fact-finding mission to every United States city with a population under 10,000. Anybody who values family life—or who lacks the stamina to cope with such a hectic pace—eventually resigns.[12]

THE TRANSFER

Another approach to making life miserable for an unwanted person in your command is to transfer him or her to an undesirable location.[13] A location can be undesirable for a number of reasons, including distance from relatives and friends, weather, or expensive living conditions. One unwanted political rival who had a gracious home near Louisville, Kentucky, was told he would be transferred to a corporate staff job in New York City. He and his wife soon discovered that a suitable replacement for their $75,000 Louisville home would cost $200,000 in the suburbs of New York. When he explained the circumstances to the executive who ordered his transfer, the regional manager was told, "Sorry, your job is now in New York." Rather than disrupt his way of life, the manager cashed in some of his savings and opened a men's clothing store in a suburb of Louisville.

GIVE SELF-SERVING ADVICE

A particularly chilling power play is to give people advice that, instead of helping them, serves your ends. When a stockbroker suggests that a little old lady "churn" her stock portfolio, he might be accused of dispensing self-serving advice. The more the woman switches stocks in her portfolio, the more commissions to the broker.

One typical type of self-serving advice took place in a business equipment manufacturing company. As described by a man close to the scene:

Darwin was the manager of a quality control department in the manufacturing section of the company. Darwin wanted a bigger empire to control, but felt that limited opportunities for advancement existed in the company. His master plan was to make a proposal to the company president outlining the importance of a corporate quality assurance department. The purpose of the "assurance" department was to guarantee quality of the machines produced by the company. The quality assurance department would have more power than the quality control department.

Darwin advanced the argument that since quality control reported to manufacturing, it could not be truly objective in its pronouncements about product quality. The top executives bought the concept. As he had planned, Darwin was appointed the quality assurance director of the corporation. He was given the authority to begin initially with a staff of six people. He reported directly to the president.

The people closest to Darwin got a chuckle out of his new assignment. This was the same Darwin who one year ago said a quality assurance department was redundant providing the quality control department was doing its job properly.

PLAY DISHONEST GAMES

A perverse way of maintaining power over others is to play dishonest games; in other words, you have an ulterior motive for seemingly honest and forthright interaction with another person or group of persons. Until people get on to your particular game, you will be able to exert control over them. The popularity of Transactional Analysis has encouraged many people to develop more authentic relationships in the office. But TA's popularity has also spurred many office politicians to play dishonest games. Two are particularly applicable to office politics:[14]

Blemish. This is an extremely simple game to play and is widely used by superiors to keep subordinates in line. All that is required is for the boss to find some small flaw in every assignment carried out by the subordinates. The game-playing boss stays one up with comments such as, "Smith, you did a great job on that report except for your conclusion. It just didn't seem to fit the body of the report."

Why Don't You. . . ? Yes, But. . . . is ideal for committee or staff meetings where the leader wants to prove that the other members are far from being perfect problem solvers. In its purest form, the game player begins by telling others about a problem he cannot solve. Those who fall for the bait begin to offer advice: "Why don't you. . . ." To each solution, the experienced game player responds with a plausible reason as to why the proposed solution will not work. The reservation is usually prefaced with "Yes, but. . . ." If the player can reject every proposed solution, he has proven his superiority by putting the other players down. Another implication is that if the game player does solve the problem, he is a veritable superman because no one else in the meeting could arrive at a worthwhile solution to the problem.

USE IMPLIED POWER

If you are tied to influential people, others will go along with your demands; they know that your connections can influence their welfare. When your connection to power is, in fact, weak, you can still exert influence if people *believe* you have good contacts with powerful people. With only slight deception on your part (devious tactics vary in degree), you might be able to capitalize upon implied power.

James worked as a clerk in an insurance office. He preferred to work at an unhurried, casual pace. His boss, Tony, preferred that he work at a much more hurried, more intense pace. One day, James mentioned to Tony that his father was president of a company that had a chain of 125 retail stores and that the company was actively recruiting people for store manager positions. Tony grabbed the bait. From that point on, he was particularly nice to James, allowing him to work at the pace he preferred.

After 6 months of a harmonious superior-subordinate relationship, Tony asked James the inevitable question, "Do you think I might speak to your father about working for his company?" James replied, "Oh, I have no influence over my father's business. He would never listen to me. We hardly talk to each other." At this point, Tony was too embarrassed to begin again placing work pressures on James. Instead, he continued to allow him to work at his chosen pace.

BE INDISPENSABLE THROUGH POOR RECORD KEEPING

A last-resort technique for hanging on to your job is to do such a sloppy job of record-keeping that you become irreplaceable. The result would be chaotic if a person who kept poor records suddenly were removed from the office. Harry, the sales order department head in a small company, tried this ploy. No one else in the firm could figure out where information was stored since Harry kept all key customer information in his head. When somebody needed an answer regarding a customer's records, he or she usually had to consult Harry—the records were so inadequate.

Harry's demise came about while he was on vacation. The president asked his nephew, a recent graduate of business school, to do an efficiency study of the department. The nephew reported:

> This whole office is such a can of worms, you would be better off throwing the old records out and starting from scratch. I recommend that we personally contact all the customers and explain that we need their help in revamping our office system. We'll lose some good will and maybe a couple of orders. In the long run, those few inconveniences will more than compensate for it. What Harry has done is no way to run a business.

Following his nephew's advice, a new business system was installed in the order department. Harry was not fired, but was demoted to a clerical position. He complained bitterly that the department would fold without him in charge. His prophecy proved incorrect. Within 3 months the office was operating more efficiently than it was during Harry's reign.

THE BOGUS INTERDEPARTMENTAL ENVELOPE TRICK

Another tactic for the little person trying to create a big impression is to imply that he or she is important because of the people who send him or her mail.[15] One way of implementing this strategy is to place the names of VIPs on an interdepartmental envelope that is used repeatedly until all the name spaces are filled. Your name is written in the space just above the name of the person who is receiving your message. Directly above your name is the name of a highly influential person. Above that person's name are those of other company bigwigs. (All names have a thin cross-out line through them.) Hopefully, the recipient of your envelope will be impressed by the list of people from whom you receive memos.

One person who tried this technique said it has one pitfall. "Writing down the names of powerful people is easy. The hooker is to find influential people in the company to receive your correspondence. It's no use trying to impress people of less importance than yourself. Yet who can send memos to powerful people if you have no genuine message for them?"

WHEN IN DOUBT, SMILE

A disarming cover-up technique is to smile when confronted with a serious problem, never really committing yourself. Smiling in this context is devious because the person who wants an answer is really being deceived. Here, smiling is used as a holding action until a counterattack can be launched against the person with the audacity to bring a delicate issue to the surface.

A CPA encountered an interesting example of "When In Doubt, Smile." He recalls with a mixture of anger and indignation. "We told the president that our audit revealed so many irregularities in the company's books, that a favorable report could not be sent to the stockholders. His response was a big smile and a polite thank you. The next day, my firm received a registered letter from the president saying that his company had decided to switch accounting firms; consequently, our services would no longer be needed."

PART V

Antidotes

Stemming the Tide of Office Politics

Excessive office politics weakens an organization and injures many innocent victims. Therefore, if you are at the top of an organization, it is worth considering what can be done to minimize political game-playing below you. If you are less concerned about the good of the organization or department, and more concerned about being victimized by politics, you might want to consider how to combat political assaults directed against you. Perhaps you are a Machiavelli or a Company Politician who thrives on political conflict. You might want to parry the counterthrusts of those who are trying to contain your manipulations. Even criminals want a strong police force to protect them against other criminals. Whatever your vantage point in the organization, stemming the tide of office politics can improve your life.

HAVE A CLEAR-CUT JOB FOR EVERYBODY

Office politics is more pronounced in departments with unclear purposes and where it is difficult to measure contributions people make. Conversely, the more definable the task in which people are engaged, the less the need for politicking. When people know what is expected of them, know how their results will be measured, and believe that what they are doing is important, the need for political maneuvering lessens. Some people play politics to impress others because they lack relevant work to use as a vehicle for gaining recognition.

Augie Pulls in His Political Horns. Media design specialist Augie spent many a lunch hour trying to cultivate department heads. He flattered them and made frequent reference to the contribution he and others in his department were making to the organization. One day, a manager asked Bill, Augie's boss, "What's Augie's problem? Why does he spend so much time licking people's boots? Maybe you can help the fellow out. He's a nice guy. Perhaps you should find some honest work for him to do."

The acrid commentary made by this third party gave Bill an idea. He gently confronted Augie with the comments relayed to him, combining the criticism with a couple of constructive suggestions. "Augie, they tell me you're spending too much time playing politics. Specifically, you're trying to impress people with your words instead of your deeds. Let me suggest that you change your approach to being a media design specialist."

"What do you have in mind?" asked Augie. "I thought you agreed the company needed improved media design."

"That could be," said Bill, "but few people even know what a media design department is supposed to do. Why don't you let it be known that your department is willing to help people with any illustrations or art work they might need. Even use the word 'graphics.' I think you would get better requests from other departments if people knew you were willing to take on straightforward work. The way things stand now, people are hesitant to request your services."

Augie dutifully let it be known that the media design department was also an art and audio-visual department. Gradually, interesting requests for useful work came to the department. Augie's contribution was now being acknowledged and he spent very little time at lunch telling people how great they were, or he was. Talking about the visual displays he was doing kept Augie busy.

HIGH PAYING AND EXCITING JOBS FOR EVERYBODY

The president of a small company that provides energy conservation services to businesses and individual homeowners told me there is almost no office politics in his company. Asked why this was so, he replied, "People are too busy and too happy in my shop to bother with backbiting or apple polishing. Everybody seems to be doing the kind of work he or she wants and we pay darn well for a company located away from a metropolitan area. There's a good spirit in the office. We all know that we're doing something very important for society."

The idyllic state of affairs described by this president is not readily achievable, but it does point to an important way of combating office politics. When people are well paid and enthusiastic about their work, they tend to concentrate more on work and less on office politics. Placed in a job that you find stimulating, you, too, might have less need to engage in political behavior.

SET FAVORABLE EXAMPLES AT THE TOP

Senior management sets the stage for the type of political gameplaying that takes place at lower levels in the organization. When top management manipulates people, discredits the opposition, and covers up the truth, similar machinations are found all down the line. When senior management plays sensible politics, a good example is established as to what kind of behavior is acceptable and encouraged.[1]

Helen Holds People Accountable. An influential member of the business community, Helen was appointed publisher of a suburban newspaper. Within 4 months, according to an insider, the petty politics that had plagued the paper in the past had substantially diminished. The decrease in rampant office politics had improved morale and made it easier for the paper to make its deadlines. Helen explains her method of lessening political activity at the paper:

When I took over the political climate was so thick you could cut it with a knife. All the good jobs were held by personal friends of Mr. Galsworthy, the former publisher. A reporter had to be extra nice to the editor-in-chief to get important new assignments. You had to buy gifts for the production room people to gain any cooperation at all. Gifts were no longer a bonus for good performance; they were a requirement for getting the paper printed.

Two weeks after I took over, I told everybody we were staring with a new slate with respect to friendships and personal ties. From now on, everybody had to prove himself in his job. After 6 months, permanent assignments would be made. Many people would hold on to their old jobs, but reassignments would be made according to ability. I said that no layoffs or firings were planned. Everybody was to write a signed statement as to what job they were being paid to perform. I asked no one for special favors and I didn't grant special favors to anyone.

A few people squirmed when I announced my new policy, but, for the most part, people sighed in relief. For the first 6 months, everybody seemed to conduct himself in a businesslike manner. Sure, we would get the occasional plea for a special favor based on personal friendships, but not to a disruptive extent. I think I succeeded in flushing politics out the paper. At least for a while.

TELL THE TRUTH

A powerful antidote to office politics would be a climate of openness and trust. A deep-rooted reason many people engage in political antics on the job is that they fear the consequences of telling the truth. You might be willing to tell your boss that his proposal is flawed with poor logic if you did not fear that he would find a way to get even (or get you fired). When an organization welcomes candor, people have less fear of telling the truth. Thus, they are freer to be less political in their actions.

Val Levels with His People. The experience of one department head, Val, helps explain how leveling with people in the office can curtail the need for playing office politics. When he first took over his department, Val noticed that people went out of their way to please him in a variety of ways in addition to turning in good work performance. Having spent a number of hours in management-training sessions aimed at helping managers learn how to level with people, Val thought his department was ripe for such an approach. He reports:

> It appeared to me that people were wasting a lot of time politicking. It was quite apparent in such things as writing memos to me, proving what a good job they had done. People were figuring out all sorts of ways to impress me and my boss. After I was on the job 6 months, I accumulated enough information about my people to have a good idea of their strengths and weaknesses. I then held an appraisal session with each department member. I also explained what promotions could be made in the next year or so. Everybody then knew where he or she stood and what chances for advancement were so long as I was in the saddle. My talks had a dramatic effect on people. One man quit because he did not like my evaluation of him, but everyone else seemed to enjoy knowing the truth. Job politics went way down and work performance went way up. Since people knew what I thought of them, politicking seemed unnecessary.

DOCUMENT YOUR SIDE OF THE STORY

Although the manager just cited dislikes subordinates trying to impress him with memos, documenting your side of the story may, at times, be necessary to prove what you have accomplished. This is particularly important when you are engaged in political warfare with another person, including your boss. A full dossier of your accomplishments can help settle a dispute as to whether you are performing properly in your job. The time invested in documenting your accomplishments is a good investment since the same information might come in handy as a career-boosting tactic (described in an earlier chapter).

Manfred Compares His Decrease to Others.   Accompanied by his wife and five children, Manfred moved from the Far West to the East to become Dean of the College of Continuing Education ("night school") at a medium-sized university. A number of faculty members and administrators in his college were opposed to the idea of an outsider being appointed dean. Slowly, they began a campaign to have him ousted. One approach they used was to let outside people know how discontented they were with their new dean. A department head under Manfred attempted a more devastating maneuver. He reported to the university president that enrollment in the college had declined 14 percent since Manfred was appointed dean.

The president contacted Manfred and told him to be prepared to defend the charges being made against him —declining enrollment and employee dissatisfaction. Manfred spent a busy week accumulating facts and figures to answer the charges. His number one defense of his methods was that his college had experienced a smaller decline in enrollment than other colleges of continuing education: His school showed a decline of 14 percent versus an average of 21 percent for other like colleges. As to a decay in morale, Manfred pointed out that absenteeism and turnover figures were lower than in the previous 2 years. Case dismissed. However, Manfred still had a long way to go to build the support and confidence of his subordinates.

STOP GOSSIP SHORT

Many political ploys begin with the spreading of gossip. When gossip is stopped short by ignoring or challenging the gossip, another form of office politics is diminished. When the gossip runs out of listeners he or she might return to productive work. A few examples follow of ways in which gossip can be stopped short:

GOSSIP: Too bad about McGee. I heard that his wife has cancer; he's having an affair; and the whole mess is affecting his work.

POTENTIAL LISTENER: That is too bad. But everybody has problems. I'm sure he'll work things out. Is there something you wanted to talk to me about?

GOSSIP: I've heard from a reliable source that the marketing department is in for another shake-up and Todd, the vice-president, will be axed.

POTENTIAL LISTENER: Could be. The company always sends out official announcements of organization changes in the management newsletter.

BREAK UP LITTLE EMPIRES AND CLIQUES

The negative side of long-standing cliques and departments with high team spirit is that, under such circumstances, people tend to become involved in political warfare with other departments. As people receive exposure to different departments, they tend to develop broader perspectives and place less importance on maximizing gain for their own department.[2] Political warfare among departments can become particularly intense when department heads are competing for a promotion.

An Oil Company Plays Musical Chairs. In one large oil company, four vice-presidents were being groomed for the president's job. Each VP was intent on protecting his own department, causing a breakdown in inter-departmental cooperation. The antidote chosen by the company was to play musical chairs at the top. For instance, the vice-president of manufacturing was moved to sales and the engineering vice-president was moved to manufacturing. All four executives were rotated departmentally twice in a 5-year period. As a result of this rotation, the four executives developed a more realistic perspective of each others' problems. An important side benefit was that the cross-training helped prepare each vice-president to become the president. When one man was chosen for the presidency, he was not beset with the problem of having recently been engaged in interdepartmental rivalries with the other three executives.

CHECK OUT PRAISE AND CRITICISM

An effective way of snuffing out one form of office politics is to determine why one person praises or criticizes another. Hopefully, the praise or criticism is factually based.[3] At other times, the comments made by one person about another are aimed toward a devious end. People tend to be naïve with regard to receiving compliments about themselves, so you have to work hard at evaluating praise aimed at you. Asking another person why he or she is dispensing praise or criticisms is helpful, but a more penetrating approach might be to investigate why a third party is being praised or condemned.

Virgil Sings the Praises of His Buddy. Late one afternoon, Virgil dropped by his boss's office to chat about some production problems. After making a few routine comments about factory activities, Virgil dropped a few words on behalf of Nick, a first-line foreman. He said to his boss in an offhand manner, "I'm getting to think this company is sure on the way up. Look at the caliber of some of our new foremen. Take that fellow, Nick, who was made foreman last year. The guy's an absolute pistol. I wish I had more people like him working for me."

Virgil's boss listened but did not react. Instead, the next day he asked Nick's boss how Nick was doing as a foreman. He was told, "Good thing Nick has an old fishing buddy in Virgil. Otherwise, he wouldn't have been recommended for the foreman spot. I promoted him against my better judgment, but Virgil insisted the guy had lots of hidden talent. In fact, the talent is so hidden, I'm thinking of recommending that the company fire him. Maybe Nick can discover his hidden talent at someone else's expense."

Cagey Virgil was trying to protect the hide of his fishing buddy, Nick. If Virgil's boss had not investigated the reason for his song of praise for Nick, he might have been deceived into believing that Nick was a capable foreman. When Nick's boss ultimately recommended that he be fired, Virgil's boss might have mistakenly attributed Nick's problems to a personality clash with his boss.

CONFRONT PEOPLE WITH THEIR POLITICAL GAMES

By now you are aware of most of the forms of politics played in the office. To defend yourself against such politicking, you might confront people with the type of game they are trying to play—particularly when they are using devious tactics.[4] To illustrate, if a coworker tells you about a job opening in another company that fits your background, you might ask, "Why are you telling me about this job? Are you looking for a favor from me? Do you want me out of the way? I'd like to know." If you find confrontation exciting and you do not mind running the risk of alienating an office politician, here are a few sample confrontations:

Situation 1: A co-worker of yours invites you to lunch on your birthday. A week later, she brings you two canceled Swedish stamps because she has heard you mention that your daughter collects stamps. The following week, she hears that you have been given an exorbitant amount of work to do. She volunteers to pitch in, so you can spend the weekend free of office work. You confront her with the question, "Why are you being nice to me? What favor do you want from me in exchange?"

Situation 2: A subordinate of yours says he has a plan to help develop Tim, one of his subordinates. The plan is have him supervise a department of hard-core unemployed trainees. You know that Tim has an upper-middle-class background and has no supervisory experience. You assume he is not prepared for such an assignment. Because of your suspicions, you say to your subordinate, "Is this a sink-or-swim setup designed to have Tim sink? Do you want him out of the way? Do you want him to fail? Are you giving Tim a fair shake?"

Situation 3: A clerk from the accounting department sits down next to you in the company cafeteria and says he has something important to talk about with you. He then says, "I'm looking for a promotion—into your department." After you tell him that you have no openings for clerical help in your department, he says, "Don't you realize, I'm in charge of auditing the use of office supplies. I know that your consumption of supplies have been a little heavy lately. Almost like you've been taking some supplies home. I wouldn't want to report my findings to upper management. Tell me again, are you sure you don't have any openings in your department for a person of my talents?"

You respond, "Let's you and I go to the head of the accounting department right now. I want you to repeat your conversation. Come to think of it, maybe we should bring along a member of the security force. You're accusing me of embezzling some office supplies. In return, you're attempting extortion. This matter is too important to drop."

EXPOSE DIRTY TRICKS

The confronter in Situation 3 threatened to expose a political game that fits the dirty-trick category. In his situation, some risk was involved since the extortionist might have had some valid derogatory information about his consumption of office supplies. Exposing a dirty trick is a direct and effective antidote to one of the most unsavory forms of office politics. Usually, the dirty trickster will be too embarrassed to repeat the act.

Grace Gets Her In Basket Stuffed. Typist Grace was happy to find employment in the steno pool of a large office as it fit in with her plans for someday becoming a legal secretary. However, her straight-laced devotion to duty and her prissy mannerisms put Grace in disfavor with other women in the steno pool. To make life difficult for Grace, on several occasions somebody rearranged the order of work in her In basket. In this way, Grace was typing her assignments out of order. Newer work was being typed before older work. The result was a number of complaints about Grace's work by attorneys in the firm.

Grace refused to accept her harassment gracefully. She typed a report about what she thought was happening and carefully reviewed it with her supervisor. The upshot was that the supervisor called for a department meeting. She angrily told the group that word had gotten back to her about childish pranks being played with others' In baskets. The pranks ceased, and Grace developed a better system for placing priorities on her work assignments. She received an excellent rating on her last performance report and is now on the way toward becoming a legal secretary.

BE IMPERVIOUS TO AN EXPOSÉ

Another person out to get you and your job has the best chances of succeeding when you have something to hide. A simple antidote against this is for you to become Mr. or Ms. Clean. People can use extortion against you only when you have engaged in some deviant or questionable act.

Arnie Stretches His Expense Account.   Sales manager Arnie imprudently used his expense-account privileges. While on a business trip, he had no compunction about buying perfume for his wife or stuffed animals for his children and lumping the cost under "cab fare." On one occasion, he spent 2 extra days in San Juan at company expense.

Fred, Arnie's field sales manager (and at least a contender for Arnie's job), asked that he be recommended for a maximum salary increase. Arnie flatly refused, telling Fred quite honestly that his performance did not justify any more than a cost of living increase. In retribution, Fred wrote the company president a memo exposing Arnie's mistreatment of expense-account privileges. An investigation resulted. Many more irregularities than even Fred was aware of surfaced. Arnie was forced to resign.

Fred did not get Arnie's job, but he did get retribution. If Arnie had had nothing to hide, he would have been impervious to the counterdevious tactics of an irate subordinate.

LET OTHERS PLEASE YOU

The ultimate antidote against having to engage in political actions that you dislike is to become so secure that you find it unnecessary to play most forms of office politics. When you are successful, competent, and confident, there is much less need for you to curry favor with others. It is their turn to please you. When you reach the stage in your career where you are satisfied with your amount of power and recognition, you can play office politics more out of fun than out of necessity. When you reach that stage, or if you are already there, you have truly won at office politics.

Notes

Chapter 1

1. An analysis of why we have office politics is found in Andrew J. DuBrin, *Fundamentals of Organizational Behavior*, Second edition, Pergamon Press, Elmsford, New York, 1978, Chapter 5.

2. A good discussion of the inevitability of power struggles in organizations is found in Abraham Zaleznik, "Power and politics in Organizational Life," *Harvard Business Review*, May-June 1970, pp. 47-60.

3. Important information about appropriate dress for males in business may be found in John T. Molloy, *Dress for Success*, Warner Books, 1976.

Chapter 2

1. Sixteen of the questions on the Office Politics Scale are quoted or paraphrased from Eugene E. Jennings, "You Can Spot the Office Politicians," *Nation's Business*, December 1959, p. 52. The questions on our scale quoted or paraphrased from Jennings are numbers 11, 15, 19, 22, 23, 25, 31, 35, 52, 56, 57, 58, 77, 84, 86, and 97.

2. Eleven items of the Scale are paraphrased from Richard Christie, *Studies in Machiavellianism*, New York: Academic Press, 1970. Christie's items correspond to the following numbers on our Scale: 2, 18, 20, 36, 39, 44, 51, 78, 91, 95, and 96.

Chapter 3

1. The source of this question is Perry Pascarella, "How Can I Keep the Boss Happy?" *Industry Week*, October 13, 1975, p. 38.

2. *Ibid*, p. 42.

3. Alan S. Schoonmaker, *Executive Career Strategy*, American Management Association, 1971, pp. 104-106.

4. The idea of identifying powerful people by asking oldtimers is attributed to Edward J. Hegarty, *How to Succeed In Company Politics*, Second edition, New York: McGraw-Hill Book Co. 1976, p. 67.

5. Schoonmaker, *Executive Career Strategy*, pp. 107-109.

6. Hegarty, *Company Politics*, pp. 187-194.

Chapter 4

1. The concept, Become A Crucial Subordinate, is discussed throughout Eugene E. Jennings, *The Mobile Manager*, University of Michigan Press, 1967.

2. Gerard A. Santelli researched the incident about winemaking.

Chapter 5

1. Robert Dodenhoff researched the incident about the paper company executive who climbed into a vat of mulch.

2. The information about matching social activities to the preferences of higher ups follows the reasoning presented in Walter H. Stern, *The Game of Office Politics*, Henry Regenery, 1967, pp. 140-147.

3. The information about White House callers is credited to Meg Greenfield, "The New Washington Power Game," *Newsweek*, January 31, 1977, p. 80.

Chapter 6

1. Rosabeth Moss Kanter, *Men and Women of the Corporation*, New York: Basic Books, 1977.

2. A good reference for an elaboration of the ideas presented in this section is Ed Roseman, "How to Become A Better Teamworker," *Product Management*, January 1976, pp. 17-20.

3. Sherryl McGomber researched the anecdote contained in this section.

4. Niccolo Machiavelli, *The Prince*, translated from the Italian by Luigi Ricci, The Modern Library (Random

House), 1940. The original book was published circa 1510.

Chapter 7

1. Research about the problem of courtesy in business is reported in Eugene H. Fram and Herbert J. Mossein, "High Scores on the Discourtesy Scale," *Harvard Business Review,* January-February 1976, pp. 5-6.

2. A complete report of the consulting program mentioned in this section is found in Andrew J. DuBrin, *Casebook of Organizational Behavior,* New York: Pergamon, 1977, pp. 272-282.

Chapter 8

1. Gerald W. Oakley researched the anecdote about Harriet and developed the basic idea contained in this section.

2. A relevant reference about the power of gossip is Michael Korda, *Power! How to Get It, How to Use It,* Ballantine Books, 1975, pp. 102-107. Originally published by Random House.

3. The basic idea contained in Use Initial Power is credited to Korda, pp. 151-152.

4. An original source of this idea is Norman H. Martin and John H. Simms, "Thinking Ahead: Power Tactics," *Harvard Business Review,* November-December 1955, p. 28.

Chapter 9

1. Thomas Busch researched the anecdote about Abner.

2. The anecdote about Jeff and Nick was researched by Arnold Smeenk.

3. The anecdote about Foster is credited to Andrew J. DuBrin, *Fundamentals of Organizational Behavior,* New York: Pergamon, 1974, p. 153.

4. The anecdote about the protege of a protege was researched by Mark Kindig.

5. The case history of Biff is credited to Verne Walter, "Self-Motivated Personal Career Planning: A Breakthrough in Human Resource Management," *Personnel Journal,* March 1975, p. 115. The anecdote is paraphrased

and Biff is the name we assigned to the anonymous general foreman.

6. Andrew J. DuBrin, *Survival in the Sexist Jungle*, Books For Better Living, 1974, pp. 42-43.

7. The anecdote about Glenn was contributed by Mark Kindig.

8. Anecdote researched by Arnold Smeenk.

9. William M. Newman, *Administrative Action*, Second edition, Englewood Cliffs, N.J.: Prentice-Hall, 1963, p. 89.

Chapter 10

1. The concept of the streetwise in relation to gaining power is credited to Ed Roseman, "The Myth of the Powerless Product Manager," *Product Management*, February 1976, pp. 33-37. The anecdote about Pam in this section is credited to the same source, p. 34.

2. The basic concept of "Make A Quick Showing" is credited to William H. Newman, *Administrative Action*, Second edition, 1963, p. 87.

3. The basic concept of "Camel's Head in the Tent" is credited to Newman, *op. cit.*, p. 87.

4. Henry L. Tosi and Stephen J. Carroll, *Management*, St. Clair Press, 1976, pp. 214-217.

5. *Ibid.*

6. The basic concept of "Collect and Use IOUs" is credited to Alan S. Schoonmaker, *Executive Career Strategy*, *American Management Association*, 1971, p. 115.

7. *Ibid.*, p. 102.

8. Wayne Strawn researched this anecdote.

Chapter 11

1. John Costello, "When You Lick em, Lick 'em Good," *Nation's Business*, March 1974, p. 10.

2. Jurgen Ruesch, *Knowledge in Action*, Jason Aronson, 1975, p. 158.

3. William H. Newman, *Administrative Action*, Second edition, 1963, p. 89.

4. Andrew J. DuBrin, "Keeping the Boss' Job," *Upstate* (Rochester Democrat and Chronicle), June 12, 1977, p. 12.

5. Niccolo Machiavelli, *The Prince*, The Modern Library, 1940, p. 61.

6. *Ibid.*, p. 82.

7. The basic idea of "Build A Monument" is credited to Rosabeth Moss Kanter, *Men and Women of the Corporation,* New York: Basic Books, 1977.

8. Robert N. McMurry, "Power and the Ambitious Executive," *Harvard Business Review,* November-December 1973, p. 142.

9. *Ibid.*, p. 141.

Chapter 12

1. Edward J. Hegarty, *How to Succeed in Company Politics,* Second edition, New York: McGraw-Hill Book Co., p. 122.

2. The central idea in this section is credited to Hegarty, p. 123.

3. The basic idea and quote in this section is credited to Terry Farnsworth, *On the Way up—The Executive's Guide to Company Politics,* McGraw-Hill (UK) Limited, 1976, p. 30.

Chapter 13

1. The anecdote about Alec was contributed by Stephen Hlasnicek.

2. Paul G. Swingle, *Management of Power,* Lawrence Erlbaum, 1976, p. 32.

Chapter 14

1. Niccolo Machiavelli, *The Prince,* Modern Library, 1940, p. 73.

2. The basic idea of Take Undue Credit is credited to Vance Packard, *The Pyramid Climbers.* New York: McGraw-Hill Book Co., 1962, pp. 201-202.

3. The example about Sam in this section was researched by Gerard A. Santelli.

4. The Smokescreen idea is credited to Chester Burger, *Survival in the Executive Jungle,* New York: Macmillan, 1964, p. 6.

5. This quote is credited to the *The AMBA Executive,* March 1977, p. 7.

6. Fred K. Kaltenbach researched the information contained in this section.

7. Ed Gundrum researched this anecdote.

8. The concept, "Death on the Vine" is credited to Norman H. Martin and John H. Simms, "Thinking Ahead: Power Tactics," *Harvard Business Review*, November-December 1955, p. 30.

9. *The Federal Political Personnel Manual* is generally unavailable but is quoted extensively in Doug Shuitt, "Federal Jobs and Politics," *Los Angeles Times* (Reprinted in the Rochester, New York, *Democrat and Chronicle*, December 26, 1976).

10. *Ibid.*

11. *Ibid.*

12. *Ibid.*

13. *Ibid.*

14. The information in this section follows closely that presented in Donald D. Bowen and Raghu Nath, "Transactions in Management," *California Management Review*, Winter 1975, p. 80.

Mark Kindig contributed the basic idea contained in this section.

Chapter 15

1. A recent analysis of this basic idea is Stephen P. Robbins, "Reconciling Management Theory With Management Practice," *Business Horizons*, February 1977, p. 47.

2. The information about the oil company executives is credited to "Playing Office Politics, or Grab For Glory," *Industry Week*, March 23, 1970, pp. 28-29.

3. The basic idea in this section is credited to Edward J. Hegarty, *How to Succeed in Company Politics*, Second edition, McGraw-Hill, 1976, pp. 189-190.

4. The basic idea in this section is credited to Ed Roseman, "How to Play Clean Office Politics," *Product Management*, May 1976, pp. 34-35.

Bibliography

Chester Burger, *Survival in the Executive Jungle*, Macmillan, 1964.

Richard Christie, *Studies in Machiavellianism*, Academic Press, 1970.

Caroline Donnelly, "Warding off the Office Politician," *Money*, December 1976, pp. 70-74.

Andrew J. DuBrin, *Fundamentals of Organizational Behavior*, Second edition, Pergamon, 1978, Chapter 5.

Andrew J. DuBrin, *Survival in the Sexist Jungle*. Books Reinhold, 1977.

Andrew J. DuBrin, *Survival in the Sexist Jungle*. Books For Better Living, 1974.

Terry Farnsworth, *On the Way Up—The Executive's Guide to Company Politics*, McGraw-Hill (UK) Limited, 1976.

Edward J. Hegarty, *How to Succeed in Company Politics*, Second edition, McGraw-Hill, 1976.

Eugene E. Jennings, *Routes to the Executive Suite*, McGraw-Hill, 1971.

"How to Survive in the Corporate Jungle," *Industry Week*, November 15, 1971, pp. 29-33.

Michael Korda, *Power! How to Get It, How to Use It*, Ballantine Books, 1976. Originally published by Random House.

David C. McClelland, *Power: The Inner Experience*, Irvington (Division of John Wiley), 1976.

Robert N. McMurry, "Power and the Ambitious Executive," *Harvard Business Review*, November-December, 1973, pp. 140-145.

Niccolo Machiavelli, *The Prince*, translated from the Italian by Luigi Ricci. The Modern Library (Random House), 1940.

William H. Newman, *Administrative Action*, Second edition, Prentice-Hall, 1963, pp. 86-98.

Vance Packard, *The Pyramid Climbers*, McGraw-Hill, 1962.

Perry Pascarella, "How Can I Keep the Boss Happy?" *Industry Week*, October 13, 1975, pp. 38-43.

"Playing Office Politics, or the Grab for Glory," *Industry Week*, March 23, 1970, pp. 25-30.

Stephen P. Robbins, "Reconciling Management Theory With Management Practice," *Business Horizons*, February 1977, pp. 38-47.

Rosabeth Moss Kanter, *Men and Women of the Corporation*, Basic Books, 1977.

Ed Roseman, "How to Play Clean Politics," *Product Management*, May 1976, pp. 32-36.

Ed Roseman, "The Myth of the Powerless Product Manager," *Product Management*, February 1796, pp. 33-37.

Ed Roseman, "How to Become a Better Teamworker," *Product Management*, January 1976, pp. 17-20.

Jurgen Ruesch, *Knowledge in Action*, Jason Aronson, 1975, Chapters 9, 10, and 11.

Virginia Schein, "Individual Power and Political Behaviors in Organizations: An Inadequately Explored Reality," *Academy of Management Review*, January 1977, pp. 64-71.

Alan S. Schoonmaker, *Executive Career Strategy*, American Management Association, 1971, Chapter 5.

Walter H. Stern, *The Game of Office Politics*, Henry Regnery, 1976.

Paul G. Swingle, *Management of Power*, Laurence Erlbaum, 1976.

Abraham Zaleznik, "Power and Politics in Organizational Life," *Harvard Business Review*, May-June 1970, pp. 47-60.

Index

Abolish their jobs, 278

Accomplishments, 90, 177-78

Accountability, 294-95

Acid tongue, 246-48

Acquire seniority, 204-206

Act on advance information, 149-50

Administrative ability, 257

Advice giving, 117-18

Allow your boss his or her pretense, 85

Analyze the competition, 178-79

Analyzing politics below, 54-56

Antidotes to office poliitcs, 294-305
  clear-cut jobs, 294-96
  confrontation, 302-304
  dismantling cliques, 300-301
  documentation, 299-300
  evaluate praise and criticism, 301-302
  expose dirty tricks, 304
  good example at top, 296-97
  gossip stopping, 300
  keep clean record, 305
  rewarding jobs, 296
  truth telling, 297-98

Ape your boss, 73-74

Appear cool under pressure, 99-102

Ask advice, 117-18

Ask impressive questions, 158-59

Ask your boss advice about personal matters, 82-83

Avoid being despised and hated, 125-26

Avoid being one of the gang, 92

Avoid disloyalty, 66-68

Avoid high-risk jobs, 185

Back stab, 267-68

Be a confidante, 152-53

Be a name dropper, 207-208

Be a runner of errands, 81-82

Be an information hub, 150-52

Be courteous, 135-38

Be deferent, 83-84

Be the department watchdog, 79-80

Be dispensable, 186-87

Be distinctive and formidable, 192-93

Be especially nice to secretaries, 141-42

Be feared rather than loved, 223-24

Be impervious to an exposé, 305

Be indispensable through poor record keeping, 290-91

Be prepared to desert a patron, 241-42

Be sensitive to human relationships, 134-35

Be a straight arrow or innocent lamb, 126-27

Be a team player, 113-16

Be street wise, 194-95

Be visible, 168-71

Become a bearer of good news, 159-61
Become the coffee baron or baroness, 122
Become a crucial subordinate, 72-73
Become a straight man, 84
Become a supplier, 120-21
Befriend a higher-up's child, 109-10
Befriend an unpopular executive, 108-109
Blackmail, 272-73
Blemish, 288-89
Blooper, 85-86
Board of directors, 227
The bogus envelope trick, 291
Boss relationships, 62-90
  advice to, 82-83
  allow pretense of, 85
  alternatives presented to, 89-90
  complaints about, 254-55
  complimenting boss, 40-41
  contact with, 75-76
  crucial subordinate, 72-73
  deference towards, 83-84
  dirty work for, 81
  disloyalty, 66-68
  document accomplishments of, 68-69
  freebies for, 77-78
  help get promoted, 187-88
  helping succeed, 63-64
  high with boss, 282
  idiosyncrasies, 76
  imitation of, 73-74
  introduce to others, 87
  listening to, 74-75
  loyalty to, 65-66
  methods to impress, 55-56
  mood cycles, 46-47
  objectives of, 70-71
  personal life of, 76-77
  politics played by, 44-45
  praise to top management, 69-70
  secretary of, 87-88
  simplify life of, 71-72

  sizing up, 38-47
  spouse of, 88-89
  teaching skill to, 86-87
  upstaging, 248-49
  watchdog for, 79-80
Boss upstaging, 248-49
Build a monument, 224-25
Build an outside reputation, 225-27
Buzz words, 157-58
Bypass for promotion, 237-39

Capitalize upon luck, 166-68
Career management, 165-90
  analyze competition, 178-79
  belief in self, 190
  documenting accomplishments, 177-78
  luck, 166-68
  mobility approach, 174-75
  path to the top, 175-77
  promotion for boss, 187-88
  promotion refusal, 189-90
  protégé system, 173-74
  risk taking, 185
  self-advertising, 182-83
  sponsor, 171, 173
  successful appearance, 183-84
  swim against the tide, 179-81
  undesirable assignment, 188-89
  visibility, 168-71
Career path, 175-77
Cater to your boss's idiosyncracies, 76
Causes of office politics, 2-21
Chain of command, 259-60
Choose the right path to the top, 175-77
Climb the social ladder, 104-105
Collect and use IOUs, 203-204
Commitments, 129-31

Communication channels, 218-19

Company founder, 257-58

Company politician, 33

Competition, 178-79

Complaints about boss, 254-55

Compliment influencial people, 93

Complimenting others, 118-20

Conduct a mass, concentrated offensive, 220-21

Conduct business as usual, 234-35

Confidante, 152-53

Confrontation about games, 302-304

Connections, 138-39, 260-61

Constructive action, 236-37

Contact a newly arrived office holder, 106-107

Control access to key people, 201-202

Control the future, 202-203

Control vital information, 146-49

Cooperate with the victor, 237-39

Counsel from others, 163-64

Counterinvasion, 221-23

Courtesy, 135-38

Cover up the truth, 268-69

Cover your boss's blooper, 85-86

Create your own job, 199

Credit and remove the opposition, 273-74

Credit for ideas, 155-56

Criticism, 232-33, 301-302

Cultivate information links, 161-62

Cultivate your boss's secretary, 87-88

Cultivate your boss's spouse, 88-89

Custom deviation, 255-56

Daydreaming, 94-95

Death on the vine, 283-84

Defeat handling, 230-43

Delicate assignments, 80-81

Develop breadth through mobility, 174-75

Devious tactics, 265-92
  abolishing jobs, 278
  back stabbing, 267-68
  blackmail, 272-73
  blunder file, 281-82
  bogus envelope trick, 291
  cost underestimating, 281
  cover up with smile, 291-92
  credit and remove opposition, 273-74
  crisis tactics, 271-72
  discrediting rival, 266-67
  dishonest games, 288-89
  distorting information, 282-83
  divide and rule, 265-66
  double cross, 276-77
  excluding competition, 274-75
  fake support, 275-76
  frontal assault, 279-80
  getting high with boss, 282
  gun holding, 283
  hanging competition, 277
  implied power, 289-90
  lying, 268-70
  negative references, 284-85
  poor record keeping, 290-91
  questioning the competition, 266-67
  self-serving advice, 287-88
  setting up others, 269-70
  sham support, 275-76
  shift responsibilities, 285-86
  shooting to kill, 266
  smokescreen, 275
  success faking, 280
  stalling on ideas, 283-84
  transfer of activity, 285-86
  travel assignments, 286-87
  undesirable transfer, 287

undue credit, 270
upsetting rival, 278-79
Discover your boss's objectives, 70-71
Discover the facts behind your defeat, 233-34
Discredit your rival, 266-67
Dispense recognition, 131-34
Display company manners, 98-99
Display loyalty, 65-66
Display the right reading material, 100-101
Dirty trick, 304; see also Devious tactics
Divide and rule, 265-66
Do your boss's dirty work, 81
Document your accomplishments, 177-78
Document your boss's accomplishments, 176-78
Document your side of the story, 299-300
The double cross, 276-77
Downward relationships, 128-43
  courtesy to others, 135-43
  handling commitments, 129-31
  human factors, 134-35
  old ties, 142-43
  personal connections, 138-39
  retaining old ties, 142-43
  secretarial relationships, 141-42
  using recognition, 131-34
Drop a few buzz words, 157-58
Dumping of people, 240-41, 260-61

Empires and cliques, 300-301
Employment contract, 227-28
Errand running, 81-82
Exchange favors, 116-17
Exclude the competition, 274-75

Exhibit eternal virtues, 166
Expense account chiseling, 253-54
Expose dirty tricks, 304
Exposé, 304-305

Fact finding in defeat, 223-24
Faking success, 280
Fear, 223-24
Federal Political Personnel Manual, 284-85
Find a sponsor, 171-73
Follow through on your commitments, 129-31
Food for motivation, 140-41
Freebie, 77-78
Frontal assault, 279-80
Future, 202-203

Get a freebie for your boss, 77-78
Get high with your boss, 282
Get your name on projects, 102-103
Give proof of prowess, 224
Give self-serving advice, 287-88
Good news signals, 159-60, 242-43
Gossip, 156-57, 300
Grab a shooting star, 173-74
Graveyard, 239
Groom princes and princesses, 219-20
Grooming of subordinates, 219-20
Group identification, 92

Help your boss get promoted, 187-88
Help your boss succeed, 63-64
High-level politics, 6-7, 56-57, 213-28
Hitch your wagon to yourself, 190
Hold a gun to management's head, 283

Improve their social life, 124-25

Indirect questions, 52

Individual distinctiveness, 192-93

Information handling, 146-64

Information hub, 150-52

Information links, 161-62

Innocent lamb, 34-35

Innocent questions, 48-49

Introduce your boss to important people, 87

Invest in your firm, 105-106

Job mystique, 214-16

Job performance, 43-44, 47-48, 55

Job virtues, 166

Keep a blunder file, 281-82

Keep your communication channels unclogged, 218-19

Keep your department lean, 223

Key people, 201-202

Key problems, 216

Laugh heartily at higher-up's jokes, 101-102

Let others please you, 305

Let someone else do your bidding, 206

Let your competition hang, 277

Listen to your boss, 74-75

Listen with grace to gossip, 155-56

Look for signals of good news, 242-43

Look successful, 183-84

Loose tongue, 244-46

Luck, 166-68

Lying, 268-69

Machiavelli, Niccolo, 125, 223-24

Machiavelli person, 32

Maintain a goodie drawer or desk top, 122-23

Maintain maximum contact with the boss, 75-76

Maintain a mystique about your job, 214-23

Maintain old ties, 142-43

Make good use of tidbits, 78-79

Make a quick showing, 195-96

Marry the boss's offspring, 110-11

Maze brightness, 194

Meetings, 94-96

Memo answering, 136

Memo sending, 103-104

Mobility, 174-75

Modeling of executive behavior, 19-20, 73-74

Money, 208-209

Monument to self, 224-25

Mood cycles, 10-11

Move out of the graveyard, 239

Musical chairs, 223, 301

Name dropping, 207-208

Need for acceptance, 17-18

Nepotism, 37-38

New activity technique, 285

Offensive power play, 220-21

Office pest, 249-51

Office politics; *see also* selected topics, Contents

accomplishments and, 90

act nonpolitically, 126-27

analyzing— politics below, 54-56

antidotes, 294-305

befriending others, 109-10

boss's spouse, 88-89

causes, 2-21

coffee and candy dispensing, 122

company manners, 98-99

complimenting people, 93, 118-20

courteous behavior, 135-38

covering up for boss, 85-86

crucial subordinate, 72-73
cultivating higher-ups, 91-111
cultivating your boss, 62-90
defeat handling, 230-43
deference toward boss, 83-84
department watchdog, 79-80
devious, dishonest tactics, 265-92
dirty work, 81
disloyalty, 65-66
downward relationships, 128-43
emotional insecurity as cause, 11-12
exchange favors, 116-17
food as motivator, 140-41
game playing in, 302-304
high level, 213-28
identify the power, 48-59
imitation of executives, 19-21, 73-74
important people, 87-88
inevitable nature, 2-21
information handling, 146-64
innocent lamb, 34-35
investments, 105-106
laughing at jokes, 101-102
loyalty, 65-66
Machiavellian, 32
Machiavelli strategies, 125, 223-24
managing your career, 165-90
medical help to others, 123-24
marriage to offspring, 110-11
memo sending, 103-104, 106-107
misfortune, mistakes, and misdeeds, 230-92
needs for acceptance, 17-18
nepotism, 37-38

organizational taboos, 244-64
path to the top, 175-76
political climate, 36-59
power gaining strategies, 133-228
power seeking, 146-228
powerful people, 48-54
praising boss to top management, 69-70
promoting the company, 107-108
recognition to others, 131-43
secretary role, 87-88, 141-42
self-advertising, 182-83
self-interest, 13-16
sexual politics, 270-71
sizing up boss, 38-47
sponsor system, 171-74
status symbols, 57-59
straight arrow, 34
strategies of boss, 44-45
strategies for gaining favor, 62-143
strategies for gaining power, 146-228
survivalist, 33-34
team play, 113-16
test for, 22-35
tidbits, 78-79
top-level power plays, 213-28
top-level strategies, 6-7, 213-28
unmeasurable jobs, 7-11
Office politics questionnaire, 22-35
Oldtimers, 50-52
Organizational beliefs, 256-59
Organization chart, 49-50
Organizational taboos, 244-64

Patron, sponsor, 171-74
Pay attention to your boss's personal life, 76-77

Peer relationships, 112-27
  acts to avoid, 125-26
  coffee and candy to others, 122-24
  complimenting others, 118-20
  exchange favors, 116-17
  improve their social life, 124-25
  medical help to others, 123-24
  supplies to others, 120-21
  team play, 113-16
Perform a vile task before an audience, 97-98
Personal life, 76-77, 82-83, 124-25
Plant a self-fulfilling rumor, 199-200
Play camel's head in the tent, 196-98
Play dishonest games, 288-89
Play I told you so, 198
Play the money game, 208-209
Play the power game, 217-18
Political climate, 36-59
Political games, 288-89, 302-304
Power identification, 48-52
Power image, 210-11
Power seeking, 3-7
Power strategies, 146-228
  advance information technique, 149-50
  bidding by others, 206
  buzz words, 157-58
  camel's head, 196-98
  collect and use IOUs, 203-204
  communication channels, 218-19
  company knowledge, 194-95
  confidante role, 152-53
  control the future, 201-203
  counterinvasion, 221-23
  create own job, 199
  fear, 223-24

  good news use, 159-61
  gossip use, 156-57
  groom effective people, 219-20
  home court technique, 209-10
  information hub, 150-52
  key people access, 201-202
  key problems, 216
  lean department technique, 223
  line responsibility, 193-94
  maintain mystique, 214-16
  money game, 208-209
  monument building, 224-25
  name dropping, 207-208
  offensive tactic, 220-21
  personal distinctiveness, 192-93
  power game, 217-18
  powerful act, 210-11, 224
  powerful title, 211-12
  question asking, 158-59
  quick showing, 195-96
  reputation outside company, 225-27
  self-fulfilling rumor, 199-200
  seniority, 204-206
  show prowess, 224
  stockpile ideas, 154-56
  vital information, 146-49
  winning big, 213-14
Powerful people, 52-54
Powerful titles, 211-12
Praise, 69-70, 118-20
Praise your boss to top management, 69-70
Present alternatives to your boss, 89-90
Promote your company's products or services, 107-108
Promotion refusal, 189-90
Protégé system, 173-74
Prowess, 224
Publicize your connections, 138-39

Question asking, 158-59

Raise questions about your competition, 268
Reading material, 100-101
Recognize when you are being dumped, 240-41
Refusal of top management, 263-64
Refuse a promotion for the good of the company, 189-90
Relationships above you, 91-111
   compliment influentials, 93
   contact new office holder, 106-107
   laughing at jokes, 101-102
   marry into the business, 110-11
   memos to influentials, 103-104
   project assignments, 102-103
   promoting the company, 107-108
   talk big, 96-97
Reputation to enhance power, 225-27
Reverse discrimination, 53-54
Rewarding jobs, 296
Risk taking, 185

Secretary, 87-88, 141-42
Seek line responsibility, 193-94
Select a compliant board of directors, 227
Self-advertising, 182-83
Self-belief, 190
Self-interest, 13-16
Self-fulfilling rumor, 199-200
Send photocopies to influentials, 103-104
Seniority, 204-205
Serve as the office paramedic, 123-24
Setup, the, 269-70
Set-up questions, 94

Sex and office politics, 270-71
Sex roles, 261-63
Sham support, 275-76
Share your accomplishments with your boss, 90
Shifting responsibilities and isolation technique, 285-86
Shine at meetings, 94-95
Shoot to kill, 266
Shrugging off defeat, 234-35
Sizing up boss, 40-47
Smokescreen, the, 275
Social, personal life, 76-77, 82-83, 124-25
Social ladder, 104-105
Sponsor(s), 171-74
Status symbols, 57-59
Stockpile a few ideas, 154-56
Straight arrow, 34
Straight man, 84
Straightforward behavior, 126-27
Subordinate relationships; see Downward relationships
Successful appearance, 183-84
Survivalist, 33-34
Swim against the tide, 179-80
Swing into constructive action, 236-37

Take counsel with caution, 163-64
Take criticism gracefully, 232-33
Take undue credit, 270
Talk big, shun trivia, 96-97
Teach your boss a skill, 86-87
Team play, 113-16
Technical skills, 257
Telephone calls, 136-37
Tell the truth, 297-98
Tell them what they want to hear, 282-83
Temper tantrums, 278-79

Test for political tendencies, 22-35

Think, act, and look powerful, 210-11

Tidbits, 78-79

Threat of negative references, 284-85

Title your way to power, 211-12

Toot your own horn (softly), 182-83

Top-level tactics, 6-7, 56-57, 213-28

Top management example, 296-97

Trade sex for political advantage, 270-71

Transfer, the, 287

Traveling sales representative routine, the, 286-87

Trigger a rival's flare-up, 278-79

Truth telling, 297-98

Try a counterinvasion, 221-22

Turnover, 258

Uncomplicate your boss's life, 71-72

Underestimate the cost for your project, 281

Undesirable assignment, 188-89, 285

Use coffee, doughnuts, and pastry to advantage, 140-41

Use the home court to advantage, 209-10

Use implied power, 289-90

Use initial power, 162-63

Use realistic compliments, 118-20

Volunteer for delicate assignments, 80-81

Volunteer for an undesirable tour of duty, 188-89

Wall Street Journal, 59, 100

Welcome that rock bottom feeling, 230-31

When in doubt, smile, 291-92

White House, 106

Why don't you . . . ? Yes, but . . . ?, 289

Win big if you want to be accepted, 213-14

Work in a crisis mode, 271-72

Work on key problems, 216

Work pressures, 99-100

World Tennis, 58

6 for success from BALLANTINE BOOKS Help yourself.